DREAMTIME

DREAMTIME

Parables of Universal Law while Down Under

Essays by Dr. Daniel R. Condron | Dr. Laurel Clark | Dr. Sheila Benjamin
Dr. Pam Blossser | Dr. Christine Madar | Rev. Paul Madar | Erin Collins
Elena Dubinski | Jesse Aaron Kern | Jesse Loren Reece
| Laurie J. Biswell | Hezekiah Condron

and Dr. Barbara Condron, ed.

Cover Design by Laurie J. Biswell
Cover Photographs
  by Laurie J. Biswell, Tad Messenger, Paul Madar, Barbara Condron

Photographs throughout text
  by L. Biswell, T. Messenger, P. Madar, Elena Dubinski,
  Hezekiah Condron and B. Condron

Special Recognition: The Universal Laws noted here are the guiding principles governing creation as taught in the School of Metaphysics course of study and by most Holy Scriptures of Earth. The phrases describing the action of each Universal Law noted at the beginning of each chapter in this book are quoted from Daniel R. Condron. For more see page 302.

© December, 2010   School of Metaphysics No. 100195
PRINTED IN THE UNITED STATES OF AMERICA

Library of Congress Control Number: 2010914627
preassigned control number
Condron, Barbara
  DREAMTIME: Parables of Universal Law while Down Under
  Summary: Thirteen real-life stories told by Americans visiting Australia during the 2009 Parliament of the World's Religions in Melbourne reveal the divine in the human, the sacred in the every day

ISBN: 0-944386-45-8
EAN: 978-0-944386-45-3

Any portion of **DREAMTIME: Parables of Universal Law while Down Under** may be reprinted or reproduced in any form with the prior written permission of the Board of Governors of the School of Metaphysics.

THE LAWS

The Laws are principles that function in our Universe. Ever-present, seen or unseen by the human eye, these unspoken agreements direct the planets and stars in the orchestra of life. They swell the tides and temper the earth. They keep rhythm beating in the hearts of young and old. They carry the voice of the ancients and the cry of every newborn. Fascination with these Laws unite science and religion, male and female, light and dark.

The Laws are egalitarian, functioning consistently for all. They apply to anyone, at anytime, at any place,– in this Universe. They are the keeper of the present where the past that was meets the future that will be. They are the impartial judge meeting all expectations with justice and candor. They are the way things have always been and will always be, in this great world of our making, these purveyors of Truth, revealers of thought. All great masters of consciousness have come to discover the Great Laws that rule our existence – as it is above, so it is below.

There are ways to live in harmony with these Laws. Health, prosperity, and peace of mind is such a one's fortune. That fortune is now yours.

Read, and learn.

If you desire to learn more about the research and teachings in this book, write to School of Metaphysics World Headquarters, Windyville, Missouri 65783. Or call us at 417-345-8411.

Visit us on the Internet at
www.som.org | www.dreamschool.org
www.peacedome.org | www.healingwall.org

THE PARABLES

Entering Dreamtime:
How Story Becomes Parable by Barbara Condron   1

One
The Law of Existence   17
I AM told by Dr. Daniel R. Condron   18

Two
The Law of Free Will   33
I Make Conscious Choices
    Parable 1 told by Erin Collins   34
    Parable 2 told by Dr. Sheila Benjamin   41
    Parable 3 told by The INVITATION Cast   46

Three
The Law of Duality   53
I Value the Aggressive & Receptive
    Parable 1 told & photographed by Elena Dubinski   54
    Parable 2 told by Dr. Sheila Benjamin   61

Four
The Law of Cause and Effect   69
I Discipline My Mind
    Parable 1 told by Dr. Pam Blosser   70
    Parable 2 told by Jesse Aaron Kern   80

Five
The Law of Attraction   87
I Am Open and Loving told by Tad Messenger   88

Six
The Law of Infinity   103
I Expand my Consciousness told by Dr. Christine Madar   104

Seven
The Law of Relativity   115
I Am Connected with All told by Dr. Laurel Clark   116

Eight
The Law of Believing and Knowing   *141*
I Learn in Every Activity
    Parable 1 told by Jesse Loren Reece   *142*
    Parable 2 told by Laurie J. Biswell   *148*

Nine
The Law of Proper Perspective   *157*
The Permanent & Lasting is Most Important
              told by Barbara Condron   *158*

Ten
The Law of Evolution   *187*
I Add to my Understanding Every Day   *188*
    Parable 1 told by Paul Madar   *189*
    Parable 2 told by Christine Madar   *197*
    Parable 3 told by Sheila Benjamin   *204*

Eleven
The Law of Prosperity   *209*
I Receive the Wealth from the Universe
              told by Hezekiah Condron   *210*

Twelve
The Law of Abundance   *232*
I Create Plenty for Everyone told by Barbara Condron   *233*

Thirteen
The Law of Completion   *279*
I Am Committed to Becoming Fully Enlightened
              told by Barbara Condron   *280*

Acknowledgements & Blessings   *302*
End Notes   *304*
Universal Peace Covenant   *308*

In the beginning the world lay quiet,

in utter darkness. There was no vegetation, no living or moving thing on the bare bones of the mountains. No wind blew across the peaks. There was no sound to break the silence.

The world was not dead. It was asleep, waiting for the soft touch of life and light. Undead things lay asleep in icy caverns in the mountains. Somewhere in the immensity of space Yhi stirred in her sleep, waiting for the whisper of Baiame, the Great Spirit, to come to her.

When the whisper came, it woke the world.

Sleep fell away from the goddess,

a garment falling to her feet. Her eyes opened and the darkness faded in their shining. The light of her body brought day into the night and Yhi floated down to earth. She traveled by thought far to the west, to the east, to north, and to the south, her mind encompassing the earth. Where her feet rested on the ground, there the earth leaped in ecstasy! Grass, shrubs, trees, and flowers sprang from it, lifting themselves towards the radiant source of light. Yhi's tracks crossed and recrossed until the whole earth was clothed with vegetation.

Her first joyous task

completed, Yhi, the sun goddess, rested on the Nullarbor Plain. Gazing upon the world she created, she knew the Great Spirit was pleased with the result of her labour.

"The work of creation is well begun," Baiame said, "but it has only begun. The world is full of beauty, yet it needs dancing life to fulfill its destiny. Take your light into the caverns of earth and see what will happen."

–Adapted from Aboriginal Myths, Legends, & Fables by A.W. Reed

ENTERING DREAMTIME
HOW STORY BECOMES PARABLE

> *Never doubt that a small group of thoughtful, committed, citizens can change the world. Indeed, it is the only thing that ever has.*
> —anthropologist Margaret Mead (1901-1978)

The SOM Australia Delegation includes (above, left to right) Paul Madar, Christine Madar, Daniel R. Condron, Vivienna Madar, Jesse Reece, Barbara Condron, Hezekiah Condron, Alexandra Madar, Pam Blosser, Sheila Benjamin, Elena Dubinski and Erin Collins. Laurel Clark served us by capturing this picture. Tad Messenger, Laurie Biswell and Jesse Kern were volunteering elsewhere at Parliament.

I knew the story of the Australian delegation was worth the telling, even before it transpired.

We were fifteen Americans, the youngest turned 3 on the trip, the oldest, 63 the day we departed. One person was born in Japan, another an emigre from Belarus. A MBA, a Montessori-trained teacher, a mother of two, a president of the 501(c)(3) educational organization which brought us together.

How the experiences in the land down under would impact our lives was a story yet to be lived. With complete conviction, I knew the trip would have a profound impact on each of us. I knew this intuitively, on spiritual levels that for most remain unseen. I also knew, if any group of people could reveal the hidden wisdom in life experience, it would be these.

From being airborne for over 15 hours to meeting hundreds of the world's citizens, all we needed was to receive Melbourne, its people and its Parliament of the World's Religions and we would change.

So it came to pass.

We were a diverse group.

My mind was open traveling to Australia. I had only been out of the United States twice in my 56 years.

The first time was when my parents and I drove to Montreal, Quebec for Expo 67. The world's fair fired my imagination and began my journey of claiming the planet as a friendly and beautiful place. People welcomed us at every pavilion we visited. They were eager to tell us of their cultures, and when common language was absent, they showed us pictures. I still remember the delightful experience of being surrounded by the sights and sounds of Canada at one of the pavilions. It was as if I was riding in a boat on the river or flying in a plane over ice caps or riding through fields. The 360° presentation was encompassing.

I experienced an awesome pride in America's exhibit. It was a geodesic dome designed by Buckminster Fuller. The busiest pavilion, the dome was as high as a 20-story building and included six inner floors filled with artifacts and Apollo space rockets celebrating "Creative America". It made me glad to be an American.

"Man and His World" was the theme of the exposition and it showed the highest hopes for humanity in the future world he would create. I was happy to see the world through its people. I was 12.

The love I experienced on my Montreal trip swept through the fertile soil of my mind planting a thousand seeds of peace, contentment, security, respect, and wonder. There amidst the wide physical diversity of colors and shapes and sizes of clothing and buildings, art and music, I learned that people are far more alike than different. Japanese laughter sounds the same as French, and the eyes speak in the language of the soul.

On our way home we spent less than 24 hours in New York City, and for years after I longed to return because I believed here was a place on earth, the place on earth, where the dream of all God's people living in harmony could happen. New York was where cultures occupied the same space, believing it possible to exist in peace with one another.

I now see clearly how these thoughts of my youth, planted at the seminal time of the stirring of kundalini energy, shaped the way I have envisioned the world ever since. Those seeds blossomed through decades of teaching the Mind and how to harmonize with Universal Law through writing, speaking, and creating. All of it was, quite literally, setting the stage for what was to come.

Decades later, my father was living his dream in San Diego. He had returned after 40 years to the oceanside site of happier days during his short-lived days serving in the Navy.

On a springtime visit, he drove my husband Daniel and me across the border to Tijuana, Mexico. It was 1994. I was struck by how easy it was to get into Mexico, no long waiting lines. We drove straight downtown. I had been to many American cities so I knew the noise and filth can mount up. What I wasn't prepared for were the shacks on the hills. Having been born in Louisiana, I had seen the kind before: modern-day huts, with open sewage, in the lonely stretches of countryside swampland. Here, they loomed over the more prosperous city life.

The poverty of spirit was thick. It was difficult for me to breathe and my gut reaction was I had to leave. It was the first time I could remember feeling this way. It came upon me, not so much from my own desire, as from an oppressive sense that I–we were not wanted there, mixed with other foreign thoughts of "wanting out".

We drove down the main street and back, taking not more than 15 minutes, then joined a very long line of vehicles, mostly trucks, intent upon entering the United States. It took 45 minutes before we approached the entry booth. I experienced such conflicting emotions. I was disturbed by what I experienced in Mexico. It was more than the physicality, it was more than the polarity in egos – the rich and the poor. It was emotional, the longing and loss, the love of life and the fear of it. It was the latter, which at the time had not yet entered the mentality of my country, that lingered with me.

Now, in the backseat of my dad's well-cared-for Cadillac, I was suddenly afraid I might not be allowed back into the country from whence I came. The questions of the border patrol, the exchanging of identification documents, seemed to take a long time. The suspicions directed to us were not personal, they were directed to everyone. Yet, I took them seriously. I had done nothing wrong, yet I was being examined as if it was possible I had. I was afraid and the fear was unreasonable.

The fear of not being found worthy of returning to the U.S., to not be admitted, was a euphemism for a higher spiritual reality of my quest, anyone's quest, to return to their Source, the place of their origin, and the boulders of unworthiness we place in our paths to being there.

I was relieved to return to U.S. soil. The desires of my youth to set foot elsewhere had left me.

Our lives are stories, parables.

I first allowed this idea to sink in when I read **As You Like It** for a college class. The play is a comedy, penned by the English playwright William Shakespeare – or perhaps Francis Bacon, as some of the stories would have it – around 1600.

> "All the world's a stage,
> And all the men and women merely players;
> They have their exits and their entrances;
> And one man in his time plays many parts."
> — Jaques (Act II, Scene VII, lines 139-142)

The idea that the physical may be more than it appears to be, that it may be an illusion of a greater reality is not a new one. This idea is at the root of all classical wholistic thought and it forms the basis of religious concepts on our planet.

Jaques' speech goes on to describe the seven stages of any man's life. They are infancy, childhood, lover, soldier, justice, pantaloon and second childhood into death. These were not new thoughts, even in Shakespeare's time, nor were they limited to the European continent. There was a development afoot that Shakespeare harnessed.

It has spread throughout the human species in its universal application like a common textbook for the maturity of humanity ever since.

Shakespeare's plays reflect a wisdom that when life is viewed as a comedy, it is easier to embrace our stories. The illusion becomes attractive, even entrancing and hypnotic. Yet in the end, even the comedy of life closes in "mere oblivion, sans teeth, sans eyes, sans taste, sans everything." There is more to life than what we can physically detect, and if we are to experience the "more" we will need to release our attachments to what enslaves our senses.

Later, in **Macbeth**, Shakespeare expresses a similar teaching from the opposing, tragic point of view. Upon hearing of his wife's death, **Macbeth** laments,

> "Life's but a walking shadow, a poor player
> That struts and frets his hour upon the stage
> And then is heard no more. It is a tale
> Told by an idiot, full of sound and fury,
> Signifying nothing!"

Well, that assessment was not at all in sync with what I believed to be the purpose of life. Yet, at 20, I was just at the beginning of my beliefs being tested. My mind was alert, my heart strong, and I believed that a tale told by a savant, sound and passionate, is worth the telling. It would require a care-full blend of daily mental disciplines in concentration and meditation applied to a developing use of visualization for my Spirit to mature, and mature it has in a similar way story-telling matured on our planet.

In the Western world, the Greeks developed story-telling and brought it to the people. Greek drama allowed males to bring to life the scope of human endeavor. Tragedies came first, attributed to Thespis in 534 BC, then comedies followed a half century later.

Tragedies started as a part of a religious festival to Dionysus, the Greek god of wine who inspires ritual madness and ecstasy. Tragedies almost exclusively dealt with stories from the mythic past. The themes were universal: love, loss, pride, the abuse of power, and the unstable relationships between men and gods. Tragedies concerned tales of better than average people suffering a transition from good fortune to bad fortune. The characters in the plays spoke in an elevated language as the protagonist realized the error of his foolish or arrogant ways. The Greek philosopher Aristotle said that tragedy purges the soul of the "fear and pity" which most people carry around. From this idea comes the concept of catharsis, still used in our world today.

Sometimes, between the acts of tragedies, short plays mocking the plight of the tragedy's characters were performed. They afforded a kind of comic relief as they were often presented by satyrs; half-human, half-goat figures. The actors wore large phalluses to provoke the audience to laughter. Some see these stories as a third kind of Greek drama. I see them as a tool the authors used to develop the consciousness necessary for a new dramatic form to be born. People needed a way to see life differently, to become familiar with concepts like absurdity and practices like self-indulgence. In this way, these satyr plays were a bridge to a second kind of Greek drama – the comedy.

The comedic play concerned average to below average people, who in the course of the play enjoy a transition from bad circumstances to good. The players spoke everyday language familiar to the majority of the audience. Whereas tragedies rose from the past, comedies were defined by contemporary figures and problems. The plays were often satirical, mocking men in power for their vanity and foolishness. As comedies evolved over time, they made light of the ordinary person's plight as well. These became the situation comedies, or sit-coms, of the television era.

The Greeks evolved their theater by expecting the audience to objectify the concept of comedy and tragedy which may well have done more to lay the consciousness-foundation for modern science than anything else. The stories of gaiety and fortune or despair and retribution were quite popular. They evolved the thinking.

As time has shown us, it is the quality of the stories we tell that makes the greatest difference. The Greek dramas laid the foundation for the kind of thinking that invited Leonardo da Vinci, Michelangelo Buonarroti, Nicolaus Copernicus, Galileo Galilei, Thomas More, and Martin Luther to participate in the human drama. The period is known as the Renaissance and people have been personally striving for that level of enlightenment ever since.

Most want the story of their lives to rise beyond comedy and tragedy. They want their lives to amount to something. They want to leave something valuable behind. Here, is where the genius of a Shakespeare made its greatest contribution.

Through our stories we come to understand the purpose of life on this planet.

The Dhammapada, the first "twin verses" spoken by the Buddha, says,

1 All that we are is the result of what we have thought:
it is founded on our thoughts, it is made up of our thoughts.
If a man speaks or acts with an evil thought, pain follows him,
as the wheel follows the foot of the ox that draws the carriage.

2. All that we are is the result of what we have thought:
it is founded on our thoughts, it is made up of our thoughts.
If a man speaks or acts with a pure thought, happiness follows him,
like a shadow that never leaves him.

To communicate thoughts, man first created pictures just like those that surrounded me those days in Montreal. I remember people remarking about the number of films shown everywhere at the expo. There were films 3-stories tall, the precursors to today's IMAX theaters. There were multiple images on different screens, a device frequently used in today's entertainment and news media. There were projectors hanging from the ceilings and movies in the round. Moving pictures were everywhere.

Pictures are the oldest form of communication. Egyptian hierglyphics of 5000 years ago, Sumerian cuneiforms dating back to 34th century BC, and Olmec writing from 1000 BC, give us images of daily life around the world in earlier times. Slowly the evidence is

making it clear that far from being primitive and uncivilized, pictures are the most direct mind-to-mind form of communication available. In today's world, pictures are assuming their rightful place as the global standard for the human race.

A picture is worth a thousand words.

For the picture, we owe a debt of gratitude to the Mind of humanity itself. Pictures are the oldest language known to man, the Universal Language of Mind.

For the words, we are indebted largely to Shakespeare.

Shakespeare's plays and sonnets show a vocabulary of 21,000 words. To place this in perspective, the average person today has a vocabulary of 2000 words, with those holding University degrees rising to about 4000. Vocabulary gives us the tools to tell our stories. Words help us describe the images in our minds and commit to our perceptions. Words give us the means to describe the thoughts about our experiences in the hope that another will receive, and understand, and that in understanding, our collective wisdom can grow.

Shakespeare's plays are noted for their content, their story lines, and their state, the words that tell those stories. In *The Merchant of*

Venice's "All that glitters is not gold", we now have a pictorial way to describe illusion, and the truth that attractiveness may not always reflect real value. When Hamlet declares he sees his deceased father "in my mind's eye", we have a way of describing the perception that comes from within Self rather than from the outer physical sense.

Star-crossed lovers, one fell swoop, naked truth, love is blind, and in a pickle first appeared in a Shakespeare play. It is thought that Shakespeare coined anywhere between 1700 and 8000 words and phrases. Bedazzled, cold-blooded, circumstantial, dishearten, ill-tempered, mortifying, and uneducated are among them. However many the actual number, he is certainly credited with contributing the most.

I find his most outstanding gift to be the usage of words. Nouns became adjectives (tradition to traditional, epilepsy to epileptic) and verbs became nouns (urge to urging, transcend to transcendence) in Shakespeare's mind. It is not so much that Shakespeare invented words as he creatively used many that already existed. In this, he exemplifies man's creative genius. The result is the freedom to tell our stories with studied nuance or flamboyant celebration, mindfully quiet or with raucous abandon. It may well be this expanded way of telling stories which opened the door to drama's third option.

To the Greek art forms of comedy and tragedy, Shakespeare created a third drama – the history. Thus he created an effective way to understand what the Hindu call the pairs of opposites in the physical world. These opposites arise from desire (comedy) and aversion (tragedy). The **Bhagavad Gita** says all men fall into this delusion at birth. We make our lives from our thoughts, comedy or tragedy, glad or sad. What we think of our lives is dependent upon our point of view.

Some years ago, I read an article that cleverly separated the word into his-story. My mind opened to all the possibilities and my point of view changed. My beliefs shifted. I began claiming the freedom to use my life by choosing my thoughts with wisdom. I was exercising the responsibility of a creator.

I had entered what the Aboriginals call Dreamtime.

Auntie Joy Murphy Wandin (left, with H.H. the Dalai Lama) is an indigenous Australian. She is one in a line of 3000 generations of men and women who came before her, a continuous bloodline stretching 60,000 years. An estimated 300,000 Aboriginals were scattered throughout the continent when the first European settlers arrived in the 1780s. They lived so far apart they did not develop a common language nor did they create a written one.

Their stories continue through word of mouth, and more importantly, through spirit.

"We believe life should be one of respect, of love, and of harmony," Joy said. "Our ancestors have passed this knowledge and wisdom onto us so that we might continue to live this way today and tomorrow."

It is a traditional custom of the Australian Aboriginal community to give permission for people to enter their country. "We invite people to share with us from a branch of gum leaves," Auntie Joy said. "By taking a leaf it means you are welcome to every thing, from the tops of the trees to the roots of the earth. It also means we have become linked symbolically and spiritually."

All Aboriginal tribes share an understanding that a dream is a journey. Like many indigenous peoples around the world, they believe we dream our way into the physical world and out of it. The spirit goes on walkabout and returns to tell the story.

Sharing our stories of our time in Australia is multidimensional. They are our way of honoring the ancestors. They are our way of putting words to the spiritual connection we experience with Auntie Joy, the Aboriginal community, and to the greater global community that is the Parliament of the World's Religions.

The stories are a way to capture a moment of Dreamtime, the sacred "once upon a time" out-of-time in which ancestral Spirit Beings formed The Creation. The Dreamtime is the story of things that have happened, how the universe came to be, how human beings were created and how the Creator intended for humans to function within the cosmos. In Dreamtime are the stories worthy of the telling, stories rooted in a sense of Universal Truth that feed the human spirit to rise, to evolve, to transcend.

These are the stories of happenings during our time in Auntie Joy's land. They are history, and they are worth telling for they are creation stories, tales of change and transformation. They tell of new experiences embraced by the elders and the flowering of wisdom in the youth. They are stories of hearts made whole, minds opened, and divine friendships formed. They are modern-day parables.

These are holy stories that teach a Mind-full way to think and an elevated way to live. They are stories from your past and your future, brought to you in the Now so you might awaken in Dreamtime.

Let the dreaming begin.∞

GROUP CONSCIOUSNESS.
IT IS WHAT WILL EVOLVE LIFE ON THIS PLANET IN THE CURRENT AGE.

When directed and high-minded – something the School of Metaphysics and the Parliament of the World's Religions are noted for – the focusing of individual intelligence toward a common aspiration generates a powerful attractor field. An elevation in the calibration of the group and all its parts results.

I have invested my intelligence, my energy, and my effort in such endeavors since incarnation. In the early years, it was relatively unconscious. As the daughter of a sometimes active minister and the granddaughter of a faith-healing Bible-based evangelist, I incarned into the field of the power of Spirit. From the beginning, the heart fire was strong in serving others. I have come to understand the value of parents who minister. It is like living with Bodhisattvas who are committed to serving until the suffering of mankind is fulfilled.

Heart fire is an internal drive, soul ambition, the headstrong might say. Heart fire is what drives someone like Greg Mortensen, himself the child of Christian missionaries, to risk his life to build schools for the youth of Pakistan (www.penniesforpeace.org). For me, it was the basis required for the mind expansion that was to come.

In my teenage years, the fire in my heart grew and smoke filled my head. The many holy scripture references to burning sacrifices on altars so the smoke can rise is an accurate description of the initiation one endures at that stage. What one learns is to keep the attention on the heart fire, to constantly feed the fire so it can expand and move up the spine to clear the head.

I didn't know this when I stood on the threshold of adulthood. What kept me going through those years were one-on-one relationships. It was a roller coaster from higher to lower heart. I experienced elation, wonder, joy, and harmony through these interactions. My heart also felt wounded in my interactions with disappointed parents, disloyal friends, impersonal teachers, and impatient acquaintances. As a result, I didn't think clearly. I often felt alienated from the religion of my past and disconnected from my more head-driven scientific present. I didn't think I belonged anywhere. My heart and my head were not in sync.

It was my head that needed clearing. The Buddhists call it brainwashing, a term the "headier" West finds ominous because it threatens the insecurity which arises in the undisciplined mind. Buddhism, being in large part devoted to disciplining the mind, is an authority on that topic. I would learn about that later in life.

My work in disciplining my Mind became conscious when I was 22. Up until that time others around me – family, teachers, employers – told me I was here to do something outstanding. Yet my heart was failing me at times when I most needed it. I was in a tailspin, a downward spiral into an abyss of my own making that I managed to aright myself from. One month later, I began taking control of my Mind in earnest.

I accomplished this through higher education at the School of Metaphysics. Study at the School of Metaphysics gave me the resources, through texts and applications, to heal my heart, then consciously feed its fire. Zarathustra taught those lessons well three thousand years ago. As the fire rose, and Kundala made her appearance within my consciousness, my head was clear of the smoke of illusion conjured by a wounded heart.

With my head cleared, ego surrendered. At last! I could heed – free of the clutter of doubt and indecision or the distortion of imagined fear – the inner calling that all Holy people hear.

First, I heard the cries of others, the suffering of the Sangha that every religion seeks to relieve. So I chose to pass on what I understand to be Truth to others, in groups. The healing of my heart was accomplished through interaction with many people, thousands of them over space and time. The beauty of this journey *is that it happened **because I chose to be with others.***

Second, the clearing of my head occurred as I separated and identified the steps in harmonizing Mind with the Universal Laws to bring about the attractor fields whereby groups of people, be they a class, a community, or a race, can experience interaction for higher purposes.

I envision those purposes as a maturing of the human race which SOM defines as Intuitive, Spiritual Man, and I refer to as homo Spiritus! This is the third stage that many masters of Spirit have foreseen. In the East, the great Chinese thinkers Confucius and Lao-tse addressed it in the 6th century BC. In Jewish and Christian thought it is the belief in the Kingdom of God. In more recent times, Tolstoy in Europe, Gandhi in India, Mandela in Africa, speak and live the Truth, as do other Light bringers, that is group consciousness.

Each individual writing here is somewhere on this journey. As you enjoy their stories and reflect upon the Universal Laws they bring to light for you, I encourage you to allow the resonant Truth to bring courage (calibration of 200 on Dr. David Hawkin's Map of Consciousness scale, **Power v. Force**) to your heart and reason to your head (calibrating at 400 MoC) so we might all evolve into Spirit (700+ MoC) – together.

> I SAY UNTO YOU, ARJUNA,
> AND TO ALL WHO FOLLOW AFTER,
> THAT HE WHOSE EYES HAVE BEEN CLEARED OF
> THE SMOKE OF ILLUSION AND WHO KNOWETH
> ME, KRISHNA, THUS AS SPIRIT ABSOLUTE;
> AND WHO THUS KNOWING,
> LOVETH ME WITH ALL HIS HEART, AND ALL
> HIS MIND, AND ALL HIS SOUL –
> HE KNOWETH ME IN TRUTH.
> AND KNOWING ME, HE KNOWETH ALL
> THINGS, AND WORSHIPETH AND LOVETH THE
> ONE AND ALL.
>
> –BHAGAVAD GITA, PART VI
> CONSCIOUSNESS OF THE SUPREME

At the close of most chapters, you will find a shaded text like this one. It will contain reflective thoughts about the universal principles illustrated in the story. The construction of these narratives are mine. With so many authors, I wanted it to be easy for the reader to identify the person whose Voice is speaking. I trust these comments will enrich your experience.

Before the parables were even written I foresaw their connectedness in the fields of time and space. This was the first time, a group of people "from" the School of Metaphysics was going to a different country to serve in all capacities: to speak, to observe, to present, to attend, to learn, to love, to share, to evolve. We were there as attendees, as volunteers, as presenters, as performers, as lecturers, as counselors, as ministers, as healers, as friends, as parents, as children.

We were engaging on all levels of consciousness and so we found ourselves giving the best of who we are and what we have to offer including our beloved Intuitive Reports. Melbourne was the first city outside the United States to host these intuitive teachings. I knew with conviction that, once written, the stories of 15 different people would come together to tell a story greater than any one of us. Like **The Silver Cord**, *a spiritual documentary based on intuitive research, I knew these stories, assembled according to Universal Law, would convey truths to nourish every soul who reads them. In the end, that's what turns a story into a parable.*

Enjoy.
Expand.
Enlighten.

–B. Condron

ONE
THE LAW of EXISTENCE

"I AM"
told by Dr. Daniel R. Condron

"For where two
or three are gathered together in My name,
I AM there in their midst."
–from **The Bible,** *Book of Matthew 18v20*

"Tahereh said – that when she heard me speak
and I asked the question – she knew
I was the person she was supposed to give the picture to.
As Tahereh was speaking these words to me,
wave after wave of shivers passed into my body."

In the early 1970's, I applied twice in two different years for a Rotary Scholarship to study abroad. Rotary International is a service organization that sponsors college students so they can study in other countries. The two countries I chose in my application, both times were India and Australia. I did not receive the Rotary Scholarship from either Rotary organization in either year.

I did, however, place a strong and powerful thought-form-image in Universal Subconscious mind that was to manifest many years later. In the year 2006, over 30 years later I traveled to India. While in India I breathed through and opened my 8th and 9th chakras. In the year 2008 I again traveled to India and again breathed through and raised my consciousness through the 8th and 9th chakras.

In the year 2009, there arose the opportunity to travel to Australia ostensibly for the Council of the Parliament of World's Religions, yet also for a rendezvous with destiny.

This time, this trip, I would be traveling with my wife Barbara and 14-year-old son Hezekiah. On the way there, Hezekiah got to visit some states he had never been in as such as Colorado and California as well as two countries, Australia and New Zealand.

After a 15 1/2 hour flight from Los Angeles, California we arrived in Melbourne, Australia, Melbourne is located in the southern part of the continent and country of Australia.

After a couple of days of finding our way around Melbourne the Council of Parliament of World's Religions was about to begin.

The Parliament began on Friday December 4, 2009 and I was to present my morning teaching on Tuesday December 8, 2009. Therefore I spent the next several days making friends, soul connections, giving love, being with my wife and son, teaching Hezekiah and connecting in the evenings with the group of 15 delegates the School of Metaphysics had sent to a Parliament of World's Religions.

Friday morning, I attended a class called *"The Breath of Life"* because breath has always been such a powerful factor in my soul growth and spiritual development. Even as a young child, while playing, my attention would sometimes go to my breath and I could not get my attention off my breath as it entered my nose even if I tried. So in a way I have been doing conscious breathing all my life. The class was led by a Benedictine monk and a Buddhist monk.

Later that same day, I attended New Thought's meeting. New Thought began in the 1900's in America and is made up of the Church of Religious Science, Unity, the Church of Divine Science and the Christian Science church. I was able to meet with the directors and leaders of these various denominations. Their main premise is that we create our lives with our thoughts. These people are doing good work in the world.

Each day we would walk about five blocks to the site of the Parliament of World's Religions which was being held at the newly constructed Melbourne Civic Center. The Melbourne Civic Center is a gigantic beautiful construction that easily served the more than 5000 guests of the Parliament of World's Religions.

The Melbourne Civic and Convention center is so large that even after entering the doorway to the building we still had 1-3 blocks to walk to get to our class.

After the day's meetings and classes Barbara, Hezekiah, and I would return by walking back to our apartment. Most of the rest of the School of Metaphysics' representatives were housed in the same building with its apartments.

The next day Saturday, December 5, 2009 I attended the 8:00 am morning observance called, Zoroastrian Daily Morning Prayers and Worship.

I chose this Zoroastrian observance because I have had a very keen interest in this teaching ever since I first heard the word Zarathustra. Zarathustra or as the Greeks called him Zoroaster was an enlightened being and world teacher who lived in Persia (modern day Iran) sometime between 1100 BC and 600 BC.

The religion of Zarathustra spread all the way through the Middle East, through Persia, into India, Babylon, Turkey, Palestine and even to China. Wherever the Persian Empire went or expanded to, there also went the religion of Zarathustra. This religion sometimes called Zoroastrianism greatly influenced early Judaism, Christianity and

Islam. At the time of the birth of Jesus who became the Christ, Zoroastrianism was the dominant or main religion in the world.

After the morning observance and teaching was over, I talked to the presenters and was given a book about the life and teachings of Zarathustra. The author was present and autographed the book for me.

I told them of the great attraction I had to the name of Zarathustra and was glad to have finally met some people of that religion. I was also appreciative of being able to be present for a Zoroastrian spiritual ceremony.

Later that morning, I attended a class that proved to be central to my next evolutionary step. It was in actuality a quantum leap forward.

The presentation was held at 9:30-11:00 a.m. on Saturday December 5, 2009. This presentation was titled *Sri Chinmoy: A Spirituality of Transformation.*

I had an interest in Sri Chinmoy and his teachings since the 1993 Parliament of World's Religions that was held in Chicago, Illinois on the one hundred year anniversary of the first Parliament of World's Religions held at the 1893 Chicago World's Fair.

Sri Chinmoy had given a morning meditation experience for everyone at the 1993 Parliament of the World's Religions. So many people attended that the room was full. The event was televised in another room so that the overflow of people could observe Sri Chinmoy on camera as he led the morning meditation. My wife Barbara and I observed Sri Chinmoy on the television. I had looked forward to being with him in person. Therefore, when this opportunity came at the Parliament of World's Religions to attend a presentation of the life of Sri Chinmoy, I chose to attend.

The following are some quotes or sayings offered by Sri Chinmoy.

We come into the World to make others happy.
If we do this our life will be worthwhile.

The most effective medicine on this Earth is Love.

Peace of the Heart

No price is too great for Inner Peace.

To serve and never tire is Love.

It is only through Inner Peace that we can have true inner freedom.

To love others before we love ourselves is a rare achievement.

See the Divine qualities in others.

Love is the Essence of God's Divinity.

Gratitude is the Essence of Man's Divinity.

The heart reads only one book – God's Love. This book is sufficient.

To surrender to God's will constantly is the most difficult.

True service and one love – heart are all I need
to manifest Peace on Earth.

Love, Devotion and Surrender are 3 intimate friends
that are always found together.
Silence and Peace visit each other.

Peace is founded on forgiveness.

Peace is found in Self-giving.

*I am a reader only of inner books. What are these books,
Love, devotion and surrender.*

*When the Power of Love replaces the Love of Power,
man will have a new name – God.*

On Earth God loves the Peace Lovers most.

*Two Lovers, the Mind and the Heart
The Mind Loves
The Heart Loves*

Live in the here and now in the Present Moment.

Loving makes the soul loving.

All of these statements or quotes resonate with my open heart and mirror the experiences I have had with the open heart, the chakras, Kundalini and offering shaktipat, the Word or energy of the Divine to people I lead in meditation.

At the end of the class about Sri Chinmoy and his life, the presenters asked for questions.

I asked the following question: "Why is it that when I go to see these enlightened beings they have already died - passed away, withdrawn from the physical body?"

The answer from the presenters was, "We don't know, that is a good question."

As they were answering from the front of the room a woman came up the aisle to me and gave me a card. I was sitting on a chair next to the aisle and the woman came from the back of the room, behind me and handed me the card. She was not one of the presenters in the front of the room. On this card, slightly larger than a business card, was beautiful picture of Sri Chinmoy with a beautiful green background of plants-trees. Sri Chinmoy was smiling serenely in the picture. I found myself drawn into this picture and especially to his eyes. It seemed very significant to me, more so than any picture I had ever gazed at or into.

After the presentation was over I got up to thank the woman who had given me the card with Sri Chinmoy's picture on it. The woman, whose name I found out is Tahereh, told me she had been carrying around this picture for over two years and it kept falling out of this little metal card case or makeup case. Each time it would fall out she would put the card back in her purse.

Tahereh said, she had the thought, "maybe I should just take it out of my purse and put it someplace else" but that something just told her to keep it in this little case in her purse. Tahereh said – that when she heard me speak and ask the question – she knew I was the person she was supposed to give the picture to.

As Tahereh was speaking these words to me, wave after wave of shivers passed into my body. The energy seemed to come down from above throughout my body with the strongest place being my heart center.

I then told Tahereh this, and said, "I know the reason I never met Sri Chinmoy while he was in the physical body. The reason is because I am not supposed to be a devotee this lifetime. I am supposed to be a spiritual master, a master teacher, and a spiritual leader."

Then our discussion was over so I walked downstairs to the exhibit area where the different organizations booths were located. I went to the **Course in Miracles** booth. I sat down in a chair in the booth. The woman at the booth was crying while talking to a man. He was asking metaphysical type questions. I began to answer some of his questions and told him the work they (**The Course in Miracles** people) were doing was good work. After the man left the woman thanked me profusely saying she had been upset because she was at a loss for words as to how to describe the **Course in Miracles**.

Then another woman walked up and Helen introduced as Kristen. As Kristen stood in front of me and I was sitting on a straight chair and we were talking I felt the energy of my heart go out to her as it does when I hug someone who will receive Divine-Heart-Love through me or when I lead meditation and my heart goes out to someone or the whole group. At those times a pure white tube of energy goes from my heart to their heart.

This time, however, something new happened, as Kristen stood before me. Not only did my Heart chakra-Love energy go into her heart, in addition, all my chakras, including my 8th and 9th chakras sent out radiant energy to all Kristen's chakras and raised her Kundalini up through the crown of her head.

I said, "Do you experience-feel what I am giving you."

To which Kristen responded, "I can feel it!" She smiled in a state of ecstatic bliss. She received everything I was offering or that was being offered by the Universe-Divine through me.

I said to Kristin, "I LOVE YOU," and Kristin said, "I LOVE YOU TOO." And we loved each other, as I offered Divine Love and she received Divine Love.

After awhile, Kristin left to take care of a seeker-customer, and so I returned my attention once again to Helen. As I was talking with her an amazing Divine Love for her arose in me and again, as with Kristen, the chakra energy of Divine Love went from my Heart center and then all my chakras into Helen's chakras. Helen immediately said she felt the energy and was having this blissful experience. The same all chakras Divine-Love experience I offered to Kristen.

This was a dramatic breakthrough because now I can offer Divine Love through all 9 chakras whereas before this I offered Divine Love mainly through my Heart chakra.

The next two days, I experienced the chakras as if each chakra was pushing out from the front of my body. I experienced these chakras as very real, even physically real. I could feel them in the front of my chest and abdomen.

Two days later, I saw Kristin at the bottom of the escalator on the second floor. She was coming down and I was getting ready to go up. We talked and I received her info-business card. Then the Divine Love-Open Heart-All chakra energy went out of me into her again and she again went into a state of ecstatic bliss. She said, "We are so fortunate to have you at the Parliament of World's Religions.

Later that same day I went to the Sri Chinmoy booth and talked to the man running it. I told him my story about Sri Chinmoy and myself. I showed him the picture. He said, "I wondered where and how you got that picture because that card-picture was only given to those people present at Sri Chinmoy's memorial service. He passed away or transcended the body-Mahasamadhi on Oct. 11, 2007, which is more than 2 years ago. This now being December 2009."

The quote on this card is the last thing Sri Chinmoy wrote. He wrote it the night that he passed away. The quote says, *"My physical death is not the end of my life. I Am an Eternal journey."* So then both he and I knew that Sri Chinmoy had Tahereh carry that card with her for over 2 years so she could give it to me and so I would receive the gift, the power and consciousness of Sri Chinmoy.

Amazing and Wonderful.

All of this occurred on Saturday and I had until the following Tuesday before I gave my teaching as an 8:00 a.m. morning observance titled, **The Still Mind, Emptiness and Divine Love.**

Several presentations on sacred sites were offered. I attended several for the purpose of receiving other people's thoughts and experiences and knowledge of sacred sites. Several years ago, I received a vision from within of how to create a sacred site. This vision was implemented on the College of Metaphysics campus in southwest Missouri. It began by identifying the intersections of the ley lines on the 1500-acre campus. This I accomplished with my body, mind and consciousness. In order to be very specific about these locations I enlisted the aid of a School of Metaphysics student named John who had learned the art and science of dowsing. He showed me what he knew and using this we could identify the exact spot where the ley lines came together.

Next, it came to me that we were to construct octahedrons to place at the first of these ley lines. Then we planted a dodecahedron, then an icosahedron and finally a tetrahedron. These forms, together with the cube form of the Center for Student Life building, used all five platonic solids.

Planting these sacred geometric forms at the intersection of ley lines created a time-space intersect that balanced, freed, and healed the energy meridians of the living being known as Mother Earth.

Thus it was that I had a tremendous interest in Sacred Sites from around the World. Many of the sacred structures, sites from around the world are located at the intersections of the ley lines of the Earth, unbeknownst to the followers or most of the followers of the various religions that claim them as their own. This I was to find to be true for at every sacred site discussion or presentation I attended, I found absolutely no discussion or elucidation on ley lines and how they cause a sacred site to be.

There was no talk of ley lines until finally after attending several of these presentations. I realized the need to offer Truth and my experience so that people could know.

So when the presenters asked for questions at the end of one sacred site presentation I asked the following question:

"Why don't we just create new sacred sites?"

At the College of Metaphysics on our 1500-acre campus we have mapped out the ley lines which are the acupuncture meridians of the Earth. Then we planted sacred geometric forms at the intersections of the ley lines. It is these intersections of ley lines that create the True Sacred Sites. All the ancients knew this and erected their Sacred Sites at the intersections of these ley lines.

The people I asked these questions of really didn't have an answer to these questions, but after the presentation was over an Australian woman came up to me and said, "Well, I'm glad to hear there is someone here who knows about ley lines. I'm a dowser," she said.

To which I replied, "Now I know why you know about ley lines."

Then she went on to tell me that the aborigines of Australia have always known about ley lines and have always used them.
One of the ways they have used them is to communicate over hundreds of miles almost instantly.

She said that in the early days of the white men settlements, that when a white woman was having a baby that in order to contact the doctor or relatives that might be hundreds of miles away the white family would have an aborigine send the message. The aborigine would send the message down the ley line of the Earth and a different aborigine hundreds of miles away would receive the message along the ley line and give it to the doctor or relative.

The aborigine have been living in harmony with nature and Mother Earth for at least 50,000 years before the coming of the white man.

So I told the woman about my experiments with dowsing the College of Metaphysics campus. She said, "When you asked that question I knew you were a dowser."

I attended a meeting of those people who desired to sponsor and host the next Parliament of World's Religions. Many countries and cities were represented from around the Earth, such as Sweden, India, Taiwan, Phoenix, Dallas, and several others.

Dirk Ficca, the executive director of the Council for a Parliament of World's Religions, outlined the requirements needed to host the Parliament of World's Religions. The meeting was very informative and showed that this possibility exists for cities all over the world.

The days of the Parliament of World's Religions continued until Tuesday, December 8, 2009 arrived. This was the day scheduled for my Teaching during the Morning Observance from 8:00 a.m. to 9:00 a.m. the title of my teaching being *The Still Mind, Emptiness and Divine Love.*

I had thought about having to condense the teaching of the ***Still Mind, Present Moment, Open Heart*** from a day-long teaching to one hour.

By stilling my mind the answer of what I was to do and how to do it came to me.

I began by telling those attending of my life and the steps on leaps in

It brings me great joy and a renewed sense of hope to present Dr. Daniel Condron and the teaching of the Still Mind, the Present Moment, and the Open Heart.

I believe in the power of the Human Spirit, and I believe in the power of this teaching to unlock the doorways to high consciousness and transcend the limitations that separate each one of us from that Spirit. In this teaching, lies many keys or secrets imperative to the unlocking or cultivation of human potential, Divine Love, and understanding of the power of Emptiness therein, and the creative potential of Space.

I have been on the receiving end of Dr. Daniel's teachings for the past two plus years. I appreciate it greatly and with deep gratitude. It is a simple teaching and therein lies its power; for in simplicity is also depth and profundity. With this in mind may you breathe deeply, with great patience, and allow your Self to receive, the universe and its infinite abundance.

This teaching has been lifetimes in the making. As for this lifetime and this day's teaching, it is 30-plus years of Discipline, Service, and Teaching in the receiving, coming through this teacher's experience of transformation. I have experienced the fact that this teacher's consciousness is transferable. What we each have learned through our lives has created who we are now and what we have the capacity to bring to the present moment and every individual directly connected to it. I have learned this teaching is an experience that at best can be a direct transfer of consciousness, from teacher to student, to the degree the student is open and the teacher is willing.
I have always found this teacher to be willing to give. May your love deepen from these teachings and the connectedness of life become more real to you every moment of every day.

– Introduction given that morning
by Jesse Loren Reece

spiritual understanding I had achieved. Then I asked everyone to say to the person on their left, the following words, "Thank you, Gratitude." Then, the second person would say the same thing, this process continued for 5 minutes. Then we sat in still mind, open-eyed meditation.

For the second steps, I instructed everyone to say to themselves, "I ask for forgiveness," out loud for 5 minutes. I explained that this forgiveness could be for themselves, the world, or whoever they think has hurt them. That is the beauty and power of this statement. It works at whatever level one is willing to receive. Then we sat in the emptiness of the present moment.

The third step of my teaching was to have the people turn to their right and say to the person "I LOVE YOU, "and then the person receiving was to say "I LOVE YOU" in return. This continued for 5 minutes. Following this everyone sat in stillness with closed eyes and received my Open Heart of Divine Love to whatever degree they were capable and willing.

They also could receive from each other or the Divine, the All or they could just open the Heart.

All these things were possible and many wonderful things occurred. Many people came up to me after the teaching was complete and thanked me and said how much they had received. Some had tears in their eyes as they recounted the details of their deeply rewarding experience. In the days afterward, people would come up to me at the Parliament and tell me how much they had received, and to thank me.

The room was completely filled for the teaching and I was

fulfilled. I can see, foresee, and visualize and perceive this new teaching spreading all over planet Earth, enlightening and uplifting the consciousness of all the people.

The Still Mind, Present Moment, Open Heart is the key to knowing the whole Self and whole mind. It is also the key to World Peace.

The next to the last day in Melbourne, my wife Barbara and I had breakfast with the Dalai Lama at the convention center as did about 200 other people. The Dalai Lama has become, over the past 50 years, the world's spokesman for World Peace. Even though he was forced out of his own country and land by invaders, he has still remained compassionate while teaching Peace.

He talked for a while of peace and compassion after being introduced by an aborigine, a member of the indigenous people of Australia.

The original people of Australia, the Aborigines, have lived in Australia for over 50,000 years. They are amazing people. The rest of my time in Australia was spent meeting the people and seeing the sights of Melbourne with my wife and son Hezekiah, age 14. Just to travel to Australia, a country and continent half a planet away, on the other side of the equator, was amazing for anyone especially a 14-year-old boy, and then to attend the Parliament of World's Religions was amazing and life changing for him. It opened up so many possibilities and ideas for him. Since thought is cause, and this whole experience has affected him and his thoughts greatly, his creative abilities will be enhanced throughout his whole lifetime.

Dr. Barbara Condron gave two presentations. She was on a women's panel of education and giving. Each of the women represented a different religion. Barbara represented Christianity. This was very well received.

Barbara also gave a presentation class on the three ***Crown Jewels of Consciousness*** that was very well attended. Those present experienced the transcendent.

All in all a very uplifting and enlightening experience.∞

About the Author

Daniel R. Condron is a teacher, educator, writer, composer, recording/ producer, agriculturist, ecologist, landscape designer, dedicated to knowing Self and mind for over 30 years. He holds a Doctorates in Metaphysics and in Divinity (School of Metaphysics), Master of Science (University of Missouri) in Agricultural Economics, and he is a Certified Biofeedback Specialist.

After 25 years of meditation, service and teaching, Daniel developed the Still Mind. After 27 years of meditating, Daniel became aware of the Present Moment. After 28 years of meditating, Daniel, achieved an Open Heart. After 29 years of meditating, Daniel experienced the Emptiness. This "Emptiness" he explains in **The Emptiness Sutra**, *a book he wrote at the end of a two-hour still mind session class he taught on the College of Metaphysics campus.*

Dr. Condron is also the discoverer and developer of the sacred ley lines of the 1500-acre College of Metaphysics campus. He has supervised the planting of sacred geometric forms on the campus.

Dr. Condron has taken spiritual journeys to India in September 2006 and March 2008. While in India, Dr. Condron opened his eighth and ninth chakras and experienced bliss. He is the author of over a dozen books including, **The Emptiness Sutra, The Purpose of Life, Permanent Healing, The Still Mind, Present Moment, Open Heart, Understanding your Dreams,** *and* **Universal Healing Truths.**

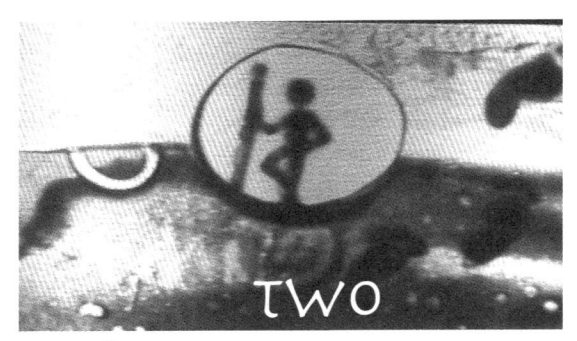

TWO

THE LAW of FREE WILL

"I MAKE CONSCIOUS CHOICES"
told by Erin Collins
12/31/09

"The great Tao flows everywhere;
It can go left; it can go right.
The myriad things owe their existence to it,
And it does not reject them.
When its work is accomplished,
It does not take possession.
It clothes and feeds all,
But does not pose as their master.
Ever without ambition,
It may be called Small.
All things return to it as their home,
And yet it does not pose as their master,
Therefore it may be called Great.
Because it would never claim greatness
Therefore its greatness is fully realized.
–Tao Te Ching 34

My experience in Melbourne, Australia was everything I knew it would be. I had wanted to travel for some time now. Traveling, meeting new people, experiencing new things is what keeps me going. It keeps life fresh and exciting for me.

Over a year ago, I had put on my "10 most wanted list" that I wanted to travel to another country for educational purposes. This meant that I did not want to travel just to lie on a beach or merely for recreation. I wanted to learn through experience.

December 7, 2008, I was invited to join fellow students and teachers of SOM to volunteer to help out at a pre-Parliament event held in Chicago. The Parliament of the World's Religions organization holds ideals that are dear to me personally. I share the vision of this organization which is stated on their website as:

> The vision of the Council for a Parliament of the World's Religions is of a just, peaceful and sustainable world in which:
>
> · *Religious and spiritual communities live in harmony and contribute to a better world from their riches of wisdom and compassion*
>
> · *Religious and cultural fears and hatreds are replaced with understanding and respect*
>
> · *People everywhere come to know and care for their neighbors*
>
> · *The richness of human and religious diversity is woven into the fabric of communal, civil, societal and global life*
>
> · *The world's most powerful and influential institutions move beyond narrow self-interest to realize common good*
>
> · *The Earth and all life are cherished, protected, healed and restored*
>
> · *All people commit to living out their highest values and aspirations.*

DREAMTIME

When I learned of the opportunity to be involved in something so great for our planet I felt no other choice but to say YES! I saw hope in that experience in Chicago. I met wonderful people, worked along side them, and learned about different cultures and religions from presenters which helped me to appreciate what they had to offer to our planet. That day is the day I learned that the main Parliament which is only held every 5 years would be held the next year in Melbourne, Australia.

Australia had been a destination I wanted to experience for many years. It was one of those moments that felt too good to be true. I knew I had to be a part of this. As the months passed other things in life came up. My youngest sister got married which meant I had to put out a lot of cash for gifts, showers, parties, a dress, travel, etc. My car stopped working and I had to buy a new one since I rely on a car for transportation. Other things came up and I started thinking that I will not make it to Australia this year. It would cost way too much.

I had a moment of clarity one day after much meditation on the subject. I realized I was limiting myself with my thoughts. Of course I wouldn't make it to Australia this year if kept thinking this way. I decided right then and there that I WAS going to Australia. I would make it happen and it would happen. I knew that's all it would take.

FOR ME TO MAKE A DECISION WAS GRANTING ME THE POWER TO MAKE IT HAPPEN.

It was such a freeing realization and very empowering. Once I decided I was going, that was it. Next thing was to figure out how.

Everything seemed to come together once I had made the decision. I made sure to save enough vacation days at work. I made sure to save enough money for the plane ticket and the registration fees for the conference. I decided to volunteer for the conference which meant I would have a significant discount on registration fees. That was another great decision. Not just because of the money but because of the opportunity of experience it would provide.

Because I was a volunteer, I was able to take advantage of the home-stay program they had set up. I was going to stay in someone's home for 8 nights and only have to pay the $50 application fee. Everything was just falling into place to manifest exactly what I wanted. I thought of an old friend I had met in previous travels. He happens to live in the large country of Australia. I found our last correspondence from 6 years ago and sent him a letter telling him about the Parliament and the trip I was planning.

It turns out that he lives in Melbourne, would be happy to see me, to pick me up from the airport, and to clear out a bedroom for me to stay in for a week. Even better than that, he took the week off of work to be my personal tour guide. We really had a great week together; renewing our friendship which I would definitely say is divine. We did everything that I had wanted to do. All I had to do was put it out there and it happened. We went on a two day road trip up and down the Great Ocean Road. We visited animal and floral sanctuaries. I saw a cricket game, ate delicious, fresh baked meat pie. I even ate a vegemite sandwich, which I can honestly say, is not very tasty. I met his family and visited with them. I really got a great taste of being a local in just one week.

For the second week in Melbourne, the conference would be starting. My friend drove me into the city to transfer me to my new friend who had volunteered to host me as a visitor to the Parliament. This was another divine friendship in the works. We were excited to meet each other from our first email exchange. We had similar taste and interests and some fabulous and stimulating conversations. I met her friends, she took me to her church where I was welcomed with open arms and again was able to immerse myself in the local culture. Now the conference was about to begin and I had already had an enriching experience of friendship and worldly observation.

DREAMTIME

My first day in the central business district of the city was incredible. First I had to take a bus and then a train and then walk along the river to arrive at the convention center. I was very nervous to be on my own, in a strange city, taking public transportation. This would mean that I only had myself to make decisions for. I was afraid I wouldn't get there. That I would take the wrong bus or not get off the train at the right stop. I reasoned with myself that what was the worse that would happen? That I would get lost? In that case, I would learn to speak up and ask for directions.

I was up for the challenge.

I am proud to say that I made no wrong turns and I arrived at the desired destination with time to spare. It was a day to see my independence shine. I arrived at the convention center for my first volunteer shift. I would be working the registration area which was the only area open on this first day.

The majority of the participants and speakers/presenters at this conference arrived this day to check in with their registration. It was a very busy day. I quickly realized that there was not too much organization when it came to the duties of the volunteers. It was pretty much assumed that I would have to be proactive and find a place where I was needed.

I found a place right away doing what I do best, talking to people, greeting them with my smile, and then making sure that this line that was the length of the convention center was in-fact, the correct line for them. How much fun that was! I literally spoke to every person in that line for hours. Some recognized my accent which would start a conversation, or we would just talk about how happy and excited we all were to be there.

Everyone was so happy, so cheerful, and helpful. It was a terrific environment. I befriended another woman who was a volunteer working the line with me. She was very funny, introducing herself with a joke. We took to each other right away. Throughout this long first day I found myself at different stations, helping wherever needed. I seemed to keep finding myself working alongside my new friend Jean. She was such a nice, older woman, who seemed to know a lot about what was going on so I think I gravitated toward her, to learn from her.

I found out later that this fantastic volunteer, Jean, was the wife of the Chair of the Council for the Parliament of the World's Religions. I realized then what this conference was made of. Every person in attendance truly wanted to be there. Every one of them was there to make a difference in our world. I spent a volunteer shift standing at a directional sign with the daily programs on it. I was asked to just stand there, smile, and be helpful. Again this job was what I was perfectly suited for.

By standing at this sign I had the opportunity to smile and talk to everyone who passed me. These were presenters, long time participants, and even people who wandered in off the street because it sounded interesting. I spoke with one woman at that sign for a good twenty minutes just about what a wonderful vibe the entire conference and its people were giving off. I talked to presenters on their way to their session. I talked to presenters on their way to listen to someone else's presentation.

I got to talking to one gentleman about the session he was on his way to and we both figured that 1/3 of all participants were presenters themselves. The people I encountered did not seem above or below anyone else. I felt all were equal and all were welcome. It was a very empowering feeling in itself to be included with this group as one of them. We were all there for a greater purpose. I am so blessed to be a part of that.

I sat and listened to a panel discussing Jesus through different religious texts.

I listened to a choir sing.

I listened to a native Aboriginal Elder tell her story and her parents' story and how their lives are affected today.

I listened to a brilliant woman speak on the art of bead work and how every creation we can make is a reflection of ourselves.

I watched a very important film on war in the name of God.

I experienced all of this right alongside some great people. It helped me to know that I can be great too, that I am great to be in such company.

This experience was everything I knew it would be. My dream come true is that people, leaders, from all over the planet can get together, share their stories, and listen all for the common goal which is peace. In Melbourne, Australia, I witnessed this dream and I have never been so excited to keep on dreaming bigger dreams.∞

About the Author
Erin Collins currently lives in Chicago, Illinois. She loves to travel, meet new people and have new experiences every day. Erin works for a medical education association and also for a public library.

"I MAKE CONSCIOUS CHOICES"
PARABLE 2

told by Dr. Sheila Benjamin

The INVITATION Real Time

I portray Mother Teresa of Calcutta in *The INVITATION*.

When we were still in the United States, the cast got together and we discussed the way that we would present *The INVITATION*. We were going to dress in street clothes as we normally might, and talk in our own voices, without adopted accents. To keep our connection with our laureate strong, we talked about bringing a physical item that would resonate with that person.

I realized, once I landed in Melbourne, that I did not bring my rosary, which was going to be my object. This opened the door for me to ask many different people here if they had one. One of the people I asked was a priest. He had one, however, he needed it for his own prayers.

This morning, the 6th of December, the day we are offering *The INVITATION* at the Unity Church, I still have no rosary.

Laurel and I decide to attend their service this morning. Turns out, the train stop we were given for disembarking is incorrect, however, guess what is right in front of us when we got off? You're right, it's a Catholic Church! They are in-between masses, so I enter and purchase a rosary, all the while inviting all of the people I meet to come to *The INVITATION* that afternoon.

I have practiced and offered *The INVITATION* dozens of times over the past four years. I know this one will be different. Delivering Mother Teresa's words as Sheila Benjamin feels as if I am reading her speech. I find in some ways Mother Teresa to be even more profound to me when I am speaking her words instead of receiving her into my thoughts first. I think it is so different because I am hearing Mother Teresa's words from a different and new perspective. Her words are the same, my experience is what has changed.

In the Peace Dome at the College of Metaphysics, The INVITATION is given in the round. The laureates interact in the center space. They are the focal point of all the action with the audience seated around them.

In the rectangular Melbourne Unity Church, each of the cast members are seated in the audience throughout the whole presentation. We are scattered amongst the individuals who came to witness the performance. In this way, they have become part of the performance. We are like them, so they can become like us. The message we want to convey is that anyone of us, at anytime, can make choices that result in becoming recognized as a Nobel Peace Prize Laureate.

A Life Worth Examining, a film Paul Madar very mindfully put together, makes its debut today. The film shows pictures of the lives and experiences of each of the laureates. It is an addition to our presentation which was stimulated by feedback that we received at the Chicago premiere a year ago. It was suggested that a way to put the play into context would make it more understandable to those not aware of the histories of these people.

Months before the cast chose words that described the turning point in each of the laureate's lives. We wanted to capture the point where each decided to devote their time on earth to service. Paul then took our narrations and put them with actual footage.

The film is very moving. It is the first time any of us have seen it and it prepares all of us for what is to come.

Dr. Barbara Condron introduces *The INVITATION* to those gathering, then, one by one, we go up to the front of the church to deliver our laureate's opening speech. Gazing upon the audience, I can tell they are moved by what is being said. I see people nodding their heads in agreement as I say Mother Teresa's words: "no one is home to receive them (children) and they go to the streets and get involved in something."

Before we leave the altar to go to new seats, we receive "the invitation" from Barbara: a copy of the *Universal Peace Covenant*.

Once all the laureates have spoken, we are seated in the audience, surrounded by an entirely new group of people. We recite in union, *"Peace is the breath of our spirit. It wells up within the depths of our being. To refresh. To heal. To inspire!"*

I can tell that the people in the audience want to read along or follow along as they look in their program expecting to find the words. They are not there. The experience of the *Peace Covenant* is first received, it is first heard. I expect this will make the *Peace Covenant* that they will receive at the end even more important.

The chairs in the church are arranged in a horseshoe formation. This leaves an open space in the center of the church where each of the people seated can easily see what is going on. This is the space that we use as we pair off with another Laureate. I have to say that I have gotten quite used to walking with Paul as the Dalai Lama (pictured at left). Freed of the interaction between us "in character", I find myself moving my vision and looking into the faces of the individuals in the audience.

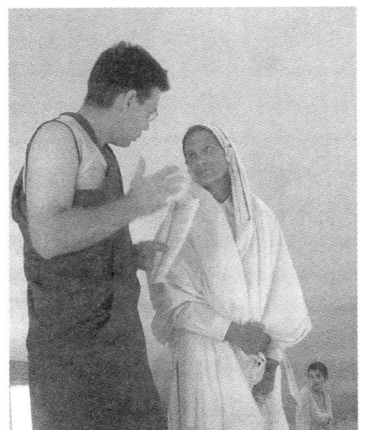

After our meeting, when Paul and I return to new seats in the audience, we remain standing. One by one each of the laureates give their final words. This is a profound moment for each of us. I watch as the audience moves their attention to each of the cast members when each speaks. This is the moment when the laureate's words and the Peace Covenant are laced together in such an artistic way.

Afterwards, a woman comes up to me in tears. She is so thankful that we are there, that I brought Mother Teresa to her. She tells me her mother worked with Mother Teresa and that she has always had a warm place in her heart for the Sister of Charity.

I speak with another woman who expresses her gratitude for her experience. She provides in-school English language courses in the United Kingdom. As we talk, she says she would have loved to see us in full costume. I tell her that I will be happy to send her a copy of **The INVITATION** on DVD. She is very happy. My expectation is that **The INVITATION** may become one of the courses in her program.

Another man wonders how we can remember the words so well. I explain that it is an action of visualization. For me, I can relate to many of the stories that Mother Teresa's words communicate. I hold those images in my mind as I say her words.

There is an expansion that **The INVITATION** experiences in Melbourne. It is more than premiering it on another continent. It is an inner expansion of Spirit. What happened at Unity in Melbourne brought what we do closer to the people. I can only imagine the difference we all will experience the next time we offer our living prayer in The Peace Dome.∞

About the Author
A charismatic speaker, Dr. Sheila Benjamin has devoted her life to serving and uplifting Humanity. A teacher of metaphysics since 1979, she lectures, designs workshops and presentations, and gives sermons to health practitioners, civic organizations, public schools, colleges and universities, senior groups as well as professional groups and businesses. She has brought Mother Teresa of Calcutta to life in the play The INVITATION since 2005.

Dr. Benjamin earned degrees in science from Southern Illinois University and metaphysics and divinity from the School of Metaphysics. A certified counselor, an ordained minister in the Interfaith Church of Metaphysics and an Intuitive Reporter, her essays appear in the books **Lucid Dreaming, How to Raise an Indigo Child,** *and* **Total Recall.**

IT IS AN INNER EXPANSION OF SPIRIT.

From the freshness of Erin's self-discovery as a creator to Sheila's deliberate, long-standing nurturing of the ideal of a life of service, these two women demonstrate the extremes life offers each one of us. When we choose, we experience freedom. When we are free, we learn how to respond, then we come to understand the true nature of Self.

Erin was inspired to overcome the limits of her own willful imagination. Through fulfilling personal desire she came to realize higher purposes in life. Through living for a higher purpose, Sheila came to new levels of Self fulfillment.

This is why the ancients taught that all roads lead to Olympus. We merely choose our route and the duration of the journey.

Those who hear the calling use their choice in outstanding ways. Their journey is well noted, studied by others, who would also choose the life worth examining. The inner voice becomes their guide, and paradoxically, the choices of the temporal mind fall away like leaves in the autumn wind as Divine Will establishes dominion.

"Thy will be done on earth as it is in Heaven." This is what it means to make conscious choices. -BC

"I MAKE CONSCIOUS CHOICES"

PARABLE 3 told by the cast of THE INVITATION

One year before giving *The INVITATION* in Melbourne, the play premiered in Chicago during the PreParliament event organized by the CPWR. This great honor became an open door for the play's natural evolution.

Someone suggested that the presentation could be more meaningful if placed in context. We were aware that the power of *The INVITATION* is the window it provides into history, for the cast as well as the audience. Upon discussing how we might make it easier for people unfamiliar with Albert Schweitzer or Betty Williams or Shirin Ebadi, we came upon the idea of a short film that could capture the spirit of each person's calling.

Being metaphysicians, we could employ the powers of visualization in this work. The script was created by the cast including Tad Messenger, Sheila Benjamin, Ryan Jones, Paul Madar, John Harrison, Pam Blosser, Christine Madar, Laurel Clark and Barbara Condron. Each had spent hours researching the thoughts and actions of the laureate they bring to life. Original cast members – Messenger, Harrison, and Paul Madar – had spent years coming to understand and know the individual they portray. This mind melding allowed for a certain intimacy to come alive in choosing the words that best describe that laureate's "defining moment."

Paul, who brings His Holiness the Dalai Lama to life, researched photos of the historical conditions existing during the time of the eight Nobel Laureates featured in the program. By arranging these images to synchronize with the words spoken, history comes alive. The pictures convey a thousand words.

In just 16 minutes, the film brings to the viewer's attention the real needs that fueled each laureate's commitment to action. The emotional impact of the highlight of their lives provides the audience with context, and hopefully sufficient impetus for future study.

The choices we make in life determine the course of our lives. They also determine the outcome for all of us. Twenty-five hundred years ago, Socrates encouraged his students to challenge the accepted beliefs of the time and think for themselves. At the time, such free thinking and self-determination were considered heresy against the state. Those convicted faced a death sentence.

While on trial for this offense, Socrates was offered the opportunity to live in confinement rather than face death. This was the circumstance that prompted this man, who had devoted his life to examining the world around him and discussing how to make that world a better place, to utter one of his most frequently cited observations: "The unexamined life is not worth living."

Certainly the challenges of Socrates' time remain in our world today. In modern technological times, anyone's life is up for examination. All forms of media, including the internet, make this possible in a way previously inconceivable. As a result what is now dawning in the collective consciousness that is humanity is the value of what we see. Increasingly, we find ourselves in a position to judge the worthiness of ideas and conduct. What kind of individual celebrates the human race? *The Invitation* gives an answer. Paul Madar's film – *A Life Worth Examining* – teaches us how such a person comes to be.

A LIFE WORTH EXAMINING

On 27 November 1895, Alfred Nobel signed his last will and testament, giving the largest share of his fortune to a series of prizes for individuals outstanding in their fields. As described in Nobel's last will and testament, one part of his fortune was dedicated to "the person who shall have done the most or the best work for fraternity between nations, for the abolition or reduction of standing armies and for the holding and promotion of peace congresses." This award has become known as the Nobel Peace Prize.

Albert Schweitzer
German theologian, musicologist, medical missionary
Nobel Peace Prize 1952

Germany 1910s

At an early age I was so fascinated with a statue of an African, his face with its sad, thoughtful expression, spoke to me of the misery of the dark continent. I promised myself to devote the first thirty years of my life to study philosophy, theology, and music, and the rest of my life in service to humanity. When I was 29 years old, I saw a magazine, a journal of missions on my father's desk. It was calling for doctors to work in Africa, and I immediately knew, this was my long sought destiny.

Linus Pauling
American scientist, peace activist, Nobel laureate in science 1954
Nobel Peace Prize 1962

United States 1950s

After the first bomb was dropped on Japan, I was asked to speak about the nature of nuclear fission. I was able to speak as freely as I wanted to because I didn't have any classified information. As I gave more and more lectures on this topic, I began to insert my own opinions about nuclear testing.

Martin Luther King, Jr.
American clergyman, civil rights leader
Nobel Peace Prize 1964
Georgia, 1950s
In the summer of 1955, Rosa Parks was arrested for refusing to give up her seat on a bus to a white man. The black community met and decided to boycott the busses. I was asked to lead the boycott and I readily agreed. It was an opportunity to fulfill my desire to cause massive social change, through love, and by using peaceful, nonviolent social protest.

Betty Williams
North Ireland office worker
Nobel Peace Prize 1976
Ireland 1970s
As it turned off the main road, a car came careening out of control and slammed into a woman and her children. I was the first one onto the scene. I remembered holding little Joann in my arms, covered in her blood and whispering in her ear, "I love you" and saying to myself, "I've got to do something to make sure that this doesn't happen to any more children in Northern Ireland."

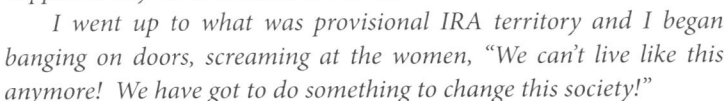

I went up to what was provisional IRA territory and I began banging on doors, screaming at the women, "We can't live like this anymore! We have got to do something to change this society!"

Within six hours, we had 5000 signatures for peace. Then I was asked to go on the television and I had the opportunity to say to the women of Ireland, "Please, if you feel like I do, join me in a rally on Saturday at the church."

In one powerful act of love, we wiped out 850 years of bad history. We just ran into each other's arms. Ten thousand women turned up for that first rally.

Mother Teresa of Calcutta
Macedonian Roman Catholic nun, missionary
Nobel Peace Prize 1979

India 1940s

Life outside of the convent walls were not unknown to me. I would hear stories from my students who would visit patients at the hospital. Hearing about the bitter poverty the people in the slums lived in. I was aware that beyond the convent walls, people died in misery, alone, and in dirty conditions.

These were desperate times. There was great hostility between Muslims and Hindus, and this left hundreds to die. In August, 1946, the fighting was so bad that the streets of the city were rendered horror zones. Water was polluted, food was scarce, and the dying were left in the streets. I heard the calling, an inner command to leave Loreletta, the convent, to serve the poor in the streets. The message was quite clear. I felt God wanted something more from me, he wanted me to be poor and to love him in the distressing disguise in the poorest of the poor.

Alva Myrdal
Swedish sociologist, ambassador
Nobel Peace Prize 1982

Sweden 1960s

In 1961, I was introduced to the work of nuclear weapons disarmament. Having completed an assignment as Sweden's diplomat to India, I was waiting for a future assignment. My boss, the foreign minister of Sweden, asked me to prepare a report on possible disarmament proposals that he might make on Sweden's behalf on his farewell speech to the U.N. General Assembly. I asked him to give me two weeks to gather material together. Thereby, I plunged myself into the debate material and writings which were coming out at the time.

Well, to make the tale brief, once I had begun, I was never able to stop the search for the whys and hows of something so senseless as the arms race.

The 14th Dalai Lama of Tibet
Exiled Spiritual and Temporal leader of Tibet
Nobel Peace Prize 1989
Tibet 1950s
In 1950, I was called upon to assume full political power after China's invasion of Tibet in 1949. The next nine years saw a full scale military take over of Tibet by China. Finally, in 1959, with the brutal suppression of the Tibetan National uprising in Lhasa by Chinese troops, I was forced to escape into exile. I slipped past the thousands of people who had gathered. Three weeks after leaving Lhasa, we reached the Indian border.

Shirin Ebadi
Iranian Lawyer, Judge
Nobel Peace Prize 2003
Iran 1980s
When I was one of many who protested against the Shah and wanted him to be overthrown, when that did happen, at first there was a great feeling of pride and joy that the revolution was going to bring about a new age in our country.

I had willingly and enthusiastically participated in my own demise!

I was a woman and this revolution victory demanded my defeat. I was asked at first to cover my hair. Never in my entire life had I covered my hair. I was ordered to be removed from my position as a judge. I had been a judge since I was 20 years of age and women could no longer hold that position.

Then I discovered that what used to be laws to bring about equality, no longer existed.

There was a group of university students who took hostages of diplomats in the American embassy. The government praised them and considered these students to be heroes, who had taken people hostages!

The laws turned the clock back 1400 years, to the early days of Islam, the days when stoning women for adultery and chopping off the hands of thieves were considered appropriate sentences.∞

I HEARD THE CALLING, AN INNER COMMAND... THE MESSAGE WAS QUITE CLEAR.

—MOTHER TERESA

The Invitation *is available on dvd, and the script is published by the School of Metaphysics. Performance rights are available at www.peacedome.org. The play is presented each fall in the Peace Dome to commemorate the dome's dedication to humanity as a universal site for peace. As a result of our experiences in Chicago and Melbourne, sound and sight have entered into* ***The Invitation.*** *The play now includes four, well-placed songs capturing the spirit of the laureate's message, a suggestion from the music director at Melbourne Unity, and each laureate holds a candle to symbolize the ebb and flow of awareness in humankind's journey toward living peaceably. These additions give a dimension to the experience of the play that is universal. It is our expectation that, as time progresses, many people around the world will bring the ideas, principles, and practices of these individuals to light thus encouraging the maturing of will in Self and in humanity.*
–BC

THREE
THE LAW of DUALITY

54

DREAMTIME

"I VALUE THE AGGRESSIVE & RECEPTIVE"
PARABLE 1

told and photographed
by Elena Dubinski
December 3-9, 2009

*"If God removes his hand,
the world will end."*
  −a Traditional African Proverb

I came to Australia with the group that represented the School of Metaphysics from the USA. Some of the people in my group have participated at Parliaments before; for me it was a first time. I had no idea what to expect, so I was open to all new experiences. And I had plenty of them!

I was very encouraged to see how representatives from many religions were saying that we have One God but different beliefs. We all have to come together in peace, with respect to each other's beliefs, to save our beautiful planet Earth. We can coexist with one another in peace! This will help to stop a lot of miscommunications and misunderstandings. It will also help stop and prevent any possible wars! We can make it happen; we just need to bring the Parliament's enthusiasm back to our countries and continue to spread it around the World! If we all get together, then we can do it!!! Let Peace prevail on Earth!

One of the most inspiring and memorable experiences that I would like to share is the construction of the sand mandala. Wikipedia defines the sand mandala as "a Tibetan Buddhist tradition involving the creation and destruction of mandalas made from colored sand. A sand mandala is ritualistically destroyed once it has been completed and its accompanying ceremonies and viewing are finished to symbolize the Buddhist doctrinal belief in the transitory nature of material life."

Day One.
I was walking on the second level of the

Melbourne Convention and Exhibition Center. My attention was drawn to the two monks doing something at a table located in the middle of the Tibetan setup. I came closer and saw that they were working on a sand mandala. The mandala was getting constructed on the mandala base with measured lines. The monks were applying colored sand through the end of a metal funnel which was rasped against another funnel. To create a different design, funnels with various sized openings were use by monks. I was amazed to see how much patience, persistence and stillness were needed to work on the sand mandala!

Day Two.

The sand mandala was getting bigger. Millions of grains of colored sand scrupulously were placed on a flat platform. Section by section the mandala was coming to a beautiful creation.

Day Three.

I was looking forward to a new day to see the sand mandala. I was trying to bring back to memory all the information that I knew about it.

Usually, the mandala has inner, outer, and secret meanings. On the outer level, the mandala represents the world in its divining form. On the inner, it represents enlightenment. The secret level depicts the perfect balance of body and mind.

Day Four.

My heart would stop beating when I was emerging all my being into the beauty of the sand mandala. I was realizing that the sand mandala teaches simply "being here and now".

Day Five.

What an amazing creation this sand mandala! The bigger it was getting, the more people it was attracting. I noticed that people were spending a longer time by the table with the sand mandala. I was noticing that their facial expressions were becoming calm and peaceful with a definite sign of bliss present. I was thinking that the sand mandala could help create a gateway to pure bliss, peace, healing and harmony in the world.

Day Six.

The completion of the sand mandala was getting close to an end. Many hours of marvelous work were about to deliver to the world a beautiful creation. Mesmerized by its perfection, I was able to see how the construction of the sand mandala would help one to reach enlightenment. How it would help one to free from all obstacles, and become filled with compassion and wisdom. I was feeling the peace and healing of this powerful work of living art which has been generated.

Day Seven.

The construction of the sand mandala was over! An amazing piece of art was presented. I knew that the mandala was created in the spirit of impermanence and non-attachment and it was waiting to be washed away.

"ALL CREATED THINGS PERISH,'
HE WHO KNOWS AND SEES THIS
BECOMES PASSIVE IN PAIN;

The destruction of the sand mandala was performed in the ceremony.

Monks were following a specific order till the last section of the mandala has been dismantled.

The sand was collected in a jar which was then wrapped in silk and transported to a river where it was released back into nature. It was beautiful!

I will remember this amazing experience for the rest of my life! ∞

THIS IS THE WAY TO PURITY."
— THE DHAMMAPADA

About the Author

Elena Dubinski was born in the city of Mosty, Grodno region, Republic Belarus-former Soviet Union, into a family of teachers on October 19, 1968. Elena and her older brother were raised in a loving family. Growing up, Elena had a wide variety of interests and hobbies. She learned how to play the violin, knitted, sewed, crocheted, and macraméd. Other hobbies include straw handcrafts, photography, cooking, and gardening. Elena loved to read and spent every available minute doing it. Also, Elena loved sport activities. She did kayaking, camping, swimming, judo, as well as rifle shooting.

In High School, Elena served as a Vice President of the High School Youth Komsomol Organization. After graduating high school with exemplary grades, Elena was admitted to the Grodno Medical Institute in 1986. In 1991 she came to America for a visit and stayed for 3 years. In 1994, Elena moved back to Belarus and in 1997 immigrated to USA. That same year Elena went back to school to continue to work on her education. In 2001, she earned a BS in Physical Therapy from the University of Indiana. In 2008, she received a MBA from Anderson University.

Currently, Elena resides in Carmel, IN with her son and mother, and works as a Physical Therapist at St. Vincent's Rehabilitation Center. Since 2008, Elena has been a student at the Indianapolis School of Metaphysics.

"I VALUE THE AGGRESSIVE & RECEPTIVE"
PARABLE 2

told by Dr. Sheila Benjamin

Sacred Selfish Service... through Volunteering

Throughout my life I have found that being of service has provided me with great fulfillment. Volunteering at the Parliament of the World's Religions provided space to meet some very fascinating individuals. I know that several of the people that each of us met through this avenue are and will continue to be friends of the School of Metaphysics.

There is a continued appreciation that I have for the work that we do especially since all of us give from a place of service and love knowing that in return our souls will be richer. This is a unique idea in our world since most are motivated by material gain instead of soul enrichment.

Dr. Laurel Clark and I met two beautiful men the first day that we volunteered. Through our conversations with these two men, I found out that they had just met. I had thought that they had been friends for a long time because of the love that they shared between them. Shekhar, the man who lived in Melbourne had just found out about the Parliament through his friend, Phiroz. It was through

Phiroz's suggestion that Shekhar came to the conference center and volunteered.

Both of these men had been born in India. Shekhar was a very gentle and kind man. You could see it in his face. He shared a heart-warming story. One of his missions is to spread peace to other parts of the world that need some help. He has a very simple but profound project that he does. He gets long sheets of paper and creates a scroll upon which he invites anyone to share their thoughts of peace, their messages of peace, their thoughts for hope (see picture, opposite page).

He said that about 6 months ago (sometime in June of 2009) there had been a very large bush fire which had taken the lives of many, destroyed homes and killed many of the animals. What he did was go into the schools in Melbourne and ask the children to share their thoughts of love, peace and hope with the children who had been in this destructive fire. The children of Melbourne drew pictures on this scroll, wrote poems and other things. After he had gotten several yards of messages he went to the area of Australia which had experienced the fire and delivered the scroll to the children of this area. As the children received the messages of love from the children in Melbourne, Shekhar filmed the children who had received these messages of inspiration, expressing their thankfulness to the children of Melbourne. He shared with us that there were children who would say thank you, my pet dog was killed in the fire, I lost my family, and stories of that nature.

When he returned home to Melbourne he shared his film with the children of Melbourne. These children were changed knowing that they had cared enough to give to others whom they had never met before. They had learned how connected we all really are.

As Shekhar was sharing what he had done, it brought tears to my eyes because it was such a small and profound thing to connect with others through our hearts. He knew that in troubled times that it is important not only for the people of the area to know that people care but that it could change everything if the heads of states and countries could receive hopeful thoughts.

His next project was to have a scroll where people could share their thoughts of peace with the leaders and people of Copenhagen,

Denmark, who would be at a summit. When he found out about the Parliament of the World's Religion coming together he wanted to have it available for all of the people who were coming together from around the world to sign. In the beginning, the staff of the Parliament thought that if they had allowed Shekhar to do this then others as well would want to do their thing so he had thought he would need to have his scroll placed outside the convention center.

As time progressed he was able to have it in one of the passageways inside of the conference center, where the heart of the Parliament of the World's Religions was meeting. The length of time that he could keep it available to those who were attending the Parliament and who were passing through this public building continued to be extended. At one point, I made a comment to him about the fact that his scroll remained available to others and he said to me, "It is now a part of the Parliament."

He was also allowed on the last day to show the film which he had filmed of the children who had experienced the bush fire, expressing their gratitude to the children in Melbourne for their messages of hope and of care. This was such an active display of the Law of Abundance and Prosperity, in the sense that Shekhar did not aggressively seek after all that he received, he merely asked the Parliament and waited for the rest of the Divine Plan to unfold. I see this as working in Harmony with the Universal Laws because his whole thought was to aid the people and heads of states in Denmark to a place of hope, peace and love and in return he was able to tell his story. His story was also told to the people of Melbourne, as there was an article in the newspaper and a picture of people signing the scroll.

As You Give, So Shall You Receive

One of my duties as a volunteer was to man the registration desk. I found that I was able to bring some stability to this area. It appeared that there were many times when the people in charge did not know what to do with us volunteers, so my initiative to seek areas where I could be of assistance helped those in charge to relax.

As I was manning the registration desk I was able to meet a lot of interesting people from around the world. You just never know who you might meet when your heart is open. That day as I was taking care of those who needed to register, I was able to help Michael Beckwith and Rickie Byers-Beckwith.

I said to Michael, "I know you, you were in the movie, *The Secret*."

He immediately turned to his wife and told me that she was leading a group of people who would be offering their music at the Sacred Music Presentation. At that time, I was unfamiliar with the Agape Choir.

I soon found out what a powerfully inspiring group of spiritual singers they are. Rickie Byers-Beckwith was especially attractive to me. I had the good fortune of being able to see the Agape Choir sing in a smaller room the day before the Sacred Music performance. When Rickie got up in front of the room she commanded the attention of the whole group. She was able to get all of us involved. One of the things that she said was that music was much more than sitting back and listening. When each and every one of us is a part of it, it fills our whole being. She got us all singing.

After listening to the Agape choir sing once again at the Sacred Music performance (at left), I went to bed that night with the music from one of the songs in my thoughts, "I want to live in a Wholly, holy way. I want to serve in a Wholly, holy way. I want to love in a Wholly, holy way." I woke up with the same words in my mind. They stayed with me all day and when I ran into Paul Madar, he had said that he too was singing the words in his head. Just sharing this with you right now activates the memory of the experience.

My desire is for the Agape Choir to get to know us because I think that we could collectively do what we all came to do. One of the members of the Agape Choir sang at the Unity Church where the School of Metaphysics presented *The INVITATION*. Faith Rivera needed to get back to practice for the Sacred Music concert, and she was disappointed that she was not going to be able to be present for the play. I assured her that I would send her a DVD of the performance so that she could experience it in virtual form. I imagine the spaces and places where this can go.

I also think that Rickie would love to hear the music on the *Hope* CD, since I know Paul Madar's compositions were inspired by different Holy Works.

What will Michael think when he reads Dr. Laurel Clark's **The Law of Attraction and Other Secrets of Visualization?**

What I received from this is that we are all connected. We can illuminate the planet in greater ways as we discover each other and make a more secure connection. With so many light bringers, doors can be open to allow many people to walk in.

Young and Old, Death and Birth

As a volunteer, I was also sent to a room where all the speakers were sent to register before they spoke. This was a place where if the speakers needed to have their presentations downloaded into the electronic system being used, they came here.

As I was volunteering, I met a group of young men who called themselves "Pedaling for Peace." When I asked them questions about what that meant, they told me they came to Melbourne from Sydney pedaling all the way a ten-hour or so trip by car. One of the men was the filmmaker and he was documenting their journey.

In this group, there were young people in their early 20's who were from different religious backgrounds. Many of these individuals were positioned in life so that they could be a big influence on the youth of Sydney. One was a tennis coach, another an archery coach, and so forth. They each were touching hundreds of children's lives.

On their way to Melbourne, they had stopped at different schools and at other places children gather to interact and teach. Their mission was to communicate a peaceful coexistence among many.

I spent a great deal of time talking to one young man whose name is Mohammed. You guessed it, he is Muslim. He told me that as they go into these classrooms they don't tell the children their names. They ask the kids to guess what religion each of them practice. The purpose for this is to test the children and to let them realize how much they may judge another for the way that they look.

Mohammed stated that he is often guessed more accurately because he is so dark and middle eastern looking, however there is a young man who looks very Asian and of Oriental descent. He is often guessed as being a Buddhist and is very much a Christian. Their desire is to open up the minds and hearts of the youth and help them become free of prejudice. Mohammed stated that one of the most surprising answers they receive comes when they ask the question: How many of us are native to Australia? He stated that often the children think very few of them are, when in reality they all are. I was impressed with the way in which they go about teaching the children. Their questions help the children to see how they rely on the information they have received with in their school education, from their parents and through media and technology.

Mohammed shares his story as to why this work is important to him. He had an older brother who dedicated his life to providing programs for the youth who were peace-filled and were high-minded. It seems that there were lots of gangs and some unclean types of activities that the children of Sydney were becoming involved in. He was a pretty powerful figure among the youth and was making great changes in the community.

The gang leaders were very upset about his work and they killed him.

Mohammed felt that he wanted and needed to carry on the work of his brother. This is how he came to do this work.

It's All Good

I wanted to attend Shekhar's film the final day of Parliament. The unfortunate thing for me was that he was showing his film at the same time the Tibetan monks were scheduled to dissolve the sand mandala which they had spent the days of Parliament creating. I had set my sights on being present for this great display of non-attachment.

Non-attachment is a constant lesson at Parliament. At any given time, there may be four or five workshops or sessions you want to attend. You may be looking forward to a session that ends up canceled because the speaker couldn't make the trip. You may miss the talk that replaced it because it was added late and not in the published program guide. Parliament is about being awake and aware. Ready to take action, willing to receive. Just like all the volunteers.

I met Shekhar because I volunteered to help at Parliament. Now I can share what I learned about him with you.

Because I attended the monks' and mandala work, I was present to encourage my young friend Hezekiah Condron's participation in the closing ritual (below).

Acting and waiting. This is the reality at Parliament. Every moment is filled with people – from all over the world, of all ages and backgrounds, and of course religions – working together with love for each other and their Maker. Every meeting is an opportunity to give to someone and to receive from them.

It is how the world can be, and Parliament shows the way.∞

About the Author

Dr. Sheila Benjamin has freely given service to her fellow men and women for all of her life. She has taught every age, encouraging the young and infirmed to excel, assisting the lame and aged to heal. A world server, she traveled with the first People to People delegation of metaphysicians to India in November 1999, then led the School of Metaphysics delegation to CPWR in Cape Town, South Africa a month later. She presented at the International Association for the Study of Dreams conference in Montreal, Quebec in 2008, and is always willing to serve in any capacity that aids people toward greater harmony.

> EVERY MEETING
> IS AN OPPORTUNITY
> TO GIVE TO SOMEONE
> AND TO RECEIVE
> FROM THEM.
> IT IS HOW THE
> WORLD CAN BE...

When to open, when to close?
When to cling, when to let go?
When to give, when to receive.
When to speak, when to listen.

All the important choices in life have little to do with lack and loss, and everything to do with answering one question, "When?"

Elena marveled at the monk's reply. Each day they came to build, knowing their creation is temporary. They embody the perfecting of present moment consciousness and every witness is touched by the beauty of creation and purification.

Sheila describes the motion of life as when to act, when to receive. That is the essence of Duality and the secret of balance. "To everything there is a season, and time for every purpose under heaven," says Ecclesiastes 3:1. Every moment is an opportunity to give and to receive. Recognizing the difference frees the Self to learn, to understand, to become, to be.

–BC

FOUR
THE LAW of CAUSE AND EFFECT

"I DISCIPLINE MY MIND"
PARABLE 1

told by Dr. Pam Blosser

"By Divine Law
are all forms manifested;
Inexpressible is the Law.
By Divine Law are beings created;
By Law are some exalted.
By Divine Law are beings marked with nobility or
ignominy;
By the Law are they visited with bliss or bale.
On some by His Law falls grace;
Others by His Law are whirled around in cycles of births
and deaths.
All by the Law are governed,
None is exempt.
Says Nanak, Should man realize the power of the Law,
He would certainly disclaim his ego.
– Sikh Teachings of Adi Granth

Big Mind Big Heart was the first presentation I attended at the Parliament.

Presented by Philip Oude-Vrielink, a student of Genpo Roshi, the founder of the Big Mind Big Heart Process, this session was experiential. In his introduction Philip told all of us to put away our pens and notebooks. This was not a session of gleaning information from a speaker to record in a notebook, but an experience to record in our brains, hearts and minds. It was an opportunity to get out of our boxes and play something different.

Philip invited us to play with him. He mostly asked questions to which there were basically no wrong answers. He instructed us to identify with one aspect of ourselves, which was The One who Seeks. We were to speak from this perspective.

He asked, "What does the self think about The One who Seeks?"

We were to speak from the perspective of The One who Seeks. The self was to be referred to in third person, as he or she. And the self was the conscious mind self.

The thought form in the room changed when Philip asked the question, "Now what happens when The One who Seeks is denied, when it gets locked in the basement?'

From studying the Universal Language of Mind in the School of Metaphysics, the language of dreams, this was a perfect symbol because the basement symbolizes one's unconscious thinking. When any of us deny a part of ourselves that's productive, when we have an experience we don't understand, these memories and impressions are stored in the unconscious part of the brain. When the memory or impression is understood, it is no longer a part of the unconsciousness.

When we were instructed to take The One who Seeks out of the basement Philip asked if we had noticed how the energy in the room had changed again. Everyone said yes.

What I learned from this session is that there is an innate part of myself that seeks. I'm grateful to have that part of myself. When I am purposeful I welcome it. When I am afraid I deny it, lock it in the basement. When I react it is a sign to me that I have just moved out of the present moment, and denied a sacred part of myself. I am not whole --- holy. I vowed to be vigilant of myself and others, to honor, understand and offer perspective.

We also imagined what Big Mind is. It's bigger than everything and encompasses everything. I see it as Awareness. Then we explored Big Heart in the same manner. Big Heart is being moved to respond to that expanded awareness. This was a valuable workshop for me. What I had been endeavoring to understand for years in neutralizing reactions seemed to all click together inside me. This workshop was the catalyst that brought it all together.

Developing a Dynamic Interfaith Movement

The Interfaith Movement in Arizona based out of Phoenix led this. It was an energetic, openhearted group that was truly inspiring. One of their innovative projects and main source of income is the sale of license plates that say on them "The Golden Rule State." Of course, it helped that the governor of Arizona is one of the organization's members. I was impressed with the spirit of the people, their joy and appreciation for each other.

Afterwards I introduced myself to Beverly, one of the panelists. She was ecstatic when I told her I was with the School of Metaphysics. Metaphysics is something she is very interested in.

Later, I saw her again. She turned to others in her group and said, "This is the one I was telling you about." One from the group Kaye, is a Unity minister. I told her about the Universal Hour of Peace and reading the Universal Peace Covenant at midnight of New Years Eve, and she plans to implement it. I plan to stay in touch with Beverly and Kaye.

Meeting Margareta

I was searching for the room for the next session I had planned to attend, "Christian Action and Witness for the Environment: What You Can do When you go Home." I walked past a room, and a smiling woman was standing at the door with a picture and a caption about big business harming small Latin American countries. I smiled back and kept walking, not thinking this was the room I was destined for. When I saw the room numbers on the next rooms, I realized the room I had just passed was the room I was looking for.

The title of the session didn't match the woman's poster, but I walked up to her and said, "This is the room I'm looking for." She gave me a big smile, welcoming me in.

I found out the friendly lady's name was Margareta Dahlin Johahnsson, pastor of Peace Lutheran Church in Danville, CA. She and Steve Harms, Senior Pastor of Peace Lutheran Church were part of a panel. Their presentation dealt with how they are aiding indigenous people in Ecuador to regain their clean environment from Chevron Oil Company. The history, as they told it, was that Chevron Oil Company went into Ecuador to drill for oil. Chevron negotiated with the government of Ecuador that they would either pump the waste and toxins from the drilling back down into the ground, a practice they do in the United States, or give the Ecuadorian government $3.00 for every gallon of oil they received from the drilling. The Ecuador government chose the latter leaving Chevron to dump the toxins and waste onto the land and in the rivers of Ecuador. Now there is no clean water in Ecuador resulting in diseases such as cancer and leukemia as well as stillbirths and birth defects. Rev. Steve and Rev. Magareta are part of a movement to speak for the people of Ecuador in the court system so the land can get cleaned up.

As the session continued, I asked myself what had attracted me to this session. It wasn't what I had expected it to be. I read over the description and bios of the speakers and for the first time noticed the friendly lady was from Sweden and had worked with children. I thought to myself, I must introduce myself to her after the session and tell her about *The INVITATION* as well as give her a copy of one of the School's publications, **How to Raise an Indigo Child**.

After the session finished, I introduced myself to Margareta. I told her about *The INVITATION*, a play the School of Metaphysics would be presenting at the Unity Church on Sunday and that I played Alva Myrdal, a Swedish sociologist and Nobel Peace Laureate. She immediately was thrilled to hear that and said that as a young girl growing up in Sweden she admired Alva Myrdal greatly.

In that moment such a deep connection was made, and it was because of Alva. Alva had brought me together with this big-hearted woman, and now because of Alva we were like sisters. All the admiration, respect and love we had for Alva was transferred one to the other.

In that moment, I knew why I had attended this session! This was the reason!

I told her more about the presentation the next day and invited her to *The INVITATION* at Unity. She copied down all the information. I hugged her, then saw her later in the corridor and gave her another hug.

The next day when we started our presentation of *The INVITATION* and I got up to deliver the first part of Alva's talk, I looked out into the audience, and there about halfway back on the left side near the door, sat Margareta and Steve. I wanted to jump up and down with joy, but of course that wouldn't have been befitting the grand lady I was representing. I would save that for afterwards. I searched out a DVD copy of *The INVITATION* to give her.

I saw Margareta and Steve many times throughout the rest of the Parliament: at the Peace Pole dedication, in the halls, at the site where the Buddhist monks were creating the beautiful sand mandala. And each time I gave her a big hug. She gave me a t-shirt the front of which was a design of a mosaic on the front of their church. It has signs of different religions as well as symbols of brotherhood and sisterhood among all people.

Appreciative Inquiry and Healing the Earth: Extending Faith beyond the Realms of Religion

Tad Messenger and I attended an experiential workshop on Appreciative Inquiry. This is a strength-based management tool that focuses on positives and possibilities. The process goes through four steps: discover, dream, design and destiny. After the introduction, we broke up into smaller groups to go through these steps. Once we got started some other people joined our group.

As we got to know each other, there were so many serendipitous and synchronistic connections. There was a musician and founder of Inner Harmony, Michael Stillwater, from Switzerland who was making a film for school children to aid them to awaken the songmaker and singer within them, and a couple from New Zealand who work with school age boys who have lost their voices because of traumatic situations. These were the very people who had joined our group late. They definitely were being led by Law because a friend had told the people from New Zealand to be sure and meet Michael Stillwater.

I was so excited to meet them too because I am going to be launching a project in Champaign-Urbana to bring mind skills of concentration, relaxation, breath and guided imagery into schools for school children. We talked about looking seven generations forward as to the effects of our efforts. Tad also told Michael about Hezekiah and his film on the Healing Wall.

Soon everyone in the group started exchanging business cards as each person explained more of what they did. I gave the woman from New Zealand a copy of the script for *The INVITATION* with the thought that they could bring that to schools in New Zealand. How quickly the attraction to know each other and be in each other's lives far beyond the time we were in Melbourne came into being! Such magnificent potential energy moving to kinetic energy!

Compassion Rising

I attended the world premiere of a film called *Compassion Rising*. It is a film about bringing the Tibetan monks of the East and Trappist monks of the West together -- work that Thomas Merton began before his untimely death. Thomas Merton was a Trappist Monk who felt moved to make connection with Buddhist Monks. He had just met the Dalai Lama and they were both looking forward to cooperating together in mutual understanding. Twenty-five years after his death the Dalai Lama visited the monastery of Thomas Merton in·Kentucky to honor his life and continue with some of the work Merton had initiated.

Michael Fitzgerald was the creator of this beautiful film. He is a cellist and much of his music is on the film. Some of the filming was done in Mammoth Cave, the world's largest cave, where monks chanted and Michael played his cello. The music is beautiful and moving.

Michael was present to introduce the film, telling that the making of the film had started out to be a six-month project but continued for over a decade, and it's still not exactly what he wants. I got to enjoy Michael's playing again as he played the cello at the closing plenary just before the Dalai Lama spoke.

I purchased a copy of the film to share with others at school. Afterwards, Dr. Christine Madar and I talked with Michael. We gave him a Peace Covenant and a brochure about the Healing Wall.

When he saw the picture of the Peace Dome he became excited. "Where is this Peace Dome?" he asked.

We told him, "In Missouri."

To that Michael exclaimed, "I want to come play my cello in your Peace Dome."

I can imagine him being part of our celebration when we inlay stones from all over the world into the Healing Wall!!!

Peace Pole Dedication

I truly enjoyed the Peace Pole dedication.

It started out with about 30 people and kept growing as people joined us after the plenary in the nearby concert hall was being let out. I especially liked waving our flags to send our messages of peace to the countries of the world.

Leaders of different faiths gave blessings before each continent. When a Mayan priestess gave a blessing I made a note in my head that I would like to talk with her.

After the ceremony when our group was gathering together, I saw her and offered her a **Universal Peace Covenant**.

She asked, "Do you have one in Spanish?"

I was glad to say yes, and Sheila got her email address, so we could send her the link. She showed us dolls she is making for indigenous children around the world. They are very cute, and I could tell she is quite proud of them.

The Still Mind, Emptiness, and Divine Love

Tad and I had volunteered to set up the book and information table for this morning observance given by Dr. Daniel Condron. We arrived early, and once we had the books and brochures laid out people began to come. We drew quite a crowd with the books, talked to many people inviting them to join the still mind practice. I saw two of the people I had invited, gave one a hug, and then suggested a book for him to pick up after the session. The room began to fill. Dr. Daniel requested the door stay open, so it was easy for latecomers to enter with little noise. Tad and I stayed out in the corridor while Dr. Daniel led the people in the still mind practices.

Afterwards, people came to the table and we gave away all the books there. People were grateful to receive them.∞

> I VOWED TO BE VIGILANT OF MYSELF AND OTHERS, TO HONOR, UNDERSTAND AND OFFER PERSPECTIVE.

The Universal Truth in My Story
Dr. Pam Blosser

The Morals in the Stories
There are universal truths in every experience if we have the eyes to see. My stories reflect the truth that Thought is Cause. Thoughts have form, structure and energy that then become physical manifestation.

The way I think and view myself has repercussions within my consciousness. With Big Mind Big Heart when our group changed our perspectives, we all noticed a change in the energy in the room and in our countenance. What I learned resulted in thinking differently; my view of myself and others had changed and the effects were a deeper compassion and understanding.

The way I think and view myself can be experienced by others. The Interfaith Movement in Arizona was a great example of the power of group consciousness. Their thoughts about what they're doing and the mutual respect they have for each other created an invigorating, attractive force, one that people want to be a part of. This thought form was palpable, and each person's attitudes about being part of the group added to the dynamic force there. When we experienced hosting Dr. Daniel's presentation, we also created an attractive force. We knew the value of what Dr. Daniel was teaching and we wanted that for others. We wanted to share the teachings from the School of Metaphysics publications. Many people were served, and many people asked if there was a School of Metaphysics in Australia.

When our ideas and philosophies are communicated clearly and powerfully they live on beyond ourselves through others of like mind. In the case of Thomas

Merton, his work is continuing through the Trappest monks, the Dalai Lama and Tibetan monks, and Michael Fitzgerald. His desires are inclusive, easy for others to pick up and carry the same mantle.

Our desires for greater connections in the physical are manifestations of a deeper longing to know and understand the inner conectedness within consciousness. This is true even if that longing is not fully conscious. I experienced such great joy in connecting with Margareta and the people I met in the Appreciative Inquiry class. This was also true as I waved the flags I held at the Peace Pole dedication because connectedness is our true nature. When we are immersed in our true nature of connectedness it is sublime. It would make sense that we would have many experiences through the Law of Cause and Effect that resonate with our inner urge at the Parliament of the World's Religions.•

About the Author
Pamela Blosser, D.M., D.D., is currently the director of the Urbana School of Metaphysics. A minister with the Interfaith Church of Metaphysics, counselor, author, teacher, musician, public speaker, and faculty member of the School of Metaphysics, Pam has devoted the last thirty-two years of her life teaching and practicing the principles of metaphysics. She served as President of the School of Metaphysics from 2001-2005 and currently serves on the Board of Ordination of the Interfaith Church of Metaphysics.

"I DISCIPLINE MY MIND"
PARABLE 2

told by Jesse Aaron Kern

In going to the Parliament of the World's Religions in Melbourne, Australia, my ideal was to further peace on earth through the School of Metaphysics' Universal Hour of Peace. I had goals of meeting new friends and people who will practice this beautiful experience with us from around the world.

The Universal Hour of Peace is the hour from 11:30 PM to 12:30 AM on New Year's Eve, which spans midnight into the New Year. The School of Metaphysics invites people from all over the planet to spend this hour doing something peaceful - with friends and family or in reflective contemplation - it's really up to the individual. My first thought was to not attend the Parliament of the World's Religions for financial reasons. However, I decided to go in March 2009, about eight months before the event, after our 24-hour Peace Dome Vigil during the first of the year. I felt quite strongly about responding to the opportunity Parliament affords.

Many of my most significant experiences while in Australia involved volunteering in a variety of capacities for the Council.

My metaphysics teacher, Dr. Sheila Benjamin (above far left, I'm on the far right), decided to volunteer and mentioned I might want to as well. I have a history of volunteerism at church, growing up as the son of a Southern Baptist minister in Texas and Idaho. I also participated in national service as an AmeriCorps Promise Fellow in 1999-2000. AmeriCorps is a domestic PeaceCorps program in the United States. The Promise Fellow position worked directly with youth to deliver needed community resources to improve the quality of their lives.

I decided I wanted to volunteer to be useful for this event and to the people attending it. As a metaphysics student and teacher who knows how to concentrate and focus, I know that I have the ability to be productive and wanted to share this with others. Oftentimes at large conferences like this, it is helpful to have a way or place to give my time and energy when so much information, through classes and workshops are being offered to receive from. The monetary discount I received as a volunteer was also helpful for me, reducing the expenses I incurred to attend the Parliament.

On Thursday, the day the Parliament began, from noon until 7:00 pm, I volunteered registering people whose organizations had booths in the Exhibition Hall. I was well received by Jo, one of the Arinex Staff, as I was using my still and concentrated mind to be focused and calm in a fairly stressful situation. The Council for a Parliament of the World's Religions hired Arinex to staff and manage many aspects of the conference from registration to coordinating the Exhibition Hall.

In this first volunteer experience, I was grateful for my mental discipline and focus. That day I met Arinex staff who I later became acquainted with and interpreted dreams for. Some of their colleagues also had questions I was pleased to answer. It was a heartfelt experience.

On Saturday, I volunteered for the Parliament staff room. Zabrina, Executive Deputy of the Staff, sent me on an errand to retrieve flowers from a flower shop near where they, the staff, were staying. I was given a map to (a foreign city, mind you) and adequate directions as well as plenty of money to make the purchase. I gladly set out on the mission and upon arrival at the flower shop it was closed.

Trusting that, by Universal Law, the person in the shop next door would have the information I needed, I walked in and asked for other flower shops in town. He smiled, and said he also works at one in a neighboring burrough of town that I could get to on the free trolley. There, I would find what I needed.

I had quite an adventure seeing a new part of Melbourne. I negotiated the trolley, asking questions of local people and finding beautiful flowers were used as gifts to special dignitaries at the plenary presentation that night, even though I did not attend the plenary.

The Youth Coffee House, which was held for youth attendees three evenings after the daily open plenary, was a productive experience of meeting lots of young people, interpreting their dreams and sharing the Healing Wall with them.

At the first Coffee House I met a gentleman named Weston Pew with the Sacred Door Trail, the only sacred trail on the North American continent (www.thesacreddoortrail.com). The trail will be a loop traveling about 180 miles around the Phillipsburg Valley in Western Montana. Stones from sacred sites all around the world will be buried at a certain part of the trail. An altar will also be built on the land which will be dedicated to all who use it. Weston said he will send the Healing Wall a rock from the Sacred Door Trail after its dedication.

At another of these coffee house events, I also met Colin Lee, a young man who, as a minister and the head of Shift International (www.shiftinternational.net), has influence with 30,000 youth in Australia. Shift International develops teenagers' personal and professional lives with life skills and employability development classes and workshop programs. Their mission is to "help young people to empower themselves to create their own future as magnificent as they dare to dream."

During the World Peace Prayer Society's Peace Pole Dedication, I held the United State of America

Flag because I was reading President Ronald Reagan's autobiography while in Australia. I also know the secret, spiritual destiny of our nation. This secret destiny is to bring about the next evolutionary stage of our race, the Spiritual, Intuitive thinker.

As a melting pot, the United States is a breeding ground for the best thinkers and people from all over the planet and from across much time and space who have come together to aid the evolution of consciousness on this planet. President Reagan aided this in giving people the opportunity to keep more of their income and thus have more resources to create with for themselves and other people the world over. This is why economically the 1980's was such a prosperous time.

During the Peace Pole Dedication Ceremony I wanted the United States' secret destiny to be honored. It was very special and meaningful to my soul to hold the United States' flag. A thought surfaced in my consciousness while in Australia – that I am studying at the School of Metaphysics to complete what I started in the Founding Father's days of our country. It is one of my most heartfelt desires and fuels me to be a disciplined student and to teach many people.

On the last day of the Parliament, I again volunteered in the staff room. This time I was asked to go with the staff to the stage and prepare for the final, mid-day plenary. Zabrina gave me the duty to take down all the Pre-Parliament banners on display in the Exhibition Hall. These 5 foot by 3 foot cloth banners were silk screened with the Parliament logo and signed by those attending PreParliament events around the world.

Before we left, Zabrina told me there were two banners in the staff room on someone's desk. I looked but did not find these additional two. Then, I found another volunteer to help me and we went about the task of collecting banners. All the while, I was looking for the School of Metaphysics banner from our PreParliament "Living Peaceably" event, which had been held at the Peace Dome in September. I did not see or come across it.

Unbeknownst to me, it was not there, a fact Dr. Christine Madar would later confirm for me.

Seventy banners in hand, I decided to try the staff room again to retrieve the missing two. Walking in the room with my arms filled, the person who knew where to find them immediately did so and gave them to me. At the time, I didn't fold or look at these two. I just put them on top of my pile and made my delivery to the backstage where they were warmly welcomed.

Later, Dr. Laurel Clark told me she had her picture taken (above) following the final plenary – with our PreParliament banner. It was one of the ones that members of the girl's choir processed to the outdoor bridge for a final CPWR group picture.

Upon hearing Dr. Clark's story, I realized our banner was one of the two that I had gone back to the office to get.∞

About the Author

Jesse Aaron Kern received a bachelor of Musical Arts in piano from Oklahoma Baptist University in 1998. He served as an AmeriCorps Promise Fellow in Oklahoma City, OK in 1999-2000, working with that community's youth. Jesse's professional resume spans positions as administrative assistant to piano teacher to his current position as a kiosk salesman of the **Des Moines Register**, *a Gannett newspaper.*

Jesse began his studies at the School of Metaphysics in 2002, earning his Respondere diploma in 2003 and the Qui Docit Discit (He Who Teaches Learns) certificate in 2010. Jesse currently teaches both the First and Second Cycle of Lessons in the SOM course of study, serves as Director of a branch in Des Moines, Iowa, is leading the opening of a branch in the Quad cities IA/IL, and is the National Peace Ambassador coordinating the SOM's Peace Ambassador Program. He is also serving in his first year as Secretary of the Board of Directors.

The Universal Truth in My Story

Jesse Aaron Kern

The moral of my story is Thought is Cause and the effect is its manifest likeness. One always has a choice. No matter the physical condition and circumstance, one has an infinite number of choices regarding the attitude held in mind during the experience.•

IN THIS FIRST VOLUNTEER EXPERIENCE, I WAS GRATEFUL FOR MY MENTAL DISCIPLINE AND FOCUS.

After we returned to the States, I asked each member of the delegation to write about their experiences. These stories are in this volume. Believing Jesse had more to say, I asked him to elaborate on his first draft and he generously made time to do so. When he sent it to me, he included this note which figured into the placement of his writing this book:

> "Dr. Barbara,
> I am writing this as a personal claiming of my birthright. Revisiting this resurfaced my self forgiveness lesson in spending money I didn't have (credit) to go. The lesson for me is to value what did occur and to always say *Yes* with reasoning. Writing this has also aided me to see the value in the trip and my choices to be there.
> O Jesse"

FIVE

THE LAW of ATTRACTION

"I AM OPEN & LOVING"

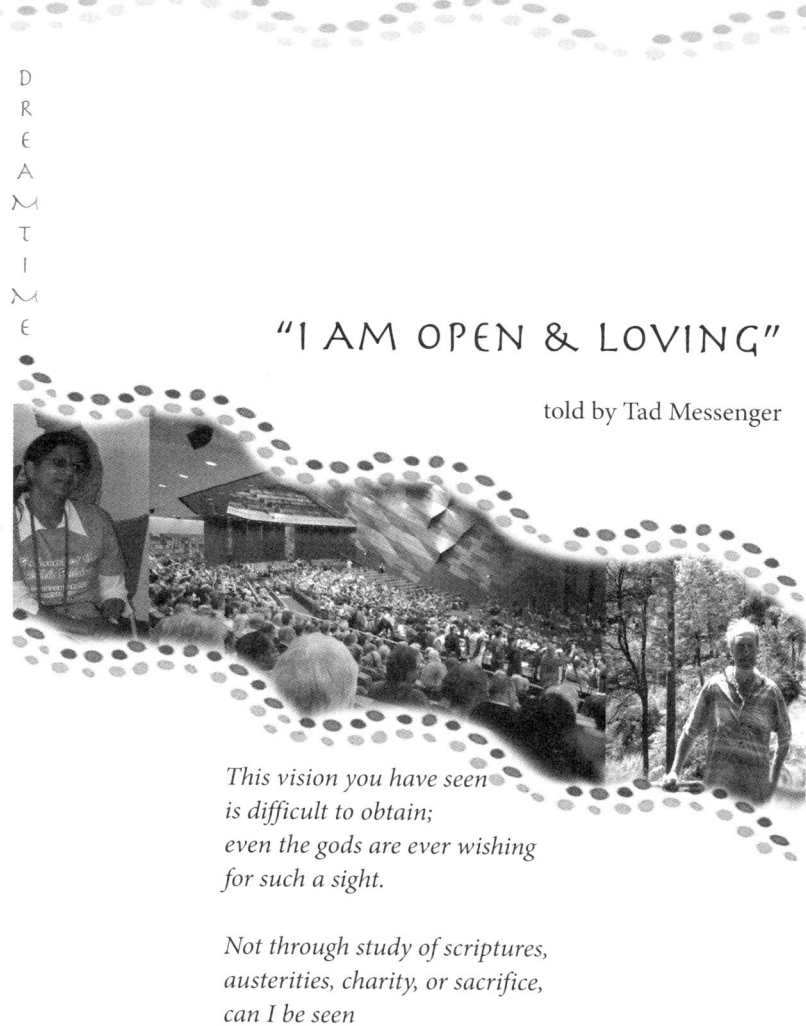

told by Tad Messenger

*This vision you have seen
is difficult to obtain;
even the gods are ever wishing
for such a sight.*

*Not through study of scriptures,
austerities, charity, or sacrifice,
can I be seen
as you have seen me.*

*O Arjuna, only by the
unswerving love of a human heart,
can my supreme state be seen,
and known, and attained.*

-Krishna in the **Bhagavad Gita**

Falling in Love – The Melbourne Experience

My experience of the Parliament for a Council of the World's Religions began with the PreParliament event of "Living Peaceably begins by Thinking Peacefully". It set the tone to meet people from many cultural backgrounds. The PreParliament event held at the College of Metaphysics especially piqued my interest in indigenous peoples when I met and formed a friendship with Grandmother Silverstar, a Cherokee elder.

I started to prepare for Parliament at a very early time. I googled a lot. I got a rough guide to Melbourne, and I recognized that I had a strong interest in the indigenous peoples and wanted to understand their connection to Earth, and the connection to a lot of different things. So, I got a book on the Iroquois Nation, and the confederacy that they built, that the founding Fathers of the United States modelled our *Constitution* upon. I wanted to learn more about indigenous people.

In planning my trip to Melbourne, I wanted to begin by experiencing the nature and wilderness of Australia. I wanted to receive and honor the spirit of the land.

With a little research I decided to rent a car and travel the Great Ocean Road that began about two hours west of Melbourne along the coast. This road led me to explore some wonderful areas. I meditated on beaches in the early mornings, walked within and above rain forests where the ferns grew 10 – 20 feet high, and the trees went upward into the sky, some were over 300 feet high.

The farms and the scenery were breathtaking. I immediately fell in love with this land. The rain forests in the Otway Range that I explored were the homeland of many of the Aborigines that lived in Australia thousands of years before the settlement from the white man's cultures of the Dutch, English, and other Europeans as well as Asians.

One experience I had on this trip that was magical involved going to a famous lighthouse. After traveling some 20 miles out of the way to go to a cape where the lighthouse was, I found out that it was closed. On my way back to the main road, I thought that this wouldn't be a waste. Something special would happen. Soon, in a eucalyptus forest, I saw a little ball in a tree. I stopped the car and saw that this ball was a butt of a koala bear. I tried to get it to turn around, but it was fast asleep. Then I noticed across the road two more butts up in a tree. They wouldn't budge either.

Then, I saw a koala bear coming down a tree. I got pictures of it and it went to the base of the tree the two koalas were in and started making funny noises. This woke them up and they looked down so I could take their picture. It was a great time walking around the forest floor with the one bear and then he decided to climb back up a tree. The wonder and awe of being with life in nature never ceases to astound me.

This land had a deep richness that spelled of ancient times, of cultures that still waited since eternity for this time of Peace and Unity. This feeling saturated over me as I immersed myself in the Spirit of Nature. This thought became prevalent in my experience of the Parliament of World's Religions in Melbourne.

Melbourne itself is a very beautiful, clean city that reflects the integrity and care that the people who live there exhibit.

There were times when I was given the opportunity to take $10,000 worth of opals out of a store without any kind of supervision so I could look at them in the light of the sun on the streets. A lady on the bus searched her purse to give me $20 worth of change so I could purchase a ticket for my passage.

After she gave me $16 worth of change, I said, "That's enough, thank you very much."

She replied, "Oh no, I can't do that. I will find $20 worth." She had the integrity and care to give.

I saw this over and over as I met the people of Melbourne. What a wonderful, beautiful, city this is!

After my two days of driving, I picked up Daniel, Barbara,

and Hezekiah Condron at the airport and we headed towards the apartments where they stayed. On the way, we stopped at Queen Victoria Market, a place to buy fresh fruit and vegetables, fish, meat, and anything else one could want.

On the way, we experienced the wonders and discipline of driving on the left side of the street, and driving from the right side steering in the car. It wasn't too difficult when I was following other cars. The most difficulty came in signaling with my other hand and using the shift lever with my left hand. I kept turning the windshield wiper blades on every time I wanted to signal a turn. All in all, we had a great and wonderful ride. The market was splendid and again reflected the quality and vibrations of the people of Melbourne.

After I dropped the rental car off near the airport, I took the Skybus back to the apartments. When I got on the bus, I sat in the first available seat next to a woman. After a couple of minutes, I asked her where she was from. She said she was a massage therapist from Tasmania. As we talked, we soon realized that we were attracted to sit with each other, and meet each other for a reason. We were both conscious of the Universal Law of Attraction.

As I talked about the SOM, permanent healing, and what we teach about "thought is cause" she became more and more excited and open. Her husband had studied in the USA at Amherst and Hobart in neurophysiology. It turned out she had relatives in Buffalo, and Rochester, New York, where I was born.

When we separated we exchanged email addresses and I told her that I wanted to send her the book, **Permanent Healing**. I sent her an email the next day because I realized I would need her address to mail her the book. She replied in an email and sent me her address. The email reads as follows:

> Good morning Tad,
>
> Thank you for your email, I enjoyed the Fleetwood Mac concert immensely. They were great!
>   Meeting you has been an inspiration and has opened a window in my mind a kind of awakening has occurred. Uncanningly, I was telling one of my clients about this experience and she asked if she could have the name of the website you gave me, asked me your

> name and as it occurs she exclaimed, "I know that name!" Her name is Simone and she said that she has attended a workshop that you were taking. A well-traveled lady to the USA and around the world. Simone does a lot of self-developing, healing etc and I think it's an integral part of the work she does.
>
> What a small world we live in when this happens. Quite amazing, it's a reminder the importance of communication. It's a great feeling to feel truly connected.
>
> Thank you for your kindness and generosity. It would be wonderful if you could come visit us here in Tasmania sometime.
>
> Enjoy Melbourne, all the wonderful people and conference.
>
> All my best wishes and Thank you
>
> Hedi

This is a wonderful story of connectedness and how small the planet is. It is also a story that demonstrates how easy it is to attract situations where we can receive stones from every country in the world for the Healing Wall, because we all know people who know people, who know people from every country in the world.

Communicate.

Ask.

Open heart.

Love.

Before all the delegates from SOM gathered together in Melbourne for our first meeting, I took the opportunity to walk around the downtown area. I had already googled opal stores in Melbourne and decided to check out four that I found most appealing.

The one I was attracted to the most before I traveled to Australia was called Lightning Ridge Opal Mine. I liked this name and this store because the best black opals in the world come from Lightning Ridge, which is about 800 miles north of Melbourne. When I walked into this store, much to my surprise, they greeted me very joyfully and proceeded to give me an education on opals.

The store had three people educate me on how opals were formed, what the differences were and how to recognize the differences between a doublet, triplet, and an original black opal, and how to cut and polish them. They demonstrated each phase (teaching is showing) and showed pictures of the peoples that live under the ground in the middle of Australia. It is so hot and dry that the surface is unbearable during certain times of the year, so people live underground.

I talked to them about SOM and about the Healing Wall. It is a family owned business and Nick, the owner, was very interested in SOM. He immediately donated a raw opal from one of the mines and he asked me if I had ever heard of Edgar Cayce.

I literally said, "Ding, ding, ding, ding!" meaning that the Law of Attraction was at work again.

I opened my case up and the first book that was on top was **First Opinion: Wholistic Health Care in the 21st Century** by Dr. Barbara Condron. I said, "This book is for you."

I started talking about intuitive reports and how we have been giving them for over 30 years. It is one of the best things the School offers. The School was built from connecting with people's souls, and teaching people how to progress in spiritual growth.

"I want one of these," he said. "Can I get one of these?"

"We have been thinking about the possibility of doing intuitive reports in Australia," I replied. "Let me talk to the people that I am with. I am with 15 other people. We are getting together this afternoon." So, we exchanged notes, and email addresses.

When the first meeting of SOM representatives took place (at a bring-a-dish dinner in the Clark-Benjamin-Blosser-Dubinski apartment) we all shared many stories of our experiences in Melbourne. I told everyone about meeting Hedi from Tasmania and Nick from the opal store. We talked of how the best time to schedule intuitive reports would be the evening after Parliament and that when we gave ***THE INVITATION*** at Unity Church on Sunday, December 6th we would probably meet more people who would like to receive Intuitive Reports.

We had time so our minds could focus. Now we needed the people wanting intuitive reports and a place to give them. Nick had gotten the ball rolling and it was felt that it would happen. A Kundalini projection strengthened the manifesting power, magnetizing the thought form.

I was placed in charge of making the details work, receiving the interest and monies. I became the first Intuitive Report Coordinator on another continent.

Among the many incredible things that happened on Sunday, December 6th at Unity Church in Melbourne, we met many Parliament people who were attending the service in the morning. Reverend William Livingston generously allowed us to print *The INVITATION* programs on the church's computer. Members of the congregation served us an exquisite meal with curry, oriental rice, vegetables, and all kinds of deserts.

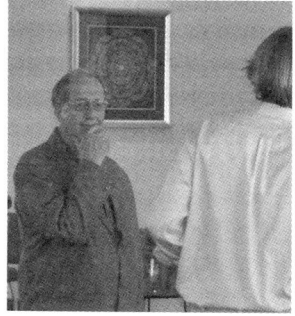

In the afternoon, we presented an unusual and unique version of *The INVITATION* which included the audience in its movement. We listened to a master didgeridu player, met more people who wanted intuitive reports and Rev. Livingston offered to make his church available for the session on Wednesday. Everything came into place and we offered our first intuitive reports to Australian truth seekers, the first outside U.S. soil.

This experience was expansive and further impressed upon me the integrity, joy, and generosity of the people of Melbourne.

Being in Love – The Parliament Experience

Meanwhile, at Parliament, on December 2, volunteers met for our initial training session and roster assignments.

I found I was working at the Registration Desk for my 16 hours of volunteer work. This was great because I got to meet many people as they came to the Parliament and received their programs. The people came from all over the world. At times I was talking to Zoroastrians, other times, Sikhs, some famous people that I knew like Michael Beckwith and his wife, Rickie, who is an incredible gospel soul singer and leader of the Agape Choir.

Most of all, I enjoyed meeting a lady named Bagya. She was from Melbourne and went to their interfaith church. She was one of those people who worked hard, fast, efficient, and was willing to do anything. As we worked together, it was amazing how much we could accomplish. There was a lot of joy that came from our relationship. And again, I enjoyed the multicultural experience of care, joy, and integrity of the Melbourne residents.

There were many wonderful sessions that I experienced. The first was led by two women. One was a Maori from New Zealand and one was an Aborigine elder from Australia. They had united in a common cause to elevate the environment and honor of their indigenous peoples. They had great joy and great vision. Miriam-Rose, the Aborigine elder had a look that was very still and very deep. I felt that she had the vision of ancient wisdom at her fingertips.

I had the pleasure of meeting many indigenous peoples including some Native Americans. The one that made the biggest impression on me was Chief Oren Lyons (right) from the Onondaga Tribe of the Iroquois (French) Nation. They call themselves Haudenosaunee, the people of the longhouses. They are the ones who, with the Peacemakers help, created a confederacy, a model that inspired the founding fathers of the United States. Their government has lasted for thousands of years.

One thing that I will always remember is Chief Lyon's look. He reminded me of what I imagine of a visionary like George Washington; a person who looks with deep thoughts that encompass not only the community, but also the world, and the universe.

"When any leader makes a decision," he said, "they first bring it to council." The council always takes into account seven generations. He mentioned the problem of the leaders today is that they don't even take into consideration their grandchildren. They only look to the immediate short-term benefits. He said his people came to make peace, to teach it and to be the peacemakers for the planet.

Afterwards, I introduced myself to him, and gave him the book, **Peacemaking – Nine Lessons for Changing Yourself, Your Relationships, and Your World** by Dr. Barbara Condron.

"I wanted you to see that others, too, honor and teach peace," I told him. I gave him the Universal Peace Covenant and he asked me to write down my name and my phone number. He said he would take this to council and then call me.

I shook his hand, looked deep within his soul, and said, "Thank you for being who you are."

There was a sense of recognition, a sense of timelessness that will forever be with me. I was in love.

God's Joy and Love Abounding

I went to two interactive sessions that were very inspiring. The first one was about working through emotional fear.

I was planning on going to a dance session on mudras. However, I realized that it would be pretty active with lots of loud music. I was in the mood for something more interactive. Immediately, I looked at the program to see what else was happening at that time. I almost literally walked into Dr. Pam Blosser from Urbana, Illinois, who was also trying to decide which session to go to. We both decided to join the one on opening the emotions.

We were asked to write down a situation where we were in a foreign land, or culture that was different than our own, an experience where we felt fearful. Then we divided into groups and discussed what we had written. Then, another situation where we only described the feelings that we had as we overcame the fears. The results were very enlightening and changing.

It was a great Taraka Yoga type change. There was a moment where everyone connected and I felt that there were many wise souls in this group that could easily be giving presentations at this Parliament. There were many exchanges of addresses and elevated thinking. It was a reflection that as many people talk and communicate with each other, they will arrive at a greater truth.

The other interactive session was on opening the heart through listening. The listening process was elevated as a very important step in communication. Too often people are thinking, or judging, or interpreting, when another is speaking and we miss not only what they are saying, but an opportunity to give a great gift – our attention. Most people want to be heard. We turned to the person next to us and one would talk while the other listened. The person I listened to was Christina, who is from Germany. I guessed her accurately to be a Cancer sun sign as she had many mannerisms like Paul Madar, a Cancer friend and sometime classmate of mine. I felt our interaction was very intimate and warm. I felt my heart beginning to open.

Then, we got a different partner and did the same thing, except more in depth. We were given a soulful question to talk about for ten minutes. After I talked to another Christina from St. Paul, Minnesota, I stopped with about two minutes to go. She asked, "Is there anything else you would like to say?" This question made my heart open with joy and love. I felt that she wanted to hear my thoughts. For one moment, I felt the experience of "Be still and know that I am God." This thought made my day.

When we talked later, she expressed that her heart had opened to me and she was in love. She is a wonderful musician, composer, a violin player who can play classical, Irish folk, and Cajun music. I later would mentally connect with her as she played her violin with other musicians. The feeling of joy and love abounded in many of my experiences at Parliament.

During Dr. Daniel Condron's giving of **Still Mind, Emptiness, and Divine Love,** he filled the room to capacity and we gave many people SOM books and Love. All the delegates decided to support Daniel and his presentation. We made flyers and passed them out to people we met during sessions and days before his still mind presentation.

As we gathered outside of his room, we kept the door open and envisioned people filling the room. Pam and I fashioned a table outside the door and filled it with seventeen different SOM books. As we talked to people and helped usher them in, I formed an energy field where people who came by would want to enter the room and experience the joy and love that Dr. Daniel was sharing and teaching. Sometimes people would walk along the corridor and gravitate toward the room. It was a wonderful, powerful attractor field.

During the panel of 10 women discussing inner peace, which included Dr. Barbara Condron, again there was much joy and love. These women had a wealth of wisdom and experience. Some were youthful and full of promise. Others were calm, disciplined and full of understanding and wisdom. Dr. Barbara was brilliant and shared her Christhood, representing the Christian faith as well as the Universal Truth.

The next day, she presented Crown Jewels of Consciousness – Three Universal Spiritual Practices. She opened with the brief version of Hezekiah's **Seventh Generation** DVD on the Peace Dome Healing Wall for the second time, made time in her presentation for all the people who have earned their doctorate in metaphysics to share their wisdom as part of an interactive group on teaching people about their dreams and answer their questions. She is truly a generous soul.

Daniel and Barbara Condron continue to be bright lights for the world. They help people to open their hearts and experience Divine Truth and Love.

Bagya (at left), my Melbourne friend and fellow CPWR volunteer, came to Dr. Barbara Condron's presentation on the *Crown Jewels of Consciousness*. I was able to give her a heartfelt hug and say goodbye.

The following day, I joined the breakfast for the Dalai Lama where people honored his 20th Anniversary of receiving the Nobel Peace Prize. His teachings the year before in Pennsylvania moved me deeply, and I continue to write about my experience there. Being in his presence has special meaning to me, and to all of the members of *The INVITATION*, for we spend much time in the presence of his thoughts.

Afterwards, I had the opportunity of escorting my dear friend Hezekiah to his apartment as his parents were going to be doing something else.

When we got out of the convention center he said, "Tad, I have never seen you so happy."

I received his love and it felt very similar to my experience with Christina. God's joy and love abounded through many hearts on that day, the last day of Parliament.

The Universal Truth in My Story
Tad Messenger

The Universal Law of Attraction is at work all the time. We attract to us, through our thoughts what we are. By opening my heart and being adventurous and curious in Australia, I attracted love, care, and integrity. I also received a deeper understanding of the elemental forces of nature through meeting many indigenous people from all over the Earth. Every story and experience I had in Australia reflected this giving and receiving of like minds. I experienced within my heart and soul an opening, a truth stated in the Universal Peace Covenant, "Living peaceably begins by thinking peacefully." That is the beginning (Alpha) and ending (Omega) of my story.•

I ENJOYED THE MULTICULTURAL EXPERIENCE OF CARE, JOY, AND INTEGRITY OF THE MELBOURNE RESIDENTS.

About the Author

Tad Messenger was born October 10, 1947 in Rochester, New York. He has a college education, which includes a B.A. in Religion at the College of Wooster in Ohio, and a B.S. in Geology from the State University of New York at Brockport. He has spent many years learning different construction skills, and helped to build the Peace Dome (a monolithic dome) at the College of Metaphysics in Windyville, Missouri in 2001.

He has studied at the College of Metaphysics for the past 11 years and is currently serving as a college graduate-teacher. Some of his primary responsibilities include directing printing productions, supporting and teaching in the Horticulture and Agriculture Department, constructing sacred forms at sacred sites on the College land, teaching as an Intuitive Report Conductor and transcription coordinator, conducting research in the areas of alternative energy, bioenergy, coordinating collecting stones from every country around the world to place on the Healing Wall in 2012, and aiding in the ongoing research of dreams.

In December of 2009, he attended the Parliament of World's Religions in Melbourne, Australia. Currently, Tad is working toward earning his Doctorate of Divinity.

THE FEELING OF JOY AND LOVE ABOUNDED... IT WAS A POWERFUL ATTRACTOR FIELD.

I have witnessed Tad transform himself into Albert Schweitzer again and again during The Invitation, much to the audience's delight. It brings to my mind a favored quote from the noted doctor: "I do not know what your destiny will be, but one thing I know: the only ones among you who will be really happy are those who have sought and found how to serve." Tad lives this every day.

When I think of Tad Messenger, an image of Hermes comes into my mind. An Olympian god, Hermes was the patron of boundaries and the travelers who cross them. Hermes is the messenger of the gods. While in Australia, Tad lived up to this divine nature, bringing together native Australian's desires for deeper intuitive insight with Americans who could fulfill those desires. Tad brought tidings of great joy to many people.

Largely through his thought form visualization and efforts, we, the collective that is the School of Metaphysics, had the opportunity to give Intuitive Reports while in Melbourne for the Parliament. We had served Australians with these reports for decades, and to now experience the richness of exchange in giving and receiving in real time, was sublime!

Dr. Daniel Condron wrote, "The Intuitive Reports were offered at the Melbourne Unity Church. Past Life, Past Life Crossings and Health Analyses were all given. People receiving them were enthusiastic about the opportunity to be present, observe, and receive intuitive reports. I served in the capacity as conductor and Dr. Barbara Condron in the capacity of Intuitive Reporter. It seemed fitting that for these, the first reports given in another country, that the inside of the church was painted pink, the color of love."

Dr. Laurel Clark who attended later said that the whole Intuitive Report session and the entire experience was very heart-centered. She wrote, "As I was observing and listening to the intuitive reports, the thought came to me, *This is an open heart experience. The church is a lovely little building, with a pink carpet, pink walls, and pink chairs. As the sun set in the evening sky, the light coming through the stained glass window cast a glow in the room. Everything was glowing pink, a soft rose pink. It was like being in the midst of the heart chakra! How fitting that Dr. Daniel was conducting this session, since he has been teaching the Open Heart for quite awhile now, and his latest book is entitled* **Still Mind, Present Moment, Open Heart**."

The reality that all three conductors and four of the reporters had made the trek halfway around the world created the incredible energy field manifesting this long time dream in every level of consciousness. Intuitive Reports in Australia transfigured the School of Metaphysics from a virtual presence (serving from a physical distance) to a real one (a healing presence). I knew I was acting on behalf of all intuitive reporters and I was honored to do so.

I want to express my gratitude and appreciation on behalf of the people in Melbourne, the student body (past, present and future!) of the SOM, for Tad's willingness to be the kind of person who practices harmonizing his consciousness every day for the greater good of the whole.

Schweitzer put it very well when he observed, "In everyone's life, at some time, our inner fire goes out. It is then burst into flame by an encounter with another human being. We should all be thankful for those people who rekindle the inner spirit."

Tad Messenger is one of these people. –BC

SIX

THE LAW of INFINITY

"I EXPAND MY CONSCIOUSNESS"

told by Dr. Christine Madar

*To what indeed shall I liken
The world and the life of man?
Ah, the reflection of the moon
In the dewdrop
On the beak of the waterfowl.*

-Eithei Dogen
Moon in a Dewdrop: Writings of a Zen Master Dogen

Resonant Moments

Gazing out the window of our large tour bus I felt safe, as the vehicle was big, and I was surrounded by American students and Irish professors. It was from this vantage point that I witnessed a most simple scene. A young woman was pushing a stroller down the street and on the corner was an armed soldier. He lifted his gun and trained it on someone, or something. The woman kept walking, pushing her baby right in front of the line of fire.

My stomach flipped and eyes opened wide. Echoes of my parents voices rang through my head, "Don't ever point a gun at anyone and never walk in front of a pointed gun." We never even had guns in our house, let alone armed guards on the street corners. Yet, my mother and father felt it was important to teach this bit of common sense, and I had received it. No one was pointing a gun at me in that moment, but the innate urge for survival, protection and safety welled up within for this woman and her child.

I felt relief when the woman crossed the street without incident and the soldier rested the gun by his side, glancing off in a different direction. I also felt a kind of sadness and despair that seemed impossible to define. The woman appeared to be indifferent, so did the soldier. People live this way in the world?

It was 1988 and I was in Belfast, Northern Ireland (right with my host, Ann Joyce).

Fast-forward twenty years.

Now it was July 2008 and I was in Windyville, Missouri on the College of Metaphysics campus. Early one morning Laurie Biswell, a COM graduate teacher, slipped in wet grass and fell, breaking her ankle. After surgery and a few weeks of recovery it was evident that she would be unable to portray Betty Williams in the August performance of *The INVITATION* at the Peace Dome on campus.

The INVITATION is a one-hour dramatic presentation that tells the story of eight Nobel Peace Prize Laureates. My husband, Paul, had portrayed the Dalai Lama for five years in *The INVITATION* so I was well acquainted with the vision, message and dream that was the driving force of this performance. Laurie had been the only person to portray the Irish peace activist Betty Williams in all the time the play had been given. Now there was an open door and Dr. Barbara Condron, the creator and director, asked if I would like to step into Betty's shoes for that August performance.

I thought about it a day or so, and decided to give it a go. I had felt a connection to Betty ever since I had heard her story. Betty is a woman who grew up in Belfast. She had witnessed, at close range, a car crash that killed three children from one family, and seriously injured their mother. The mother was pushing her baby in a stroller when the incident occurred. The driver of the car had been shot dead in a shoot-out he had instigated with British soldiers.

I have tremendous respect for Betty Williams. Her efforts, along with Mairead Corrigan rallied hundreds of thousands of people to march for peace in 1976 and 1977. She brought Protestants and Catholics together to form a common goal for a different, better life in Northern Ireland, free of the tyranny of battles, death and fear. These two women earned the Nobel Peace Prize in 1976.

For six years, *The INVITATION* brought my brief, benign experience in Belfast to the forefront of my attention. In 1988, it was as if I had experienced a portal, an opening, into the collective consciousness of the people in Northern Ireland. Now, it felt as if that portal was opening again, with new light and new perspectives, as I prepared to join *The INVITATION* .

I had nine days to learn lines and the simple staging of the performance, which is given in the round, upper chamber of the Peace Dome on the College of Metaphysics campus. Interestingly, one of those days coincided with the 33rd anniversary of the horrific car crash that changed Betty's life. On August 10, 2008, I sat alone, after running my lines in the Peace Dome, contemplating the resonance of time and space, people and events. I was only eight years old in 1976. In 1988, it was through the eyes of a twenty year old that I watched the woman, her child and the soldier in Belfast cross paths. Now, at the age of forty all of these things were related.

Since *The INVITATION* had come into being I had occasion to revisit my own, brief yet simple moment in Belfast through new eyes. Learning to embody Betty Williams, helped me to understand why the pain I felt that day was tangible. It was not imagined, and it was linked to the history of an entire culture.

When I thought deeply about it, the resonance of Ireland in late 20th century echoed thousands of years of human warring. The round chamber of the Peace Dome is conducive to magnifying thoughts. My consciousness expanded through time and space. The effect was most profound because it heightened my awareness of the present moment. It was an enormous honor to be the conduit for these energies to manifest in this current time period.

So, in August of 2008, I stepped into Betty's shoes and, among other things, these shoes led me and 14 others to Melbourne, Australia, a year later.

I am particularly fond of relativity.

I enjoy understanding how and why things, people, places and experiences relate to one another and how my own experience evolves in the process. More than that, though, understanding the resonance of an experience, whether within one lifetime or among many, is the essence of understanding the journey of the Self.

I said yes to Betty, thinking that it would be one month, giving Laurie time to recuperate and pick up the role she had been in since 2002. Her recovery was slower than anticipated thus giving more time for *The INVITATION* to develop with the current cast.

A unique opportunity opened up when *The INVITATION* was chosen to be part of a pre-Parliament event that the Council for a Parliament of the World's Religions (CPWR) was hosting in Chicago on December 7th, 2008.

I had heard stories for years about the 1993 Parliament in Chicago. Because it was located in the United States, many SOM students volunteered and hosted a booth. Dr. Daniel Condron and Dr. Barbara Condron gave major presentations and the School of Metaphysics presented a cantata about prayers from different faith traditions. A much smaller delegation made the trip to attend the 1999 Parliament in Cape Town, South Africa and we had missed Barcelona because it was too close to our own building and dedicating of the world's Peace Dome.

Now activities were revving up so that the 2009 Parliament in Melbourne, Australia would be a success. Attending this pre-Parliament event was my first introduction to any CPWR event.

Notably, this was the first time this cast (pictured below) would be performing **The INVITATION** outside of the Peace Dome. Chicago was turning out to be a resonant moment in more ways than one. Some of the teachers in SOM were talking about traveling to Melbourne, Australia, the city hosting the 2009 Parliament. Dr. Barbara Condron was envisioning presenting *The INVITATION* at this Parliament. We talked about this each time the cast met to prepare for Chicago. It was a bold idea at the time.

My husband and I drove to Chicago with our then 4-year-old and 2-year-old daughters, along with all the other School of Metaphysics teachers and students involved. We prepared in the morning for the late afternoon performance.

The INVITATION was well received and those in attendance recited the *Universal Peace Covenant* spontaneously after the cast exited. Nothing like that had transpired at previous performances. Aligning with the Parliament energies was bringing out a new dimension for **The INVITATION**. Immediately after we finished, dinner was served to the 200 plus people in attendance and evening entertainment got underway.

One of the most remarkable things about that night was how easily our daughters folded into the activities. The room was vast and they spent most of the time in the back, running, dancing and playing. At times they moved amongst the tables, going to people they knew. Everyone they met was warm, gracious and embracing.

Hezekiah Condron, who was 13 at the time, was with us as well. He is Daniel and Barbara's son, and a true brother to Alexandra and Vivienna. The three of them often experience big events like traveling to Chicago and attending the pre-parliament together. Kie was having a great time, helping with the girls, meeting the featured didgeridu player Warren Clements, and taking a lot of pictures.

I remarked to one of the attendees that it was evident the people there were accepting of the children. All of the kids were happy and joyful, a reflection of the group consciousness. Many, many people made a point of thanking us for bringing the kids. There were a few other youngsters there that night. I remember thinking that there should be more kids at events like these. It is the kind of thing that feeds someone's soul, regardless of age.

The conclusion of the event was an emotional crescendo of music and dancing. It was uplifting and thrilling.

Time and again I noted the dates for the Melbourne Parliament. They were posted on a bigger-than-life image onstage. The Melbourne event would be held in exactly one year. I allowed my attention to follow the energy into the future and received the vision of presenting *The INVITATION* in Australia. If a pre-Parliament was this fulfilling, I could only imagine what the real deal might bring.

It is now early 2010 and the story of how 15 School of Metaphysics delegates traveled half way around the world to participate in the 2009 Parliament in Melbourne, is, as they say, history. This book is a testimony that speaks to that inner and outer journey for everyone involved.

On the drive back from Chicago it was cold, dark and quiet. Alexandra and Vivienna were sleeping in the backseat and Paul was deep in his own thoughts while driving. As I gazed out the window at the starry night I felt my heart pounding. I was reflecting on the pre-Parliament event, remembering the people, the joy, indeed the whole energy of the previous evening.

Time and again, I returned to the mental picture memory of looking at the giant screen projection of the Melbourne logo with the dates December 3 – 9, 2009. As I observed the reaction/response of my body to this memory I noted that the energy was heart centered, not nervous solar plexus energy. It was becoming clearer that perhaps I was supposed to be the one to make sure that the School of Metaphysics would be at the Parliament.

The cast of *The INVITATION* had started to dream about presenting in Melbourne. No one had stepped up yet to say, "Yes, I will make sure this happens".

Before that evening, the thought of traveling to Australia with such young children was daunting. I had been privileged to lead an SOM delegation to India nearly a decade earlier. The thought of keeping the home fires burning while others made a trip to Australia was reasonable, acceptable, even practical in my eyes. As my heart continued to talk, my mind began opening to the possibilities of actually going to Melbourne.

Eventually I said out loud to Paul, "I think I am supposed to lead this delegation to Melbourne."

In his understated way, Paul's response was, "I do, too."

Once the words were spoken out loud I knew I would follow through. As the hours and miles sped by I imagined different ways to manifest the dream of giving *The INVITATION* in Australia.

This is a good time to talk more about *The INVITATION* and how it was created. The premise is this: what would eight Nobel peace prize laureates say if they were to meet and discuss the *Universal Peace Covenant*? All of the lines the laureates speak are taken from their actual acceptance speeches and put into a conversational context. This means that every time *The INVITATION* is presented, history comes to life and things happen that are not possible in the physical realm.

For instance, Shirin Ebadi, an Iranian woman and the 2003 laureate converses with Alva Myrdal, a Swedish woman who was awarded the Nobel Prize in 1982 and passed away in 1986. These women never did meet, yet in *The INVITATION* their worlds join. Mother Teresa walks with the Dalai Lama, Betty Williams meets and talks to Dr. Martin Luther King. King was a model and inspiration for the peace marches in Northern Ireland in the mid-1970's and, as is well known, his life ended abruptly in 1968.

As an audience member, people are required to stretch beyond linear time into the dimensional realm of consciousness known as Universal Mind. Universal Mind is the meeting place for consciousness without the limitations of the physical world. Subconscious memory exists here, as does the present moment. The intention of *The INVITATION* is to highlight Truth, as it has been brought into the world through the peace laureates.

At the annual meeting of all the directors of School of Metaphysics branches, it was agreed that we would send a delegation to the 2009 Parliament. The vision of the Parliament is to bring people, of all faith traditions, together for ten days of cooperation, peace and harmony. We wanted to present *The INVITATION* in this venue because it is a living example of people from all faiths, bound together through time, space and the quest for peace. Indeed, the *Universal Peace Covenant*, created by SOM teachers and students in 1996-97, was inspired by the 1993 Parliament of the World's Religions held in Chicago. Giving *The INVITATION* at a Parliament, convening on another continent was an obvious way we could honor the stimulus for this performance at its source.

As our minds stretched a year into the future, we decided to host a pre-Parliament event on the grounds of the College of Metaphysics. This would ensure that ALL the School of Metaphysics students could partake in the Parliament activities, whether they were traveling to Australia or not. We decided early on to include a special performance of *The INVITATION*. It turns out this was a pivotal choice.

The day-long "Living Peaceably Begins by Thinking Peacefully"

DREAMTIME

event began to take form. It included speakers from many walks of life, speaking about their perspectives of what it takes to live peaceably and think peacefully. Many different faith traditions were included on the "Perspectives of Peace" panel discussions. The Missouri State poet laureate was willing to create a poem in honor of the event, and the creator of *A Complaint Free World* grassroots movement, Will Bowen, was chosen as our keynote speaker.

During this time our original hope for presenting *The INVITATION* at the 2009 Parliament was shifting. We were focusing on other opportunities within the city of Melbourne. As these doors opened in our minds, field director Ivy Norris invited a woman named Gina Pearson to speak at the "Living Peaceably" event. Gina was unable to attend, however, she generously gave suggestions for other speakers. One of those speakers was Dr. Lawrence Carter, dean and head pastor of the Martin Luther King chapel at Morehouse College in Atlanta, Georgia. Suddenly the resonance with *The INVITATION* and Parliament was becoming more obvious.

Over the next few months, through connections with Dr. Carter, the School of Metaphysics befriended Rev. John Strickland, a Unity Minister in Atlanta. Rev. Strickland's intuitive response to the vision of *The INVITATION* was to fall in love with the idea. It turns out one of his best friends had been the minister of Unity of Melbourne until recently. Rev. Strickland was happy to introduce us to the current minister, Rev. Bill Livingston.

We asked if we could give a special presentation of *The INVITATION* at their church on the Sunday during the Parliament week. It was to be a day devoted to welcoming Unity church members from around the world into the local church. Rev. Livingston was gracious in extending us the opportunity we wanted. As such, *The INVITATION*, was given for the first time in Australia on December 6, 2009. It was one day short of the December 7, 2008, anniversary of that pre-Parliament event in Chicago that sparked this evolutionary path.

This time *The INVITATION* was presented early in the afternoon. The church was filled, and a new element was introduced into the performance. A short film (read the script in Law 2 section), documenting the time period and history of each laureate in the show added depth and an emotional component that rounded out the message of *The INVITATION*.

Here I was, on the other side of the year living, breathing and experiencing amazing resonance.

The timelessness of Universal Mind was real to many that day. Much had happened in those 364 days. "Living Peaceably" had manifested with great success, children had grown and changed, new students had entered the School of Metaphysics, Spiritual Focus Sessions had been hosted at the College of Metaphysics. The details of daily living was magnified through each person. Yet, standing in the Unity Church it felt like no time had passed, at all. I could have turned left and been in Chicago and turned right to find myself in Melbourne. The connecting link was Betty Williams, a woman I have never met, and a woman who has carried me so far.∞

About the Author
Christine Madar has a gift for connecting people with the resources they need. She has earned her Doctorate of Metaphysics, is an ordained minister in the Interfaith Church of Metaphysics, and serves as one of the intuitive reporters for the School of Metaphysics. She received her B.A. degree in Anthropology from Colorado College, her advanced training as a massage therapist from the Boulder College of Massage Therapy, and has long been fascinated by how the Laws of Relativity and Infinity work in people's lives. In addition to organizing international delegations and major peace events at the College of Metaphysics, she teaches the correspondence teachers as well as the College's healing class. She is a wife and mother of two great souls, ages three and six.

The Universal Truth in My Story
Christine Madar

Everything happens for a reason. Our thoughts, choices, feelings and experiences lead us through life. The more conscious you are of these, the more you can embrace infinity. Honor the reality that one thing leads to another, that your life events are related to your past, your future and to other people through time, space and consciousness. It is true that understanding the resonance of any experience, whether within one lifetime or among many, is the essence of understanding the journey of the Self.•

> I ENJOY UNDERSTANDING HOW AND WHY THINGS, PEOPLE, PLACES AND EXPERIENCES RELATE TO ONE ANOTHER AND HOW MY OWN EXPERIENCE EVOLVES IN THE PROCESS.

Since 2005, my mind has been wrapped around the exponential realities that is POWERS of TEN and the profundity that the human being rests in the middle of infinite universes. Christine's story is one of geometric proportions. It is a story that spans the globe, from the unexpected experiences of a young American woman in Belfast in 1988 to the married mother of two who gives an Irish woman voice in a play on the other side of the world from both of those countries in 2009. It is a story that spans time, from another Irish woman from the 19th century who returns to open the door for Christine to become Betty Williams. That woman is Laurie Biswell, who originated the part of Betty in The Invitation. Now an American woman, Laurie Biswell is the one who cares for Christine's 2-year-old daughter Vivienna while she and her husband Paul (who portrays His Holiness the Dalai Lama) present the play in Melbourne. Sound confusing? Infinity can seem that way to the temporary, conscious mind. That's why Christine's story was placed here. She makes the Law of Infinity accessible, and that is quite an accomplishment. –B. Condron

SEVEN
THE LAW of RELATIVITY

"I AM CONNECTED WITH ALL"

told by Dr. Laurel Clark

Grandfather Great Spirit
All over the world the faces of living ones are alike
With tenderness they have come up out of the ground.
...Give us the strength to understand, and the eyes to see.
Teach us to walk the soft Earth as relatives to all that live.
–Sioux Prayer

In the Presence of God

I attended the Parliament of the World's Religions in Chicago in 1993.

At that Parliament, I learned a little bit about religions I had never heard of before: the Sikhs, the Zoroastrians, the Brahma Kumaris, for example. I met people who were doing interfaith work in some of the cities where we have SOM branch centers. So, as the 2009 Parliament of the World's Religions approached, I was anticipating an enriching experience.

My Ideal for this Parliament was to be in the presence of God through my interactions with other people. I wanted to allow the Creator's light to shine through me, and for this purpose I entreated the Creator to use my mind, hands, voice and heart. I wanted to connect with the Divinity in each person I met. Even though the prospect of travel to Australia was intriguing, sightseeing was not my top priority. I was there to meet people.

I had offered my services as a volunteer to contribute to the Parliament and to have an opportunity to make connections with people. My flight arrived in Melbourne on Monday. The Parliament was to begin Thursday evening. Tuesday and Wednesday, two days prior to the Parliament beginning, I was fulfilling some of my volunteer duties. While some of our group went exploring Melbourne and visited the beach, I was organizing registration badges and preparing registration materials.

One of the first people I met is a woman named Linda, from Chicago. She gave me a big hug and smile, saying, "How nice to meet someone from the United States!" We encountered each other many other times during the week of Parliament events. She is a minister in a New Thought church in Chicago, and she will be joining us for the Universal Hour of Peace. She attended Dr. Barbara Condron's class on the ***Crown Jewels of Consciousness*** on the last day of the Parliament. She is also very interested in intuitive reports. This was an auspicious beginning, one example of many wonderful people with whom I connected as a volunteer.

One of the tasks involved moving program books from a pallet into a room. There were about 4,000 books weighing a few pounds each (with over 600 offerings, the program books were sizable!)

They were delivered by a truck and deposited on pallets on the floor of a large gymnasium-type room. They needed to be transferred to another office-like room that could be locked overnight.

About eight of us were moving the books in the beginning. After awhile four of the people left, having finished their volunteer shift for the day. That left two young men, a college-age young woman, Dr. Sheila Benjamin, and me.

Then two older men arrived, both originally from Bombay, India. Phiroz currently lives in Bombay and is head of an organization that raises money to give to organizations that serve the poor. Shekhar lives now in Australia and is involved in a project to have people write letters of gratitude and peace on a long scroll of paper that he delivers to government leaders or people in need. The two men had just met.

When Phiroz and Shekhar joined in the project to move books from one place to another, the young men disappeared. Shekhar suggested setting up an assembly line, with two people lifting the books from the pallets, handing them to one person in a line who would then hand the books to another, give them to another and then the last person would stack the books where they needed to go. The project was a little tedious with the repetitive motion and huge volume of books, but once we had a rhythm established it seemed to move quickly.

The young woman said that it didn't seem very efficient to do it the way we were doing it, and it was not ergonomically correct to do the same motion over and over.

Shekhar smiled a warm and radiant smile and said,

"Ah! But think of how many people's consciousness is on each book when we do it this way. And the people who receive the books will receive all of that consciousness. That's what this is all about, isn't it?"

I told him I agreed. I also let him know that I am with the School of Metaphysics and that we teach about the power of thought. Later in the day I pulled out a piece of paper from my pocket and showed him the affirmation I had been carrying with me and saying for a few weeks:

"My thoughts are pure. I control my thoughts with love and respect."

He smiled and asked me if I had ever heard of the Brahma Kumaris.

I told him that I had heard of them; in fact, that I had heard of them at the 1993 Parliament of the World's Religions but didn't know anything of their philosophy.

He said, "We believe that there is one God and we are all brothers and sisters. We are kind to one another, and see the soul in each person. By developing soul consciousness we can love one another and fulfill our duty to God."

I asked him how they develop soul consciousness, and he said, "through meditation and silence. Meditation is the way." His peaceful presence and radiant smile showed me that he practices what he was speaking.

Shekhar had just learned of the Parliament, and wanted to have the delegates sign a huge scroll of paper, with thoughts of peace and prayers for caring for the Earth, to send to the upcoming summit on climate change in Copenhagen.

Two days before the Parliament he was told that he could have a space outside the convention center.

By the time the Parliament started, he was allowed to have the scroll inside the Parliament venue, in a prominent area in the main lobby.

By the final day, he was given a room to present a film he made when he presented one of his scrolls to a group of children whose homes had been destroyed by a massive fire in Australia. Other children had written messages of hope to these children, and Shekhar filmed the two groups of children meeting.

Phiroz told me that his name is Persian, even though he is from India. Laurie Biswell, one of the School of Metaphysics delegates who also was volunteering, had met Phiroz and given him a copy of *Universal Peace Covenant*.

I asked him what language is spoken in India, "Hindi?"

"Yes," he said, "Hindi and English are both official languages but there are many other languages, including Urdu, and Bengalese, and others."

"Could you translate the *Universal Peace Covenant*?" I ventured.

He said he would love to. He named seven languages that he could translate or have someone else translate it!

I enjoyed getting to know these men. Both were very personable and kind. A simple example is the way they made it easy for Americans and Australians to remember their names. Shekhar said, "shekhar, like salt and pepper shaker." Phiroz said, "To pronounce my name it's like rose, the flower, with 'fee' at the beginning."

I received into myself the warmth of their smiles, the kindness of their hearts, and the generosity of their spirits as a gift I brought home from the Parliament.

The Jyorei Healers

It is easy to get around in Melbourne, with its great public transportation system and walking bridges to cross the river. We were staying at some homestay apartments, about a 20-minute walk from the Melbourne convention center.

When I am in America, I spend a lot of time in a car, driving from city to city. I also sit a lot at a computer. So, although I enjoy walking, it is not a part of my everyday life as it was in Melbourne. It was a pleasure to walk to and from the convention center, until a toe that had been a little sore became more and more painful.

For the first couple of days of my stay, before Parliament began, I walked a lot, and often quickly, to arrive on time for volunteer duties. The second day I needed to make four trips to the convention center, walking back and forth from our apartment eight times. The convention center itself is about a block long, so once inside I was also walking quite a bit.

A couple of weeks before the Parliament, I had given an all-day seminar, standing in high heels for about eight hours straight. This seemed to be the stimulus for the sore foot. When walking around the airports to get to Melbourne, I had noticed my left toe was a little painful. By the second day of the Parliament I noticed that my foot was becoming more and more painful every time I walked. Going up or down stairs was particularly difficult. I had to keep telling my friend Sheila that I couldn't walk as fast as she because of the pain.

I could handle the pain, but I was hoping to be free of such a distraction for the days of the Parliament. I did some healing work of my own, and was fortunate to be shown some stretching exercises by Elena Dubinski, one of the women who was sharing the apartment with us. She is a physical therapist.

On Friday, the first full day of the Parliament, I had finished two volunteer shifts (which involved running around the convention center, picking up and distributing digital recorders, meaning more walking on my already-sore foot!) and went to the exhibition hall. I wanted to see if there were brochures on the New Thought Alliance table for the upcoming performance of *The INVITATION* to be given the following Sunday at the Unity Melbourne.

I was heading out of the convention center to meet someone when a young Japanese woman approached me and asked if I was interested in healing. I said yes, and she said, "Come with me." I told her I was on my way to meet someone, and she said, "only five minutes." I started to ask her if I could come back the next day, and she looked down at her paper, repeating, "only five minutes." I realized she hardly spoke English, and was reading the words from the paper.

She seemed very sincere so I decided to follow her. There, at the front of the exhibit hall, was a booth with folding chairs lined up in two rows, one row of chairs side-by-side facing another row of chairs side-by-side. It almost looked like a train or subway. There were a few young people sitting in chairs on one side. The woman motioned me to sit down in a chair and she sat across from me. Then she told me to relax, close my eyes, and to put my hands on my knees.

Almost immediately, I felt a tingle that was subtle at first, and then I could feel it pulsating in the toe that had been giving me so much pain. It was soothing and energetically balancing. After a short while, she told me I could open my eyes. An older woman who appeared to be a mentor came over. She asked me how I felt. I said that I felt very relaxed and refreshed, and could feel the tingling in my toe which was no longer sore. I thanked them both and they smiled and graciously nodded. They did not ask for donations, nor did there seem to be any place to give a donation. They offered the service freely.

As I walked away, I was amazed at how the healing seemed to draw the pain right out of my foot. I could walk freely and easily for the first time in weeks.

After leaving the hall, I encountered Dr. Barbara Condron and Hezekiah Condron. Hezekiah was not feeling well. He had some kind of cold or flu and was ready to go back to the apartment. I told them about the Jyorei healing so Hezekiah went to receive it. Afterwards he felt much better.

In the days that transpired, I visited the booth several times as did my friends and colleagues. One day, the young man who was offering the service began with a prayer of gratitude for the spiritual master who taught this form of healing. He asked that I give thanks to his master as well. I gladly complied.

I learned that the group is from Japan, from a school where they are learning a healing method that is spiritual. The energetic healing is designed to align the self with spiritual wholeness. They believe that when there is spiritual wholeness, it brings balance to the rest of the system. I asked why they were there – for practice? For service? The mentor said yes, they were there for both purposes.

There was quite a large group of these young people, who were all very gentle and open, radiating love, with warm smiles and an eagerness to aid anyone who came by their booth. I appreciated their presence and their kind service.

Zoroastrians as Stewards of the Earth

I first heard about the Zoroastrians at the 1993 Parliament of the World's Religions. I learned that there are very few Zoroastrians in the world today, and that most of the people and their scriptures were wiped out, destroyed by conquerors. This is the fate of the Tibetan Buddhists today and has been the fate of many peoples throughout history.

After the 1993 Parliament I did some research on the Zoroastrian religion and read what I could find of the scripture, the Zend Avesta and Gathas, but what I found was spotty. So at the 2009 Parliament I wanted to attend some of the teachings to learn more.

I was very impressed with a panel I attended entitled, "Zoroastrianism: Its Stewardship for All Creation, The Animate and Inanimate." In an hour and a half I learned more about Zoroastrianism than I have in twenty years of looking for writings translated in English! I would like to share some of what I learned with you.

The panel included a learned scholar named Dr. Homi Dhalla who is the Founder and President of the World Zarathusti Cultural Foundation. He holds an MA from Harvard and a PhD from Mumbai University. He lives in Bombay, India, and travels to speak at many international conferences. Others on the panel were Rashna Ghadialy, an American Zarathusti of Pakistani descent who was raised living the practices of Zoroastrianism, Homi Gandhi, moderator, who is the co-chair of the Federation of Zoroastrian Associations of North America and representative to the United Nations, and Pervin Mistry who graduated from the University of Bombay and is a student of comparative religions and author.

Homi Gandhi began with an introduction explaining that Zoroastrianism is the oldest monotheistic religion (some sources say it began 3500 years ago; some say it is much older) and is often cited as the originator of all current monotheistic religions. The prophet was named Zoroaster, and a person who practices the religion is known as a "Zarathusti." The God is called Ahura Mazda, translated as "Wise Lord," Ahura meaning "Lord" and Mazda meaning "Wise." Mr. Gandhi said that man is given a central role to move Ahura Mazda's creation forward, that we are responsible as human beings to move Creation forward to a blissful state. Part of our responsibility is to eradicate evil and to support goodness.

Good and Evil are key concepts in the Zoroastrian faith. Both are seen as spiritual forces; therefore, evil cannot be destroyed by physical means such as weapons. Only by spiritual means can goodness prevail: a "spiritually illumined mind resists evil."

As partners with Ahura Mazda, human beings are seen as stewards of creation, which was the topic of this panel.

Dr. Homi Dhalla gave a very clear and complete presentation about the principles of Zoroastrianism and its relationship to caring for the earth. Although I scribbled copious notes as fast as I could, he said much more than I was able to record! He explained that the scientific West doesn't see us as partners with nature. Zoroastrianism views Nature as animate and imbued with transcendent divine essence known as Fravashi. All forms of life have a right to live and grow. A prayer from Yasna 12.7 says,

> "I pray for the good of the life of all living creatures which Ahura Mazda has created."

Dr. Dhalla described levels of Creation, which include the creator and the material creations they govern. Everything originates from One Almighty Creator, Ahura Mazda. As in many scriptures, it is written that a Divine Word caused the manifestation of the Universe. All the kingdoms of Nature are known as Arda Fravash (see chart). Fire is given a central place in the Zoroastrian religion and worship because it is seen as the light of Ahura Mazda.

The key concepts of Zoroastrianism that relate to man being a steward of Nature are these: There is a Divine plan or cosmic order and man is responsible for the preservation of that order. Two other concepts are non-violence (man is a trustee of nature), and harmony which Dr. Dhalla described as "moral ecology," moral connectedness and interdependence.

The principle of moderation is stressed. Dr. Dhalla cited these

Arda Fravash

All Creations (Ahura Mazda)	Mankind
Good Mind (love)	Animals
Divine Law	Fire
Divine Kingdom	Metals
Holy Devotion	Earth
Perfection	Water
Immortality	Vegetation

two scripture verses to illustrate the importance of gratitude and generosity: "A rich man who is always anxious to have more of everything is accounted poor." And "May the chosen ones of Mazda be supporters of the created world."

Some solutions were suggested: education, national and international legislation, human beings assuming individual responsibility as trustees of nature, and economic development that considers future generations. Free will is an important element in the Zoroastrian religion; thus, human beings need to be responsible for their choices and intelligent use of the will.

Another element of the Zoroastrian faith that is important to the stewardship of the Earth is the idea that "every atom enshrines within itself a living, conscious divinity." The unity of all souls sustains life; one cannot injure a part of creation because everything is connected.

Pervin Mistry referenced specific ways that ancient Persians practiced conservation and good stewardship of the earth. It is important to be responsible with mining because the earth as a living being needs minerals, just like we need minerals in our blood. Earth is viewed as an archangel who needs to be respected. The ancient Persians believed that burying bodies of the deceased polluted the earth and burning them (cremation) polluted the air. Instead, they used a Temple of Silence, a large area where bodies were exposed to the rays of the sun (in a hot desert climate) to disintegrate or be consumed by vultures. This method is still used in some parts of the world where it is legal.

Other ancient "green technology" included using cold water from underground streams and cross ventilation systems to cool their dwelling places. There are modern-day Iranian dwellings that still use some of these methods for cooling with natural sources rather than electricity.

Rashna Ghadialy gave some practical ways that people living in cities can practice conservation in alignment with the Zoroastrian principles of care of the earth, care for people, and a fair share for all. She summed it up as, "stop the throw-away mind-frame." Thinking ahead, up to seven generations ahead, is a way to be responsible. She stressed the importance of "conscious consumer behavior" and simple practices like growing as much of your own food as possible.

At another session, I learned that in Zoroastrianism, altruism and progress are valued. To progress Ahura Mazda's creation, man is seen to have three duties: to make an enemy a friend, to make a wicked person righteous, and to make an ignorant person wise.

The principles of Zoroastrianism are simple, and can be summed up in a verse from Yasna 40.2: "Good thoughts, good words, and good deeds."

The Peace Pole Dedication

My relationship with the World Peace Prayer Society began in the mid-1990's.

I gave a talk on the Universal Language of Mind at a World Festival sponsored by an organization called the Unity-and-Diversity-Council. Dr. Daniel Condron was originally scheduled to give the talk, but he was called away on a family emergency, so I represented the SOM in his place. At the Festival, there was a flag ceremony, with prayers for peace said for each country of the world, in that country's language, as young people walked across a stage carrying the flag from that country. By the end of the ceremony, the flags were in a stand, stretched across the stage.

A man named Masahisa Goi in Japan founded the World Peace Prayer Society. Following World War II, praying to avert a third World War, Mr. Goi received a vision in meditation for people around the world to spread the universal message and prayer for world peace, "May Peace Prevail On Earth". Knowing the power of thought, Mr. Goi recognized that "words carry vibrations strong enough to inspire, heal and transform the human heart as well as the Kingdom of plants, animals and all creation."

The School of Metaphysics teaches the Universal Truth that "thoughts are things," which explains the Universal Law, "Thought is cause, and effect is its manifest likeness." The mission of the World Peace Prayer Society aligns with the teachings of the School of Metaphysics, so students and teachers of the School of Metaphysics have chosen to plant Peace Poles with the message, "May Peace Prevail on Earth" on the College of Metaphysics campus and at School of Metaphysics branch locations.

Representatives of the World Peace Prayer Society from around the world have participated in the Universal Hour of Peace, have joined in reading the *Universal Peace Covenant* to bring in the New Year, and read the covenant in 2003 when the Peace Dome was dedicated on the College of Metaphysics campus.

During those days of initial contact with the World Peace Prayer Society, the SOM developed a relationship with Deborah Moldow who was director at the time. I had the opportunity to meet her in person in Puerto Rico at a meeting of the Alliance for a New Humanity.

When the SOM was preparing for a pre-Parliament of the World's Religions event earlier this year, I made contact with the current director, Fumi Johns Stewart. I wondered if someone from WPPS would like to come and offer a flag ceremony. Fumi Johns Stewart said that the flags are large and expensive to transport, and they need a long time in advance to prepare for such a ceremony. However, she indicated that she wanted to help us and would wrap her mind around someone who could participate.

Fumi connected us with Grandmother Silver Star, a Native American woman who lives near Columbia, Missouri, close to the SOM World Headquarters. She sent her blessings to us by email on the day of the pre-parliament event.

While in Melbourne, I received an email from Fumi, saying that she was getting ready to fly to Melbourne for a Peace Pole dedication, and was thinking of me and the School and wanted to send her regards. She did not know that I was in Melbourne! I emailed her back, saying that I looked forward to meeting her in person.

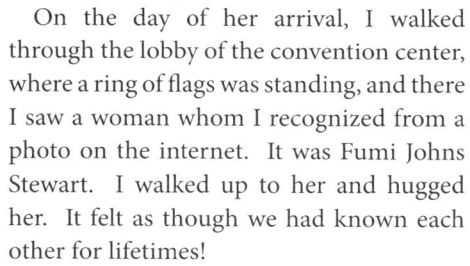

On the day of her arrival, I walked through the lobby of the convention center, where a ring of flags was standing, and there I saw a woman whom I recognized from a photo on the internet. It was Fumi Johns Stewart. I walked up to her and hugged her. It felt as though we had known each other for lifetimes!

The Peace Pole dedication was held in the evening. A group of about 40 people gathered in the lobby area where the Peace Pole stood, surrounded by 192 flags from each country of the world. The flags were hand made, and Fumi told us that it takes about a year to make a flag. Each one is infused with the consciousness of people who pray for peace in the world.

Fumi instructed everyone to choose two flags to hold and to wave when the prayer, "May peace prevail on Earth" was said. I chose the flags of Turkey and Iran, since I know people from these two countries and have heard personal stories of anguish about the need for peace in these places.

The ceremony included someone to pray a peace prayer for each continent, in the native language of that continent. Then the prayer, "May peace prevail on Earth" was said for each country, followed by a musical refrain, with everyone singing, "May peace prevail on Earth" while the flags were held overhead.

At one point, a plenary session that was taking place concurrently let out, and hundreds of people flooded the area where the dedication ceremony was taking place. People selected the flags that were still in stands. A woman from Turkey came up to me and said, "That's my flag," and I gave the Turkish flag to her. A man came up to me and said, looking at the other flag I held, "Do you know that's the flag of Iran?" I said yes, that I had chosen it because I've learned quite a bit about Iran since studying Shirin Ebadi who I portray in a play. His eyes lit up, "You know Shirin Ebadi?" I told him I did not know her personally, but had learned about her life and work.

He said he was glad that someone had chosen the Iranian flag because his country needed peace. I offered him the flag, which he accepted. He told me that he is a professor of theology at a university in Iran. I said that I had heard it was difficult to travel out of Iran, which I had heard from a woman who wanted to come to the United States and could not get a visa year after year. He said that he had no difficulty getting a visa to Australia. We exchanged business cards and I hope to stay in touch with him.

Sheila Benjamin, who was also attending the ceremony, was holding four flags, so she gave me two of hers, Sri Lanka and Kyrgyzstan, and I finished the Peace Pole dedication ceremony with those in hand!

The College of Metaphysics has mini flags from all the countries of the world, a contribution from a Chicago benefactor of the Peace Dome. The Peace Prayer Society's flag dedication ceremony inspired me to learn more about the flags and the countries to which they belong.

School of Metaphysics influence at Parliament

I felt honored to be able to attend presentations given by Dr. Daniel Condron and Dr. Barbara Condron at the 2009 Parliament. Both of them had presented at the 1993 Parliament in Chicago, placing the School of Metaphysics, the educational institute we claim as our alma mater, on a world platform.

In Melbourne, Dr. Daniel presented one of the morning observances. Every morning, from 8 – 9 am, a variety of meditations and worship observances were offered. I had attended several of these, and noticed that some people arrived late, since evening activities often ran late and many people traveled from quite a distance to get to the convention center.

Daniel kept the door open to the room where he was giving his presentation entitled, "The Still Mind, Emptiness and Divine Love." It rained heavily that morning, and people arrived slowly, but seeing the open door invited them to come in whenever they arrived. By the time 15 minutes had passed, the room was full and then overflowing, with people sitting on the floor!

Daniel led the participants through several exercises on love and forgiveness. People appreciated it. I spoke with a man afterwards who said he drove an hour and a half to get to the session, and he was upset that he got caught in traffic and arrived late. By the time the session was over, he felt much more calm and relaxed. As it turns out, he is a documentary film-maker and was partly responsible for Ronda Byrne's success in making the film, *The Secret*. (You may or may not know that Ms. Byrne is from Australia.) He was attending the Parliament to do a documentary on a monk, and thought that Daniel's teachings would be a good thing for him to experience.

Dr. Barbara Condron had two venues. She was on a panel of women speaking about peace in their faith traditions. Dr. Barbara was representing the Christian faith, and she spoke about the influence that her grandmother had on her life as a model of Christianity. She entreated people to be an example for others.

Barbara also, on the last day, gave a presentation on the *The Crown Jewels of Consciousness* which she identified as concentration, meditation, and visualization. She described in clear images how the mind is constructed, and everyone was attentive as she showed the Mind Triangle diagram.

Then she had the audience separate into smaller groups, gathering to discuss dreams. These were led by Dr. Daniel Condron, Dr. Sheila Benjamin, Dr. Pam Blosser, Dr. Christine Madar, and myself. The participants, who by the last day were ready to talk and full of questions, welcomed this.

In my group, we spoke some about dreams and also about other aspects of metaphysics, including intuition and how to keep it alive. One participant said that he used to be guided by strong inner voices that seemed to have gone away. We spoke about the importance of concentration and meditation, to be quiet in the outer mind in order to listen to the inner mind. The daily distractions of noise, cell phones, traffic, and being "busy" with activity keeps the mind busy. This made sense to him and the others in the group, and many were interested in knowing how they could pursue a School of Metaphysics education.

Dr. Barbara showed a clip in both of her presentations of a film made by her son, Hezekiah Condron, about the Healing Wall. This is an endeavor inviting people from around the world to contribute native stones to be embedded in a relief map of the world on a wall surrounding the Peace Dome on the College of Metaphysics campus.

Unity of Melbourne

Rev. William Livingston is a Religious Science minister who pastors a Unity Church in Melbourne. He is a musician who plays jazz piano and has studied metaphysical and spiritual literature for many years. A kind and warm-hearted man, he welcomed the School of Metaphysics to his church for a presentation of ***The INVITATION***. This was part of a day-long celebration, including a special service with a guest minister from a Unity church in California, a sumptuous lunch-time feast, an ice cream truck, and a presentation after ***The INVITATION***, from Indigenous musician and story-teller Jeremy Donovan.

Paul Madar, who portrays H.H. the Dalai Lama in *The INVITATION,* produced a short film that served to introduce the program. It features photos of the historical conditions existing during the time of the eight Nobel Laureates featured in the program, along with a voice-over of each laureate describing their "defining moment." The film brought to everyone's awareness the real needs that spawned each laureate's commitment to action.

Rev. Livingston also offered his church as a place for Dr. Daniel Condron and Dr. Barbara Condron to give intuitive reports after the Parliament was over. This is the first time that intuitive reports have been given in a country other than the United States. The people receiving the reports, and those who were observing, were transfixed, completely attentive and still.

As I was observing and listening to the intuitive reports, the thought came to me, "This is an open heart experience." The church is a lovely little building, with a pink carpet, pink walls, and pink chairs. As the sun set in the evening sky, the light coming through the stained glass window cast a glow in the room. Everything was glowing pink, a soft rose pink. It was like being in the midst of the heart chakra! How fitting that Dr. Daniel was conducting this session, since he has been teaching the Open Heart for quite awhile now, and his latest book is entitled ***Still Mind, Present Moment, Open Heart***.

Koala Consciousness

I couldn't get that koala out of my mind!

The last day of we were in Australia, we went on a tour of the Great Ocean Road. Our tour guide, an engaging and knowledgeable man, drove into a wooded neighborhood to see if we could see some koalas.

Koala bears are cute and cuddly creatures, right? Not so, we learned from him. First of all, koalas are not bears; they are marsupials. Secondly, they are actually quite mean. They have sharp claws and teeth and are anti-social. They live in trees and like to be alone. If two koalas have to share a tree, they sleep on different branches.

The fact that kept preying on my mind was this: Koalas spend most of their time sleeping. They sleep eighteen to twenty hours a day. In the four to six hours they are awake, they eat. They eat the leaves of the eucalyptus or gum trees in which they live. They eat all the leaves and the trees die, so then they need to move on to another tree.

The guide showed us, in the distance, forested areas where entire sections were dead from the koalas that had eaten all the leaves from the trees. This stimulated some questions in my mind. Why would a creature destroy its habitat and its food source? What is the purpose of such a creature?

It also stimulated me to think of people I've known who live like that … sleeping for long hours, using up their resources and the resources others provide for them. As the guide talked about the koalas, I thought about this, and for weeks afterwards, the thought-image of the koala kept coming to mind.

When I spoke with a woman who knew the story of koalas, she said, "Maybe they exist so that we have a metaphor to understand how important it is to respect what we have and give instead of taking."

I did some research and learned that the eucalyptus trees are poisonous to most species. The koalas are able to digest and use the nutrition in the trees, but they have a low nutritional content. This is why they spend so much time sleeping and eating: they have very little energy because they receive little nutrition from their food and have to eat a lot.

This brought to mind the verse from the Bible, from Isaiah 55: "Why spend your money for what is not bread, your wages for what fails to satisfy?" In the Universal Language of Mind, we understand food as a symbol for knowledge. Just as food nourishes the physical body, knowledge nourishes the soul.

Perhaps the koalas can teach us how important it is to choose soul-nourishing knowledge. There is a glut of information in the world. Why spend our time watching movies or reading books that fill the mind with ideas that have little meaning? We can choose to focus on that which aids us to become more whole, more connected with the Creator and other people.

Another lesson I learned from the koalas is to be open to considering the purpose for everything that exists. Maybe the koalas serve a useful function when they destroy the gum trees. Perhaps the trees would overrun the habitat if the koalas weren't there.

One lesson I am learning from the koalas is to use everything that is available. The koalas don't need to drink water, because they receive hydration from the water in the eucalyptus leaves. They are able to use these trees that other species can't. I think the reason why I kept thinking about the koalas is that it brought to my attention how much I value leaving something better than the way I found it. It stimulated me to realize how important it is to aid others, to contribute to the environment rather than using it up.

Koalas are animals. They just do what they are compelled to do by instinct. We are spiritual beings. We can choose. I choose to improve the lives of the people I touch and the place in which we live.

I am grateful to the koalas for illuminating my thinking!•

About the Author
Dr. Laurel Clark has been a teacher with the School of Metaphysics since 1979. She is an ordained minister in the Interfaith Church of Metaphysics and frequently writes articles on the application of Universal Law and spiritual principles in everyday life. Her interest in interfaith relations began as a child, having been raised with no formal religion while being taught spiritual principles by her mother who was raised as an Orthodox Jew and her father who was raised in the Congregational church. Laurel is the author of several books including **Dharma: Finding Your Soul's Purpose** *and* **The Law of Attraction and Other Secrets of Visualization**.

The Universal Truth in My Story
Laurel Clark

> *"Do not neglect to show hospitality to strangers, for by this some have entertained angels without knowing it."*
> – The Bible, *Hebrews 13:2*

When I was growing up, I was a quiet, thoughtful child. I spent a lot of time in silence, listening, observing, and thinking. When playing by myself, if I was playing with dolls, I imagined the conversations silently rather than speaking them out loud. I was called "shy," a label which I accepted and adopted. I was uncomfortable in social situations and often avoided going places where I thought there would be crowds.

It was after becoming a student of metaphysics that I unraveled the truth. I actually love people. I love meeting them, engaging in meaningful conversation and learning from them. The "shyness" was in fact a desire to learn from other people, to listen to them. It reflected a desire to learn through observation. It was also a recognition that talk can be purposeful. The conversations that brought me discomfort were those that seemed "surface," talking about physical things only.

I loved my experience at the Parliament of the World's Religions because it gave me opportunities to meet people of all kinds. People from many different countries, people of different faiths, people with different occupations and interests. People united with a common ideal of wanting to understand one another and bring about global peace and healing.

Meeting people is an enriching experience. I look at every encounter as an opportunity for me to grow, to become changed, to receive something that stimulates me to look at myself and the world from a different perspective. It is a way to develop deeper understanding of universal truth.

I still appreciate the thoughtfulness I had as a child. What does this person bring to me? What have they stimulated in my thinking? How has this interaction enriched me? How am I changed as the result of my communication or meeting with this person?   At the end of each day at the Parliament, I reflected on my experiences with thoughts like these.
It seems amazing to me that we all live in this world, descendants of one spiritual origin, and that individually we make such different choices. By interacting with one another, we learn about what is universal among the differences. Other people can inspire us. Those we admire may become role models. People stimulate us to imagine how we might reach beyond our own habits or limitations. We become aware of needs and are moved to fulfill them, drawing out understanding.

We grow through our relationships with others.

> MY IDEAL FOR THIS
> PARLIAMENT WAS TO BE
> IN THE PRESENCE OF GOD
> THROUGH MY INTERACTIONS
> WITH OTHER PEOPLE.

Laurel Clark's stories demonstrate the compassion and generosity inherent in the experience of relativity (below she connects with Rev. John and Brenda Strickland from Atlanta, Georgia). When Laurel enters into your life, she is aware that forethought has brought the two of you together. For however long you stay, when you part, Laurel carries the essence of your meeting with her wherever she goes. She shares the experience of you with others.

This is an outstanding harmonization with the Law of Relativity that makes her an outstanding president for the School of Metaphysics. Laurel is a living example of relativity, and the following entries support this claim very well. –BC

Continuing Connections

...through visits

Rev. John Strickland is minister of a Unity Church in Atlanta, Georgia. Dr. Christine Madar made connections with him prior to our trip to Melbourne. He attended *The INVITATION* at the Melbourne Unity, and as we were waiting for a bus to arrive to take us back to the convention center, we had an interesting conversation with him and his wife Brenda, learning how they became involved in Unity and how they met one another. He spoke to Dr. Barbara Condron about the possibilities of presenting *The INVITATION* at his church in Atlanta.

I made a short visit to my sister Claire who lives in Atlanta at Christmas time. We attended Rev. Strickland's church, and just before the service started I said hello to him and introduced him to my sister. To my surprise, he announced our presence during the church announcements, and also talked about the School of Metaphysics and *The INVITATION*, inviting his congregation to learn about it and re-stating his desire to present it at his church. After the service was over, he said that they are planning a trip to Missouri during the summer (he used to be the director of Silent Unity and he and Brenda lived in Kansas City) and wants to come visit us at the College. I let him know how much we would welcome their visit!

...by phone

Rev. Linda Oglesby is one of the first people I met when I arrived to volunteer two days before the Parliament began. She was at the Melbourne Unity and attended Dr. Daniel's morning observance. I saw her several times during the week, and when I learned of Dr. Barbara's presentation on *"The Crown Jewels of Consciousness,"* I invited her to attend. She did, and appreciated it. She lives in Chicago and will be joining the Chicago School of Metaphysics for Universal Hour of Peace. She had intended to come to observe the intuitive reports at the Melbourne Unity but was not able to come, so I feel certain that she will have intuitive reports through the SOM now that we are back in the United States.

I have also discovered that there is a Brahma Kumari meditation center in Chicago and a Zoroastrian center near the Bolingbrook School of Metaphysics. We have invited them to participate in the Universal Hour of Peace and Mary, from the Brahma Kumari group, will be joining us in reading the *Universal Peace Covenant* and is going to try to come in person to offer a prayer from their faith tradition.

This is just the beginning. The spirit of Parliament is to build understanding by getting to know other people, listening and learning from them, to build a world of peace, healing, truth, and love. This is something we can do every day, with the people in our communities wherever we are! •

...by email

Dear Shekhar,

It was wonderful meeting you at the Parliament. We moved registration books in an assembly line for hours ... with Phiroz and my friend Sheila. I wrote about the experience and about your wonderful project, the scroll with greetings from the Parliament folks, in an article that will be in a School of Metaphysics newsletter. I did not have a camera, and I am wondering if you have a photo of yourself that you could send to me as an email attachment that I could use to illustrate the article?

Thank you for all the good work you do in the world!
Blessings,
Laurel

Laurel Clark, President School of Metaphysics
www.som.org

From: Shekhar Kamat
Date: Mon, Jan 25, 2010 at 1:03 AM
To: Laurel Clark

Dear Laurel,

It was good gathering of like minded soul. Finally letter has progress to 60mt x 1mt both side fully covered with messages of good wishes. The roll has been sent to New York and I am waiting for time to present it to Secretory General of UN. Hopefully it can been displayed so that world leaders can read messages. I have attaches some picture of letter. I hope it will serve your purpose. Sorry for delay. I have just now completed a short film on the letter. It will be posted on my temporary website in 3 weeks time. www.goodwishes.org It was joint effort me and Maryjean. All the best.

With love and regards
Shekhar

Dr. Homi Dhalla became a manifestation of the Law of Relativity for several in the SOM delegation. Laurel attended the session she writes about here, and my son and I attended his "The Many Faces of Peace". A simple, truthful thought he quoted from the Washington Post struck me quite deeply, "Unless we teach children peace, someone will teach them violence." Having dedicated this Parliament experience in the service of Hezekiah, our 15-year-old son seated beside me, I was thrilled to receive Dr. Dhalla's well-researched presentation of the constructive steps being taken by artists (Michael Moore, George Clooney, Sara Atzman), educators (Queen Rania of Jordan, Shirin Ebadi, Ed Husain, Wangari Maathai), musicians (Harry Belafonte, Bono, Ravi Shankar), religious leaders (Dalai Lama of Tibet, Desmond Tutu, Ami Khaled), athletes (Michael Jordan, Evander Holyfield), and statesmen (Jimmy Carter, Vaclav Havel, Junichiro Koizumi) in the cause of forging a culture of peace.

In 75 minutes, Homi showed 130 slides conveying the depth and breadth of peace effort on the planet. When his presentation moved to peace projects around the globe, I knew I wanted to give the last copy of the **Peacemaking** book I had brought to Australia to this man.

Twenty minutes later, I was seated at a computer reviewing the details for Multifaith Views of Peace panel scheduled for the next day. I heard a voice in the next room, and looking up I saw Dr. Dhalla. I was thrilled. I introduced myself and shared our work at the Peace Dome.

Smiling, he asked, "Is this connected with this?" He held a copy of the Universal Peace Covenant in his hand.

I laughed, "Yes!"

"A young woman, Christine, I believe, gave me this and told me about your work. I will include it in my presentations."

It was most evident that Laurel, Christine, and I were working together as one voice speaking with Homi. We were acting in the service of connecting the Peace Dome with Dr. Dhalla's extensive peace studies, and the School of Metaphysics with Harvard University. The Laws of Relativity, Infinity, and Proper Perspective intersected in that moment.

–BC

… EIGHT

THE LAW of BELIEVING & KNOWING

"I LEARN IN EVERY ACTIVITY"

PARABLE 1
told by Jesse Loren Reece

The Mind, the mind, the mind–
This is the beginning and the end of it all.
The quality of one's life depends on nothing by the mind:
If one's words or deed come from an impure mind
    then suffering surely follows.
If one's words or deeds come from a pure mind
    the happiness walks with him as his own shadow.

–***Twin Verses*** of the Buddha
The Dhammapada

I originally joined the delegation set to attend the Council for a Parliament of the Worlds Religion's while I was studying at the College of Metaphysics.

In the summer, I moved to Louisville, Kentucky, eight hours east of the college campus which is located in southwest Missouri, near the center of the continental United States. I moved to Louisville for the purpose of directing the School of Metaphysics center that is located there.

After arriving in Louisville, I very quickly took to my new duties there as the director. I found the activities involved with directing very freeing. They seemed to offer me an opportunity to become new.

I had in my awareness of the need to accumulate some financial resources in order to fund the trip to Australia for the Council meeting among other things. I thought I would have an easier experience with making money than the experience I produced. I borrowed some money and scrapped together what I had and made it work.

Sunrise on Sunset Boulevard

The moment I left for the trip I felt free, it became very easy to release the many attachments to things in Louisville and yet still feel connected in a small way. I traveled to Los Angeles, California, first. With a 28-hour layover, I rented a vehicle and saw the coast line.

I drove up Pacific Coast Highway because the name sounded familiar. I turned right on Sunset Boulevard. Again, because I had heard the name before. On my right, a mile or so down Sunset Boulevard I saw the Self Realization Fellowship, which was founded by Pramahamsa Yoganada. I had heard of the center and had always felt inspired and reverent whenever exposed to the lineage of teachers connected to the ancient Kriya Yoga teaching taught through the SRF. They were advertising service in the morning at 9 am. I parked the car in a parking lot up the street, did the last of my spiritual exercises and went to sleep.

It was colder than I had imagined it would be in California. Now, I know to always pack at least one warmer outfit when traveling.

I went to the service in the morning, it was very scientific, very enlightened. I felt deeply connected to my Self in a renewed way. Following the service, I spoke with the monk who had given the teaching earlier. We had a lot in common, a similar life path I suppose. He reminded me of the silliness of consumption in finite experiences, and the beauty of living for the attainment of Self Mastery and mental freedom. He was jovial with light-hearted wisdom, a student of life.

Desires Change

I went to the beach from there, swam a little and then walked up to a volleyball game in progress. I had wanted to play some beach volleyball and saw this as an opportunity to fulfill my desire.

I moved on after having played for an hour or two, heading up to the pier where I found outdoor gymnastic equipment that a few years earlier would have simulated me to consider moving there just to play on it daily!

After meditating, starting with a pier of crowded people and ending in a dark silence of ocean with small distant voices, I headed to the airport. I slept for a few hours and was awakened by some of my travel mates wondering about the guy in the corner sleeping who turned out to be me! We laughed at the attractive nature of the moment, given that there were any number of places they could have stood in a very large section of the LAX airport that at that time had many more people than it had hours earlier when I had chosen my place to sleep.

On the plane to Melbourne, Australia I sat next to a young German man studying at Princeton. He was doing the final research for his Doctorate in Aerospace Engineering; 26 years young, same age as me. I asked him some questions and introduced him to Theosophy, the combined study of philosophy, science, and religion, showing him my assigned book reading called **Time, Space, and Self** by Norman E. Pearson.

Later at the Council, this same book aided me in making friends with the folks at the Theosophical Society booth. The man wanted me to donate the book to their society. I informed him that I needed it to complete my assignment. It was a humorous exchange.

Home is Where the Heart Is

I was picked up from the airport by Jaquiline Cox, who is a friend of a friend. She lives in Melbourne with her husband and daughter. Over the next two weeks, I felt like I was living with old friends. They provided me with a carriage house, meals, tours and a family atmosphere the entire time I was in Melbourne. It was unique in my life to merge in with a family, so well, so fast. In another life, I would have stayed for awhile.

I received so much on my train rides every morning and evening, and sometimes in-between. I would walk from the Cox's house to catch the train just up the road. I would ride into the city, a half-hour trip total, including walking and riding. The whole daily travel routine had a subtle meditative quality to it; contemplative as well, since contemplation comes out of meditation that makes sense.

I am realizing as I write more of why I was changed so deeply during this trip. I received some much needed contemplation and meditation time, I had become so action-oriented in Louisville that I'd lost touch with some of the deeper reasons for all the activity in the first place.

Real Mental Connectedness

When I met up with the delegation that I was a part of, I saw everyone differently. We were all halfway across the planet, on a different continent. We had all seemed to let go of a lot of mental baggage. Maybe it was just me and that was the lens I was looking through. Either way, the experience was unique.

Jesse Kern and I deepened our friendship through working together on many assignments, mostly volunteer activities at the Council. The delegation became much like a family. We worked so well together in a totally different country. Our many combined years of mental discipline made for a dynamic interconnected organism.

We were always running into each other. Melbourne is a big city, and we were constantly "running" into each other. Granted, for the most part we did travel in the same circles around the city, yet keep in mind the Parliament had over 5000 attendees. I would just stand in the main walkway, or sit and receptively await someone I knew.

They always came.

I am just realizing how connected we were as a group.

No cell phones.

It was real mental connectedness. We worked together well to host reports and travel throughout the city together to meet in new places using new modes of transportation available, all coming from different places, and all arriving on time.

One time Dr. Christine Madar sent me to the road from the Unity Church where we were giving a performance of *The INVITATION*, a play Dr. Barbara Condron wrote involving Nobel Peace Prize Laureates. I went to the street because Christine figured the Condron's needed assistance in finding the church. She was accurate. It was a clear perception on her part. Stuff like that happened often.

I met many people over the course of the two weeks in Melbourne.

I meditated longer and enjoyed my spiritual exercises with greater peace. The Cox's allowed me to use their internet access daily to check emails and communicate with the School of Metaphysics center in Louisville. That was neat. I felt like a world-traveling, metaphysical director, and for a couple of weeks I was. The center had maintained while I was away, no noticeable outward growth, nothing outwardly lost. Two weeks with the director on the other side of the world. That showed me that what had been built in Louisville, both before I arrived and after, was presently stable. This I needed to see.

The whole experience overall, the many new faces and changing scenery, the sense of family in many different ways, all the stimuli for imaginings of what I would do, where and when, in so many different ways, was very fun.

When I returned to Louisville in the weeks that followed multiple people informed me that I seemed lighter, more heart-centered, and more radiant. I experience gratitude when I think of the experiences and the people on that trip.•

Jesse Reece is the Director of the Cincinnati School of Metaphysics, where he teaches and studies mind, consciousness, and Self. Jesse played college basketball at Missouri Baptist University where he studied biology. He has completed a two-year, full-time study of mind and consciousness at the College of Metaphysics in Windyville, Missouri. There he spent much time working with the garden, orchards, and livestock while styling mind and consciousness with the Doctors of Metaphysics who reside and teach at the college. Jesse has been practicing daily mental disciplines including concentration, meditation, and breathing exercises daily for over four years. He has completed the First Cycle of study as one part of the four-tiered study in the School of Metaphysics.

> I AM REALIZING
> AS I WRITE,
> MORE OF WHY I
> WAS CHANGED SO
> DEEPLY DURING
> THIS TRIP.

"I LEARN IN EVERY ACTIVITY"
PARABLE 2 by Laurie J. Biswell

Being present at the World's Parliament of Religions was like being in the presence of the many faces of God.

I had only imagined what it would be like to be at this event. I had heard the stories of those who attended the parliament in Chicago in 1993. I knew that I could receive from people from all walks of life. I wanted the opportunity to be in their presence and share their stories. I appreciate learning the Universal Language of Mind so when I learn about a religious practice I can see how the differences in religion are just different perspectives of the same thing.

I am reminded of a story about six blind men who were asked to determine what an elephant looked like by feeling different parts of the elephant's body. The blind man who feels a leg says the elephant is like a pillar; the one who feels the tail says the elephant is like a rope; the one who feels the trunk says the elephant is like a tree branch; the one who feels the ear says the elephant is like a hand fan; the one who feels the belly says the elephant is like a wall; and the one who feels the tusk says the elephant is like a solid pipe.

A wise man explains to them:

"All of you are right. The reason every one of you is telling it differently is because each one of you touched the different part of the elephant. So, actually the elephant has all the features you mentioned."

What I experienced the most was the truth spoken in the Universal Peace Covenant that All people desire those things that make for peace. I believe this conference is a way where everyone can share their vision of how peace can come to be. I experienced this in those who presented, the volunteers, and through people I met briefly in the halls.

Eight Crossing of Paths

I arrived in Melbourne, Australia on December 1st, 2009. I met many wonderful people on my way to Australia.

One of my first meetings of those who were attending the Parliament was a couple I met while waiting for the bus to take me to the place where many of the delegates were staying, the Short Stay apartments. I was unfamiliar with the bus system and wanted to know if I was going the right way. The couple said they were going to that very place.

We began to share our stories of how and why we were attending the Parliament. I decided to help them with their luggage. The gentleman was grateful because he had a sore back. As we traveled the twenty-five minute trip from the airport I got to know the couple more. I shared with them the **Universal Peace Covenant**. They shared the many trips they had taken and I enjoyed the moment of hearing of their wonderful tales from the other Parliaments they had attended.

We parted ways when we arrived at our destination, yet it would not be the last time I would see them. Out of the approximately 5500 attendees and the many people around the city, in the eight days to come I would meet this couple on seven different occasions. I discovered this couple is on the Board of Trustees and works with the volunteers for the Council.

After meeting with the delegates, I traveled to my home stay where I would be living while I was in Melbourne. I decided to home stay because I wanted to experience what it's like to live in Australia. I was greeted by my adopted family with wonderful smiles.

Rev. David Horsey met me at the train station in the small suburb of Hampton. He was very charming when he explained to me how he thought I was a bloke (meaning male) because of my name. In Australia, "Laurie" is known as a male's name. After aiding me to the passenger side of the car (I several times went to the driver's side of the car as they drive on the left side of the road) and having a fun chuckle, he drove me to his house. I got settled in, then helped his wife and daughter make puppets. It was very much like being at home!

Dreaming of Being a Jain

On my second day, I reported to volunteer. I met a small group of people and enjoyed helping put together what would be the place for those attending the PWR to receive the catalogue of presentations. The books were thick and we moved a lot of them, stacking them under the tables for easy delivery in the upcoming days. I later found out that Dr. Laurel Clark, just the day before, had moved them from pallets into the room. I understand the power of individual attention, and each of those books received ample attention as they passed through many hands, like an old fashion water brigade, to their final resting place.

I met many wonderful people as a volunteer. One lady and her mother, were very generous. I shared with her the Universal Peace Covenant. She fell in love with it. We continue our correspondence today. It was like meeting someone I have known many lifetimes before. We had an immediate sense of long time relations.

I also met a woman who I had corresponded with before arriving in Melbourne. We met on Facebook. It was a pure joy to meet her face to face. She practices spiritual disciplines and is very gentle in her presence. I believe it was my interaction with her, combined with the Jain art I saw on the wall the next day, that entered into my consciousness and contributed to the dream I had on the third night I was in Australia.

In my dream, I was practicing the faith of Jainism. I was careful to watch my steps and walked very cautiously in order not to disturb any living thing.

I met with Dr. Barbara Condron who encouraged me. I then met with Ivy Norris who did the same. I was on an empty street that partly was familiar and partly a new area I recently had walked in Hampton.

Every breath, I noticed I needed to have a mask.

I learned to interpret dreams as a student at the School of Metaphysics in the United States. In recent years, I have worked with Dr. Condron who directs the education development through www.dreamschool.org and who teaches on the College of Metaphysics campus where I live. Ivy Norris is my teacher in the Third Cycle Doctorate of Divinity Program study at SOM. The presence of both of these women in my dream signifies the movement in Superconscious Mind occurring at the time of this dream.

The dream was a reminder to be consciously present with my experiences. Each moment I had at this event was precious. The strength of Jainism is the reverence of life. How we effect every living thing is important in a Jain's life. Karma is a basic belief for the Jain, a concept they live by, therefore how others are treated is important. I am more awake about how I interact with others these days at Parliament. With the family I am living with, with the volunteers, and with the people we are serving.

I know being in Australia is feeding my Superconscious Mind. I am supposed to be here and I am glad I came. I am forging new territory in my life, setting new goals. I know this will alter the way I see myself, and I want to direct my energies toward that new self image. The dream helps me focus on assimilating my experiences.

I am glad I have studied dreams since I was 13. As a Dreamschool Scholar, I am pursuing certification as a dreamologist and have found my knowledge of dreams very helpful in understanding the rich symbology in the religious cultures at Parliament. I know the volunteer work I do back home in the States as the Chief of Staff of dreamschool.org will help many to understand themselves and their religion.

These experiences in Melbourne, Australia will echo in my life on many levels of consciousness for some time to come. Living on the underside of the planet for a time expanded my awareness in ways I had yet to imagine. I learned of new cultures, and had an opportunity to see how others think.

I traveled mostly by tram. It seems Melbourne has a tram or train going to almost any destination. The tram structure was set up fairly simply, however, I found myself many times further away from my destination than desired. This gave me an opportunity to ask for directions.

Everyone I met was friendly. They were compassionate, and anytime I needed help, help was there. Through dozens of small interchanges, I was able to share the **Universal Peace Covenant** and my reason for being in Australia. Oftentimes these interactions, brought smiles to, as the covenant says, "the one giving and the one receiving." We found commonalities and in some cases sparked interests.

I always believed the world is a friendly place. Now I know.•

> I MEDITATED WITH A PRAYER: "IS IT IN MY BEST INTEREST TO GO TO THE PARLIAMENT OF THE WORLD'S RELIGIONS IN AUSTRALIA?"

The Universal Truth in My Story
Laurie Biswell

The moral to my story actually comes from how I got to Australia in the first place. The openness that I experienced during my trip was a direct result of the gratitude I had for even being there.

I had never traveled outside of the United States or seen the ocean this lifetime. After attending and volunteering at a pre-Parliament event in Chicago, I decided I was going to go to Australia. I did not know how, I only expected and believed that it was where I was to go. From the costs of repairing a recent injury to my ankle, my finances were low. I decided that going to Australia would be a testament to everything that I had been learning at the School of Metaphysics.

After my trip to Chicago, I put a mental tool I learned called a 10 Most Wanted List to work for me. I meditated with a prayer: "Is it in my best interest to go to the Parliament of the World's Religions in Australia?" I then visualized the trip, the people I would meet, the places I would see, and the emotions I would feel.

Several months passed as I prepared for my trip. I started to research what I would need to go – plane tickets, a place to stay, passport, registration, food & tram fares. I didn't yet know where the funding was going to come from. I believed, yet the belief needed action.

As the weeks and months passed, I began to witness small doubts. "Stay the course, " I would tell myself. Then great excitement came, as there was a price break for airfare tickets to Australia. I received a great gift of a fullly-paid, round-trip ticket from Los Angeles to Melbourne. I knew that doubt or fear had no place in creating and receiving my desire.

I am very grateful for that moment. In this one act, I was able to confirm my commitment to going. However I was still in belief.

My belief turned into knowing one night when I was returning from the main building on the campus of the College of Metaphysics to my room at the Gatehouse. It was dark, yet I saw in the seat next to me a big black bag. It was full of brand new clothes, my size. I did not know where they came from at the time. In that moment, I knew beyond any doubt that I was going to Australia!

Now I had sufficient motivation to act on that affirmation that I could find ways to fulfill my studies and duties as a divinity student and work part time to raise the remaining funds I needed for the trip. The details began to manifest. I worked several weekends as an independent contractor as a brand ambassador at a local department store. I started designing websites for pay, which initiated a new business venture I had been thinking about for some time. Acting on my desire to go to Australia caused me to fulfill other long held desires for financial freedom. My mom bought a ticket for me from Oklahoma City to LA in return for website work. The Australia financial need gave me the boost to actually stick my neck out and become a businesswoman. That fulfilled another dream I had been dreaming for a while.

The moral of this parable is: establish a clear goal, determine your purpose for that goal, and take action on it.•

EVERYONE I MET WAS FRIENDLY.

PARABLE 8

Laurie J. Biswell is a 37-year-old, red-headed female who loves nature, kids, and God. She is currently chief designer and programmer of the School of Metaphysics website, dreamschool.org. As a College of Metaphysics graduate teacher, she understands the importance and influence of dedicating one's life towards service to others.

Laurie is a diverse individual. She has a creative, magnanimous spirit that has the ability to set her mind to one thing and to find connections between that and all other things. It is in this light that she has volunteered during the teachings of the Dalai Lama in Madison, Wisconsin, a pre-Parliament event in Chicago, Illinois, and at the Parliament of the World's Religions held in Melbourne, Australia (seated at center, in picture below). the value in giving to others completely from the heart and thus experiencing the Universal Truth of "as you give, so shall you receive." Her immediate future ideals and goals include earning her Doctorate of Divinity, understanding the power of her influence, and creating a personal business that will help others to communicate around the world.

"I want everyone to understand and know the powerful meaning of their night time dreams. Each dream is like a message from God, describing who you are."

I ALWAYS BELIEVED THE WORLD IS A FRIENDLY PLACE. NOW I KNOW.

Laurie and Jesse are outstanding examples of Spirit-filled thinkers. They have managed to sustain the wonder that arises in our Divine nature. It is a quality I have observed in the very young and in the very wise. Wonder opens the mind to possibilities, to new ideas, new people and their practices, new situations. It enables the outer mind to receive, and receiving is the necessary first step for the learning that leads to soul growth and spiritual progression.

The Australia experience was a manifestation of Spirit-led thought for Jesse and for Laurie. They believed they could make the trip which immediately activated the Universal Law of Divine Birthright (Laws #1 and #2 in this writing) on their behalf. They also had faith, that if it was meant by their Real Self for them to go, opportunities to do so would arise. Through this power of imaging, the Laws of Duality, Relativity, Attraction, and Infinity were called into action.

Faith grew into knowing as they learned of new ways to prosper. The financial investment for the trip was a concern for most of us traveling to Australia, and this was true for Laurie and Jesse. Both received special fares on their flights and found no-cost places to stay; Jesse through the personal means of family friends and Laurie through the CPWR home-stay program. As Parliament volunteers, registration fees were waived. Both were also in the company and service of the many presenters who came from all over the world. Choosing to attend Parliament was an intelligent choice. Choosing to volunteer their service was a mindful one.

By far the greatest trip Jesse and Laurie took was the one from believing to knowing – the journey of learning through experience.

NINE
THE LAW of PROPER PERSPECTIVE

"THE PERMANENT & LASTING IS MOST IMPORTANT"

by Barbara Condron, DM, DD

I died as a mineral and became a plant,
I died as a plant and rose to an animal,
I died as an animal and I was man.
Why should I fear? When was I less by dying?
Yet once more I shall die as a man, to soar
With angels blest; but even from angelhood
I must pass on: all except God doth perish.
When I have sacrificed my angel soul,
I shall become what no mind e'er conceived.
Oh, let me not exist! for Non-existence
Proclaims in organ tones, "to Him we shall return."
–Jelaluddin Rumi

Melbourne, 12.03.2009.
The lights in the plenary hall are dimmed and my eyes go to one of the two large screens on either side of the stage.

Someone's hands are moving in the projected image. A circle is drawn, then the hands move in symmetry, creating the spokes on a wheel. I am intrigued, then realize it is a dharma wheel, a symbol for Buddhism. My mind acknowledges the monks' chanting on stage and I am delighted!

Then the hands sweep the image away.

I wait for another image to appear, expecting the screen to come alive with a closeup view of the action on stage or to go dark in anticipation. It does neither.

The hands continue to create. This is when I realize the work is not recorded. It is live.

My eyes search for the creator of such beauty. Is it male or female? Behind the stage or on it? I find what I am seeking when I notice a man dressed in black standing in what looks to be a booth made of wood and material. His gaze is turned downward, his arms reaching before him and moving with the music on stage. When the Aborigine plays his digeridu, he paints two fish that turn into a design that reminds me of a celtic knot and eventually turns into someone on walkabout. I am mesmerized by his mastery and my hands want to participate.

The remainder of the evening, I study the sand master creating the symbols of our world's religions. My heart swells into my throat and I realize a profound forgiveness has overtaken me. To understand why, I must take you with me to a fall evening in 1975, to the School of Metaphysics in Columbia, Missouri.

Columbia, 09.14.1975.
I had been studying metaphysics for three months, learning theory and application of Mind's potential through concentration, meditation, and visualization. Tonight, my classmates and I are gathered to receive intuitive reports that will identify a significant incarnation to the present one we are living.

The well-lit, comfortable living room is hushed though filled to standing room only. "Barbara," says the man with the silken voice made raspy by too many cigarettes.

I step forward to take my place before the man and the 30-something woman with long dark hair.

"Ready?" the man's voice is kind, his smile genuine, the twinkle in his eye a curious mix of light and mischief.

I nod, resolutely nervous.

"You will search for the identity of the entity referred to as Barbara Gayle O'Guinn – "

It begins. I hold my breath.

"You will search for the identity of the entity referred to as Barbara Gayle O'Guinn, and relate a significant incarnation for this entity."

The moment is priceless. The woman is being asked to travel time, looking for me in another form in another place. In the 21st century of science fiction turned fact, computer-generated 3-D neuroscience, such realities are no longer beyond our imagination or our reach. In 2009, they are commonplace. In 1975, in the heartland of the United States, entertaining even the idea of alternate realities is beyond most people's present lives.

The woman begins to speak–

"We see this one as female..."

I have entered into a territory I know nothing of, at a time before written, recorded history. The skepticism in my left-brain journalist identity recedes and the right-brain seeker of truth comes forward. I am about to learn how the purpose of my current life was forged by choices made centuries earlier in Mayan temples.

How an American girl raised by Christian fundamentalist parents in the Bible belt of the country came to be open-minded enough to study mind and consciousness is best told elsewhere. Suffice it to say, a strong inner urge, a calling of Spirit, had its hand on my life from the beginning and this moment of revelation was bringing awareness of that calling into my conscious mind.

I had no way of knowing just how much this intuitive report would resonate with my current life. Only living life - making the choices in the present would make that known.

What I heard that night centered me in a profound way. It was beyond whether I believed in reincarnation or not. I would spend several years developing the will power required to move from believing to a state of knowing concerning that question.

What centered me was the simple, quiet profundity of one sentence. Although the entire significance was relative to my present attitude and needs, one idea struck a chord so deeply within me that I would be dancing for 34 years to its tune. That line was:

> *"We see also this one to be somewhat disturbed within self for not living up to what would be considered perfection."*

Here was the seed of discontent, my constant companion for as long as I could remember. Could its roots lie buried far beyond my parents and the religion of my youth? Might my yearning for things to be different, for peace and joy to prevail in all circumstances arise from another time and place? Could my experience of being consistently thwarted in attempts to make life so, be owing to a karmic obligation of my own making?

These were the first questions I had to answer. By taking the proverbial monkey off my parent's back for the way they raised me, I could accept the responsibility for my choices. My parents wanted a child, any child. I, the Spirit that I Am, wanted them as my parents. Some think the idea that we return to earth is cause for irresponsibility – procrastination, or worse. I have not found this to be true. When I stopped playing the victim of circumstance, I had only myself to blame, and that was incredibly liberating.

The lifetime - the story, if you will – related that I had been chosen to manifest religious ideals in every aspect of life. Hearing this resonated with my beliefs in the present life. It touched a longing that was not fulfilled in my life at that time. Since I was 12, I had been aimless in my religious pursuit. Experiencing the weight of Christian judgement as condemnation rather than reconciliation, I let it alone whenever possible. I was not receiving a Past Life Profile for religious reasons. I was receiving it as part of my studies in Mind and consciousness. This made all the difference for it allowed my mind to be open before making judgements.

I had left the temple studies when my authority was tested, when I was expected to and failed to pass on the knowledge. Upon hearing this, I acutely felt I had let myself down. I had sold out by settling for less. I did not yet have the answers. I did know I was not going to repeat that mistake again.

Several weeks later, when the director of the school offered me the opportunity to teach the correspondence course to a woman living in Texas, without hesitation, I accepted. That was better judgement. I have been teaching ever since. That has been sound judgement.

Melbourne, 12-03-2009.

So here I am, sitting in a convention hall, the sights and sounds of the world's religions surrounding me and the intense feeling of forgiveness wells up from within.

I am overtaken by the wonder of creation in the sand master's hands. How did he ever come up with the idea of using light to project the created image? How many minds is he opening? How is his art aiding the messages in prayer and song to touch the hearts of those present?

I admire his work, and am grateful.

The Mayan incarnation has been on my mind for several months. It returns for my review with cosmic precision.

The Peace Dome, 08-15-2009.

"Dr. Barbara, what was the significance of your first Past Life Profile?" Emily asks.

Because I have stayed with teaching in this life, I have experienced the synchronicity between teacher and student that mirrors the more prevalent human experience of parent and child. Like children, students have impeccable timing in the life of the parent/teacher.

My mind rests upon the scene before me. Emily and Leah,

students from Springfield and Dallas, respectively, are painting the Healing Wall on the East side the Peace Dome under the direction of Doug, a master artisan from Oklahoma City. This is the same Healing Wall that is showcased in Hezekiah's documentary, *Seven Generations*. This day, over 50 students from nine states have gathered to prepare the dome and campus to receive hundreds for our PreParliament event September 5th.

I am digitally capturing the day, and the sight of people of all backgrounds building friendships as they create together, warms my soul. Our day started before sunrise as we gathered at the Peace Dome to read the *Universal Peace Covenant* together. This is a daily discipline, a prayer, given by students and faculty who desire to participate each morning. This morning's prayer is enthused by the multiplication of voices.

Morning meditation follows and the attitude for the day is set into motion. People are everywhere. Painting signs, clearing fence rows, draining pools, planting flowers and greenery, trimming trees, mowing lawns, preparing meals to serve everyone.

This is the first time color has been added to the Healing Wall. It is in response to many inquiries and I anticipate it will aid others to visualize our planet in their mental projections of love and light. It will also make it easier for people to imagine the map filled with native stones from around the world.

For the Healing Wall, this change is history and I am committed to capturing it.

These are my thoughts as Emily's question enters my mind. As I begin to tell the story of what I did and did not do during that past life, I observe my telling. In my mind, I realize I am viewing this past life differently than before. Until this moment, I have judged leaving the temple as a mistake and the weight of that error has created a stigma in my estimation of the value of art and music. Quite simply, as I had judged it, I was given an amazing opportunity that I threw away because I felt I was less than what the task required. In my unworthiness, I turned to art and music for self expression.

It is the present moment, of witnessing the transformation in the Healing Wall, that awakens my consciousness to a higher Truth. The current thought is deeper than the application of greens, blues, and browns to bring the water and lands of the Earth to life. What I am seeing in my mind's eye is the artistry of bringing pieces of the Earth together. The newness in this thought is the tie to my own devaluation, *my own prejudice* against my work.

"*These things I hold against you, though, you have turned aside from our early love.*" The verse from the **Book of Revelation** floats through my mind.

Far from a further condemnation, this moment is one of redemption and salvation. I am receiving how I have in this lifetime learned to use art and music and theater for a higher purpose. The book covers and pictures in magazines and on the web flash before my eyes. Some are of my making, some of those I have encouraged, while others are joint ventures.

The Cantatas are musical presentations, always with holy scriptures at their heart, that I have with the help of dozens forged over the years. Beginning with the Christmas story through to the **Book of Revelation**, we have set the scripture to music and written songs interpreting their meaning in the Universal Language of Mind. We often laughed about how the melodies would stick in your head, arising when reading the scriptures. I can accept the many ways these endeavors have strengthened the spirit of those invested in the work, thus accomplishing what I failed to accomplish in the previous life.

Then there are the two projects of the past decade – *The* **INVITATION**, the play focusing on an imagined meeting of eight Nobel Peace Prize laureates created as the Peace Dome was being constructed, and *The Silver Cord*, the presentation of the journey of one soul through time brought to life through intuitive research into past lives conducted through the School of Metaphysics. At the time of creating them, they were very different in my thinking, almost mirror images of one another.

The INVITATION is an expression of imagination, something that will never happen because most of the individuals are no longer on the earth. The script comes completely from two sources, the laureates own acceptance speeches, and the 577-word *Universal Peace Covenant*, penned in 1996-7 by a dozen spiritual teachers.

The Silver Cord is an expression of memory, the conceptualization by ten people of past life experiences revealed through Past Life Profiles, Crossing of Paths, and Family Profiles. The extemporaneous nature of this presentation was performed only once in the Peace Dome and then, again, for the camera, resulting in the first spiritual documentary based upon intuitive research.

Each project is unique in its offering, and bold in its execution. Whatever imperfections may exist in the delivery of the idea, paled in comparison to the need for the message to be imparted. Such clear-sighted dedication was what I had lacked as Quaradon, my name in the Mayan incarnation.

The Healing Wall at the Peace Dome, 09-05-2009.

A few weeks later, I stand with Grandmother Silverstar, as she blesses our Healing Wall as only one in the line of indigenous American people can. Of the Cherokee and Oglata Lakota People, Grandmother is an Elder Peacekeeper of the 52,000-year-old sacred Star Knowledge Medicine bundle.

I receive the impact of honor in her blessing. It speaks to my own ancestry, stirring the Cherokee blood that flows through my heart. The Healing Wall is the catalyst, the reason we have come together. It is artistry with a purpose and that purpose is a great one: to heal.

In preparing my message about the wall for those assembled at our "Living Peaceably begins by Thinking Peacefully" day, I have spent many hours preparing the healing room inside the Peace Dome. Working with others, we fashion it to tell the story of the stones we have already received, the ones we have yet to obtain, and the reason for the endeavor. A large eight-foot by four-foot relief map is anchored to one wall. Three dozen stones are affixed to the countries of their origin offering the viewer the image of the project we are undertaking. On the facing wall, surrounding a large yoga diagram of chakras, nadis, and postures, are framed stones that resonate with each of the chakras that connect mind and body. It is while working on this exhibit, that a new level of the Healing Wall makes itself known.

As my eyes focus on the representation of the human body's energy patterns, the triune nature of God rises in my mind's eye. I perceive healing as Shiva's dance. Shiva is sometimes called the Lord of the Dance in Hindu teachings. Partnered with Brahm, the creator, and Vishnu, the preserver, Shiva is usually called the destroyer. Together, these three represent the triune nature of creation.

Through my spiritual practices, I have known Shiva to evolve in what he represents. As the wisdom eye opens, Shiva appears to change. He is as likely to be the purifier as the destroyer, and in his higher forms is the transformer. Shiva's stories teach us about healing and wholeness, about the transient nature of the physical existence, and the purpose of our lives.

In the presence of these godly thoughts, the work of many years falls into place. In the intuitive research conducted by the School of Metaphysics, Intuitive Health Analyses have been offered to those requesting them for 50 years. These are similar to the work of Edgar Cayce in America in the early 1900s. I began intuitive reporting in 1977. For the past 15 years, my husband Daniel and I have pioneered what he has coined intuitive prosearch, an active intuitive engagement for advanced thinkers. Two of the reports arising from the prosearch are the Healer's Portrait and the Transference of Energy Report.

The Healer's Portrait identifies one's intuitive thumbprint of understandings which make him or her a healing presence for others. The Transference of Energy Report describes how one is using and recycling creative energies through the chakra system thus revealing his or her healing capacities. These two reports, along with the Health Analysis, reflect the triune nature of God. Here are expressions of the Father, Son, and Holy Spirit in Western theology and Brahm, Vishnu, and Shiva in the East.

In a more modern, scientific sense, I can see this triad in light of Dr. David Hawkin's Map of Consciousness. Dr. Hawkins is the author of many books beginning with *Power vs. Force* which explore the evolution of consciousness on our planet. These three intuitive reports calibrate in progressive levels of consciousness endeavor. The Intuitive Health Analyses describe the mental, emotional, and physical challenges to wholeness that one is experiencing, often due to unrecognized karmic obligations manifested in one's genetic make-up. Most of these function from 0 to somewhere around 250 on the Map's scale. The Healer's Portrait elucidates the individual's intuitive healing ability, working unconsciously in most yet profoundly powerful as an attractor field, functioning from 250 to 600, the level of peace. The Transference of Energy Reports afford education on the transformations that arise in states of enlightenment, functioning from there upward. Through these three means, the evolution of healing that leads to and activates wholeness within the individual can be known.

All of this work comes together in the Peace Dome and its Healing Wall, and both of those are symbols of humanity's greatest desire – peace – and the means to bring it about – healing.

Healing, the pursuit of wholeness, has been a theme throughout my life. Incarning in the household of a faith healer whose touch allowed the deaf to hear, the lame to walk, and the chemically addicted to release their chains, insured healing would be a part of my conscious thinking throughout my life. Yet, what I have learned over the years about healing and wholeness was driven by more than my familial background. It came from an inner drive to know how healing occurs, and why sometimes it seems to fail.

How could I teach or even encourage someone to heal when evidence said it does not always work? It seemed to be religion without science. This bothered me, greatly. As my report noted, I tended to deny myself the right to make errors. It may well have been this denial that prompted one of my first realizations concerning my

Past Life Profile. This was the focus of the relevance of that life to my present life. In the past life, it was described like this:

> "We see this one to view this passing on of information as a great responsibility and to be overly concerned with this one's doing this in a correct manner, and therefore, after great inner turmoil and much time upset in arriving at a decision, we see this one to withdraw from these temple duties and withdraw from this study for this one feels the lack within self to adequately demonstrate these qualities and project the proper information to others as this one would see to be in a perfect manner. "

Even after I left the temple studies, peace eluded me:

> "We see this one to find great pleasure and release of anxieties through these two forms. We see also this one to be somewhat disturbed within self for not living up to what would be considered perfection. "

My greatest insight into perfection came within the first year of receiving this report. I was teaching the Beatitudes from the **Book of Matthew** to a beginning class in metaphysics. *"Be you therefore perfect as your Father in heaven is perfect."* As I read the words, my mind opened in Shakespearean fashion. What if perfect is meant to be a verb here, as well as a noun? My mind opened with this thought. How might this change its meaning?

I spent many years using this simple idea to transform my consciousness. Because "perfecting" included the word symbolizing the ideal desired – "perfection", it became easier to hold my goals holy. I was perfecting - changing, evolving - for the higher purpose of perfection. This was a way to implement one of the suggestions given in that past life report:

> "See this one also to have error in attitude regarding the perfection of self in all activities. Suggest to this one that perfection is not required in experience upon the earth

plane, but only the performing of the activity to the best of one's ability."

I knew where I was headed, and I now knew how to get there. *"I hold this against you, though, you have turned aside from your early love.* **Keep firmly in mind the heights from which you have fallen"** is the remainder of the *Revelation* passage.

When I studied the **Bhagavad Gita,** a particular passage opened my eyes to a new level of understanding. Arjuna, the protagonist which corresponds to Jesus in Christian teachings, is challenging Krishna's (his highest Self, or I Am) counsel to engage in battling the unruly parts of Self. Arjuna reasons that if knowledge is superior to the practice of deeds, why should he undertake such actions with potentially disastrous results? In his response, Krishna counsels in part:

"Do your duty, to the best of your abilities, for the Lord, without any selfish motive, and remember God at all times - before starting a work, at the completion of a task, and while inactive."

Years later, I taught the Beatitudes again. I researched the Greek origin of the word "perfect". The original Greek word used in this passage was *teleios* meaning complete or whole. This gave me the Christian origin of the same idea in the Eastern teachings of yoga, or union. Both relate to the higher presence, that God represents. Through devoting my whole Self to my endeavors in the moment, I am able to transcend the karmic bonds that have held my soul earthbound. My spirit is set free, my consciousness resurrected in I AM, the heights that are the kingdom of Heaven.

Melbourne, 12.05.2009

All of this karmic work of 35 years culminated on Saturday afternoon at the Parliament of the World's Religions.

Each day, in reviewing the offerings at Parliament, I took 14-year-old Hezekiah into account. I knew this was his event in so many ways. Traveling halfway around the world, meeting new people, learning of different cultures, making new friends, attending his father and I, and premiering one of his films. We worked together to choose events he would find of interest. He was accommodating and so I took the opportunity to introduce him to other film makers, youth, and music.

Music has been a large part of my life. I have a natural ear for singing and a talent for composing, although lacking the sufficient skill to reproduce melodies at will on a keyboard. I saw this lack of talent as an area for forgiveness of Self, and one prompting an application of effort to produce a present life skill. My limitations did not stop me from loving the work.

Hezekiah, however was another story. I sang to him before he came into the world and by the time he was two he was wont to bemoan, "Mommy, don't sing!"

I was heartbroken, although it never carried me away. I wanted to sing to him yet would stop at his request, never forcing my singing on him. I cooperated. I chose to see this as an interesting turn of events – that something so important in my life, something that I knew could make a difference in this new soul's life, would be rejected. I knew that soul was aware of the place music holds in the thinking of the mother he chose so it made little sense in my conscious mind. How strange a lesson, I thought.

It took over ten years for Hezekiah to show a significant interest. Largely due to a young master teacher named Matt Valois, Hezekiah learned to love music at age 12. It didn't come through me, it didn't have to. It came when he was ready because I was willing to allow.

Because Matt had ignited Kie's passion, I felt free to place some theater and singing into our Parliament curriculum. On this day, we attended the Carnaval Spirituel presented by Indradyumna Swami, a traveling guru who circles the globe teaching the message of the *Gita*. From the beginning, Kie and I were enthralled. From Bharata Natyam, an ancient form of divine dance from South India, to "The Dance of the Warrior", illustrating the development of martial arts, to "Yoga Moves", the Carnaval was a spiritual feast. The theater presentation of the *Gita* captured Hezekiah's imagination, and he now says it is his favorite of all the scriptures.

Following my profound experience of forgiveness in the

presence of the sand master, now I found myself experiencing the joy of expression through art forms as expressed through the eyes of a Swami. Here is the elevation I so desire. Dance from devotion and free of provocation. Song from spirit and free of ego. Theater from truth and free of weakness. Here were the transcendent forms possible.

Then came "The Art of Happiness", Swami's 15 minutes of teaching, encouraging group meditation for connection with spirit. I admired the ease of the transition, how the art forms were intelligently used to prepare the audience to receive the message.

The full illumination of the purpose of expression was now known.

> *"We see this one presently to also have a desire to reach out to others and to pass on to them the knowledge and experience this one has reached, and to do this in such a way as to always express with enthusiasm and a positive attitude to where these will respond and recognize the value of those things that this one seeks to give."*

My Past Life Profile went on to say that my purpose in choosing the current lifetime was *"an extension of desire that has not been fulfilled in the past and the need at present time to completely express during the present period."*

Again, all the pieces are reconfiguring in my consciousness, a new yoga is forming in the levels of my consciousness. For years, I have quarreled with myself over the value of art and science. Even when I championed it, art was always the lesser in my dualistic thinking. Believing was always less valuable than knowing, the light worth more than the darkness. This is changing, rearranging in my thinking.

I do not yet have the answers I seek. I do know, I will no longer judge art, singing, dance, theater as lesser forms for conveying Truth, for in the history of the world, these are the forms which have made Truth palpable and doing so have placed it into the collective unconscious of the evolving human species. Certainly, with Shiva's eye open, art and science can unite so humans may ascend to the heights from which they have come, asserting their divine birthright.

I also know, today, in the presence of the teachings of one of my favorite Holy works, I have begun making a new marriage in Heaven.

Later that evening I serve as Hezekiah's scribe, recording his thoughts from the day. Part of his entry reads:

> "Mom's favorite part was listening to the music and watching the man design in sand. He was at center stage the entire time and reformed the sand constantly - hands, doves, religious symbols, man and woman, yin-yang. He was responding to the music."

When I started typing Kiah's handwritten journal for this book these words leapt from the page. I realized how this seed has sprouted in his fertile mind within weeks of the experience. By Palm Sunday, 2010, Kie will be creating his version of the sand art during a cantata performance in the Peace Dome, directed by his mother.

A large part of the Parliament experience for me was experiencing the Holy Spirit. The Holy Spirit, or Kundalini energy as I have learned to describe it through my adult studies, was present through the music in every tradition. The full, low tones of the Aboriginal digeridu and matched by the chanting of the Tibetan monks. The simple, repetitive melody of the Islamic calls contrast with the intricate accapella harmonies of a small chamber choir. The high, airy songs of the Hindu dancers rise next to the soul-stirring American choir that entreats everyone to lift their voices to "let me love, let me love in a holy, wholly way."

Music is the place where human beings allow the presence of the Holy Spirit.

My Spirit was stirred many times during Parliament. When I heard Rickie Byers-Beckwith's Agape International Choir sing, my Spirit leapt to its feet, swaying and echoing their melodies and words. This is gospel music at its finest, and gospel is meant to move the Spirit and touch your heart. I was reliving my youth with a happier, healthier outlook. Those gospel songs were *"Nobody Knows the Trouble I've Seen"* or *"Amazing Grace"*, songs of longing and lack.

The Agape songs ignited the spirit to, in the words of the *Universal Peace Covenant*, "transcend whatever separates us". When Rickie explained that the almost 100 strong choir had just come together since arriving in Australia, that only about 40 were core members from the States and the rest were volunteers who had joined on in the last couple days, I stood in appreciation and a bit of sadness, for if I had known the opportunity was present, I would have been there.

It was this thought that made me realize just how important music has always been in my life. As a child, my Christian parents taught me many hymns. My mother played the piano by ear. Her sister, the woman I saw as my grandmother growing up, played the organ. Everyone in the family sang. Singing was a strong means of communication in our household and as an adult I have often realized how different the world would be if life was a musical. If we were each wont to break out into song when we feel our theological or intellectual passions rather than argue them or even take up arms, what a different world we might create!

The Power of Prayer around the World enters into my thinking. This is the name of a musical cantata presented in 1993 at the Parliament of the World's Religions in Chicago. Prayers drawn from the Holy scriptures of the world were set to music by divinity scholars at the College of Metaphysics, creating the framework of the piece. Hindu, Buddhist, Confucian, Taoist, Jewish, Christian, Moslem and Interfaith are represented. What surfaces are the similarities in the yearning, through cultures and religions, for relationship with the creator.

In this moment, surrounded by the Parliament of 2009, I am realizing the truth about the arts. Throughout history, music has been the means to awaken the inner Spirit. For this reason, it is largely seen as a universal language that all people speak, or understand. Therefore, the message can be carried on the music.

I am reminded of a scene from Sir Richard Attenborough's Academy Award depiction of the life of **Gandhi.** Gandhi is a young lawyer in South Africa where British apartheid is in force. He speaks in favor of nonviolent noncompliance during a public meeting. Those in favor are entreated to stand, which all eventually do, except for the few British law enforcers who are present. Perfectly timed, the strains of *"God Save the Queen"* are played, which, because of the soldier's proprietary beliefs, obliges the Britons to also stand. The message is clear on many levels.

This is what art, well crafted, does. Art celebrates Spirit, sometimes softly and quietly, and sometimes loudly and passionately. Art challenges prejudice, questions authority, and heals the wounded. The arts – be they fine or performing – have always been the vehicle for humanity's progress. And in modern times, when education budgets are limited, what are the seemingly expendable subjects? The arts. I have known many teachers of the arts who financed their student's education through personally providing them with needed materials. The arts are all about personal sacrifice, and giving the work your all. That's why Michelangelo was able to finish the Sistine Chapel ceiling.

I have believed in the power of art all my life. In my youth, I considered my own talent good, never outstanding. It was as if the universe was conspiring to give me just enough of the arts to know yet not make it my life's passion. From this lack of personal recognition, came the opportunity for great insight which humility brings.

In the 1980s, as a teacher of mind, art and holy scripture became a tool for enlightenment, reason, and Self-mastery. By engaging the minds and talents of dozens of people over the years, Christian stories from the birth and death of Jesus to Jonah's trials to the *Book of Revelation*, have come to life through music and drama. The **Power of Prayer** was our overture to the world's holy scriptures. Through uniting art with scripture, a greater truth can be seen. These ideals are upheld in the music presented here.

The Carnavale Spirituel is the best example of this I have ever witnessed. The entire concept of the presentation is whole. Physical brawn and prowess is celebrated as martial artists tailor their expertise to the strains of Hindu music. This is matched by the hatha yoga movements of two others. Two women place their eyes, hands, and feet in the careful mudras of traditional Hindu dance that signify the return to the divine.

There are 108 movements in the Bharata Natyam. Each one the expression of a disciplined mind focused on story. At one point, the dancer's right hand is in the Katakamukha Hasta, the 3 joined fingers symbolizing the sacred syllable Aum. The left hand's fingers are in the Alapadma Hasta, the rotating lotus of spiritual light. The eyes are directed toward the Supreme Lord. The left leg is lifted for the swift ascent of consciousness in one step from Earth to Heaven. In Bharata Natyam, state of consciousness and content of consciousness meet and Heaven comes to Earth.

The entire ensemble presents a pantomime of the story of Arjuna and Krishna as told in the **Gita**. Hezekiah was enthralled as the man-turned-into-horses galloped across the stage. Then the story is told again, this time through the song and dance in today's style, as a young woman finds her true love, as her own inner Self.

Following the arts, Swami Indradyumna comes forward to speak to the crowd about consciousness. His voice is gentle and strong as he imparts the truths that are universal, the same truths spoken by Gautama, Jesus, Lao Tzu, and other great Masters before him.

In this moment of wonder, a prejudice that has bound me

for thousands of years crumbles. This is not a prejudice against others. Nor is it a prejudice against religion, or *for* science as I had concluded just days ago. This is the prejudging that art is somehow not good enough, less than the direct conveyance of truth. I have been functioning within the framework of a consciousness that is polarized by good-bad, remnants of the young thinking influenced by the values of those around her. Art is wonderful, I was taught, especially for a female, yet art is not as good, not as profitable, not as respectable as more stable, service careers.

So the focus in my consciousness has not been art. Though many would look at my life - the books written, the plays and films produced, the songs composed and recorded, and so forth - and judge otherwise. The Truth of the matter, my truth in the matter, is that striving to meet a higher calling has revealed art to me in its glory. Where prejudices in my youth might have caused me to turn away from the Carnivale, the wisdom in my saging gives me the eyes to see and the heart to understand. The prejudices against the continuity of life reflected in reincarnation dissolved in my 20s enabling my mind to open to the relative Truths conveyed in of all things – a spiritual carnival! What joy!

At this Parliament, I have reached a point in my awareness where art is on the uprise, an easier venue for conveying those Truths that apply to us all. This is a venue where the giver's self-discipline and self-restraint can meet the receiver's acceptance and allowance. I met a master of the arts today and I received his lesson wholeheartedly.

I am so grateful.

This is why I have come to Parliament. It is another golden nugget to add to my already bountiful collection of unanticipated treasures.

I am eager to return to the work awaiting me. Two months before departing for Australia, I set into motion my future. I announced I would be teaching a class at the College of Metaphysics, over three extended weekends, beginning in January. We would cover text in the *Bible*, the arc I call *"The Temptation"* which begins with Jesus and Satan in *Matthew 4*, moves to the man and woman in the garden in *Genesis 3*, and concludes with the woman and the dragon in *Revelation 12*. It is a powerful study that can aid people to readdress beliefs that have outlived their usefulness and upgrade their level of awareness towards bringing forth the Christ within.

At the same time, two dozen of us will embark upon a 2010 updated version of the **Power of Prayer around the World**, the cantata presented at the 1993 Parliament of the World's Religions in Chicago. This will be the first step of three as well. These steps will lead to the creation of the multimedia presentation of the *Book of Revelation*. Today, I find myself more dedicated to this effort than ever before.

And if it is to be, we may well be presenting the *Revelation Experience* at the next Parliament somewhere in the world in 2014.

Namaste, Swami Indradyumna, I hope we can give to others what I have been able to receive from you. In Lak'ech Ala K'in.

College of Metaphysics, 01.15.10

At the first gathering for the **Power of Prayer around the World Cantata**, Hezekiah decides to join us. Before he has stayed on the periphery, preferring to film rather than participate. He attends the auditions and the keynote which informs the group of the history and meaning of this cantata. He sings and dances with us. It is the influence of Parliament.

The next day, he tells me he wants to make sand images. He can use the overhead projector to shine the light up on the wall or on a screen and he will make the symbols with his hands or a brush. "Tad has said he will help me," Kie says.

"That's a great idea, Kie," I am delighted and surprised that he remembers and is inspired by something he saw at Parliament.

When I read his journal entry, I receive a deeper understanding of his offer to participate. He is giving something he knows his mother will favor, and I am grateful for the opportunity to be this in his life.

Unlike many women, my imaginings did not revolve around nurturing the young. I have observed that this openness, although at times disconcerting, has for the most part enabled me to honor Hezekiah as a soul. It leaves me free to teach and guide him in the same way I teach and guide others, regardless of age or parentage. Being without prejudice of who he may become, I find I can better respond to the choices he makes in the present.

The significance of that Mayan lifetime suggested,

> "...there is no need this one feels insecure, for the finding of security in what this one presents is gained through the continuous application of those principles received, this one will form the security this one requires and will be able to share with others in the proper approach."

When I first learned that Mind could be explored and consciousness developed, I wanted to understand that vast frontier. Concentration, meditation, and visualization have been the practices I received to do so. Through these, I have come to move from states of believing to states of knowing. This transition has made all the difference in discerning Truth of a universal sense.

I am keenly aware that most people on Earth have little workable knowledge of the consciousness that forms their beliefs. This is why reincarnation remains a belief to embrace or reject. It is also why the discussion of experiences like the ones I relate here hold widespread importance.

I am also aware that some will reject what is said here as a good story, wild imaginings or even demonic possession. The greater Truth lies in the story. The capacity to image a whole creation and embody it.

I have chosen a most fortunate time to live. I have at my fingertips the philosophies of the world, the ideas of the greatest thinkers of all time, the masters of consciousness as we know it. In that light, interfaith is a wise choice. It is not that having the world agree on certain ideas makes them truth, rather it is the independent rising of Truth through diverse cultures that did not know one another that makes the Truth easy to identify.

When I received that Past Life Profile so many years ago, the conductor asked this question: *What type of religion did this one follow?* The answer came back:

> "We see this religion as being the worship of one particular God or deity, and this being represented in certain symbology. We see also there to be other deities which would be considered lesser in effect in status which are represented in smaller stones. We see there to be much symbology represented within this religious practice and this to not be clear to all individuals. We see this one to have reached only a certain point in understanding the representation of this symbology and not to have continued beyond this point due to the qualities that have been given."

In this life, I have continued beyond the point. A nightmare at age six set my course to eventually learn to interpret dreams. Mastering the language of Mind, has made it easier to talk with God, and to listen. I am awake and conscious of life. I realize I am a symbol for Hezekiah, the mother archetype in his life, a representation of his own highest Self. Just as he, as my son, is a symbol for the ideal I nurture of what it means to be intuitive, Spiritual Man. I receive that duty without attachment, for I know it will last but a short while.

Like the sand that moves under the master's touch or the grains arranged by the Buddhist monks, this life, these thoughts, this existence is temporary.

Religion is the pursuit of what is immortal, eternal, everlasting. It is a valuable expression of the exaltation of man, a door that leads to illumination.

I am reminded of a lovely young lady from Japan who is a member of the World Spirit Youth Council, an international youth movement sponsored by Children of the Earth, a nonprofit UN-NGO founded by Nina Meyerhof. The young lady's name is Yuka Saionji. Yuka was one of eight young people speaking on the youth panel Rev. Terrence had invited Hezekiah to attend. As I listened to each of them share their stories, the reality of Indigo children maturing unfolded before my eyes and I had a profound sense that the future of the world is in very capable hands.

Yuka's enthusiasm radiated from her infectiously as she explained just how easy it is to determine that people of all religions can find ways to agree and to cooperate. "It's like this. If I ask John" she pointed to a man seated on her far right, halfway into the audience, "to point to the exit, he will do so." John obliged by standing and pointing behind him to the south and a bit west.

"If I ask Karoline", a member of the panel from Germany who was seated to Yuka's far left, "to point to the exit, she will point in the opposite direction from John. If I ask, the lady standing in front of the door to point to the exit, she will point directly to it (west).

"Do you see? They are all correct. I can go by any one of them and find the exit. The exit does not move. It is where it is. So the pointing of the way is a matter of perspective. Where the people are in relationship to the door.

"When we focus only on the hand and finger we lose sight of where we are headed. When we move our attention to where the hands are pointing, we can better see where we are going.

"Spirituality is the same. We are all pointing to the same thing and eventually we will all get there! We will all make it so we might as well cooperate!"

Yuka lives what she teaches. She is a deputy chairperson of Byakko Shinko Kai, an organization dedicated to world peace and raising the consciousness of humanity. Byakko believes in the divinity of all humanity and hosts interfaith events such as the Symphony of Peace Prayers, where a diverse group of religious leaders lead more than 10,000 participants in harmonious prayer. Youthful wisdom supports the reality that consciousness continues over space and time. Old souls seeking to complete their lessons in the earthly schoolroom abound in today's world. The beauty in my eyes is the availability for connection between them. That is what the

World Spirit Youth Council affords.

In searching for a picture to post of Yuka, I learn of her parentage. Her mother is Masami Saionji, the spiritual leader of the Movement of Prayer for World Peace initiated in Japan by Masahisa Goi. These are the people behind the Peace Poles that Dr. Laurel Clark references.

At age thirty-three, Goi attained oneness with his divine self. A few years later, in 1955, he founded the movement to transcend all religious, social, ethnic and political barriers through a single divinely-inspired prayer. "May Peace Prevail on Earth" is recited for every country on the planet each time a Peace Pole is planted. Goi considered Masami his adopted daughter and subsequently, his successor as chairperson of the movement.

Byakko Shinko Kai, which Yuka references, is a spiritual organization that originated in Japan over 50 years ago. The words mean White Light Association. Byakko is dedicated to world peace and to raising planetary consciousness through encouraging solid, easy to practice spiritual techniques and the commitment to one's higher spiritual goals.

Yuka and her siblings support their mother's work. She reminds me of Alexandra Madar (her hands in mudra at right) and her sister Vivienna, sisters of fortunate rebirths. Here for divine purposes.

College of Metaphysics, 01.28.10

Most of my first 28 years was spent wanting to be someone else in some other place. I dreamed of traveling around the world, to distant romantic places. My grandmother would tell a story about me as a little girl, packing my suitcase and sitting by the window, gazing outside.

When someone asked me what I was doing, she said I replied, "I'm traveling on the train!"

I visited over half the United States before I was 14, and at 12 I stepped into Canada to visit the World Expo in Montreal with my parents. Visions of the world filled my head and the U.S. pavilion - a geodesic dome - planted a seed as Kundala was stirring in my consciousness. That entire experience I would appreciate more fully when the Peace Dome grew from a seed decades later at the College of Metaphysics.

When I went to the university to study journalism, I didn't know about foreign study programs so whatever education opportunities may have been present passed me by. Within six months of graduation, something happened that transformed my thinking about traveling on the planet. That something was the reality of intuition, astral travel, and the reports given by the School of Metaphysics. I decided the first night I witnessed them that, if it was possible and I was found worthy, I wanted to be the vessel through which this kind of wisdom is disseminated. A little over two years later, I gave my first public reports in Wichita, Kansas with Joseph Harpine as my conductor. That was 1977.

In those days, those of us studying metaphysics in the heart of the U.S. looked forward. We talked often of spreading SOM teachings around the globe. We believed we would publish books and speak before large multiracial, multicultural, multigenerational audiences. We thought we needed a broadcast station to reach more of the world, and figured we would call it KSOM. We wanted to publish a magazine and give media interviews. We dreamed of school branches around the world with everyone on the planet receiving intuitive "readings".

As a graduate student and field director for SOM, opening schools in Louisiana, Mississippi and Alabama, my thinking shifted dramatically. Through the combination of SOM study and practices and public intuitive reporting, the personal desire for travel left me. In its place were the very real inner level experiences throughout times and places, many of which are not available in the present time on this planet.

I began to experience what it is to create without attachment, to manifest free of ego. Others' experiences became as my own, and I was grateful for the opportunity for accelerated learning. Lak'ech

Ala K'in, I am another Yourself, the Mayan version of "Love your neighbor as yourself" became a reality in my consciousness. I shared of the abundance we produced, encouraging my students to teach and lead in new places. Some did. They moved to existing branches in places like Berwyn, a surburb of Chicago, and Kansas City. They opened schools in Mobile, Jackson, Baton Rouge, and Memphis. We often laughed that "the South was rising again!" and Intuitive Reports played a major role in introducing Florida, Texas, and Tennessee to SOM.

By the 90s, my learning was unfolding in new cities. Daniel Condron and I began seeding cities like Houston with the Intuitive Reports and public speaking in broader venues like the 1993 Parliament, then our lives took a significant turn as a great soul chose us as parents. The report tours turned into Spiritual Focus Sessions and the pioneering of Intuitive Prosearch. The lecture opportunities turned into student weekends at the College, an educational day at universities called POWERS of TEN, and The Still Mind, Present Moment, Open Heart teachings.

I stayed close to SOM headquarters for over a decade, passing by opportunities in Barcelona, Johannesburg, and Delhi. I had no regrets for the intuitive reporting transported me through time and space in a most fulfilling manner. When Daniel began traveling a few years ago, I observed and studied my thoughts concerning his travels, asking myself if I, too, wanted to travel abroad. I didn't. I realized, then, how much I was at peace with being who and where I am.

I realized my earlier desires for travel had been fulfilled. I had written books, one being translated into foreign languages. I had spoken before multiracial, multicultural, multigenerational audiences. I had appeared on media from the BBC in England to *Asahi Shimbun* in Japan to *Deccan Chronicle* in India. I had edited SOM's magazine *Thresholds* for a decade and given intuitive reports for people on six continents. In reaching out with my mind through these venues, I had drawn hundreds of occasions to meet thousands of people from all over the world. The capacity to move in time and space around the world had made it easy to fulfill the desires I created.

What remained was service, using my life in the service of others. Intuitive Reporting is the height of this kind of service. And it was a gift to find myself offering reports in person on the continent of Australia.

I understand cycles in life, perhaps moreso because I honor the spiral of humanity's spiritual evolution. This is growth beyond the progress of civilization. It is measured not by standards of living and possessions. This growth is measured by ideals accomplished and lives transformed through love and compassion, truth and reason. As I write this, I stand on the threshold of a cycle, one astrologers identify as the second Saturn return. Seeking to understand Self, I have reflected upon how the culmination of this cycle might resonate with the responsibility I experienced in 1982 as President of SOM. I was surprised to find a spiritual Parliament on the other side of the world providing the measuring rod. The resonance came simply, in the form of the offer to represent Christianity on a peace panel. In the context of this chapter and its reincarnation theme, this would probably strike most Christians as incongruent at best. Although I must say that I have met many Catholic priests who are quite enlightened in this area of spiritual discernment.

Let it be said here that my understanding of the purpose of religion is tied to a reality where we have been Christian, Buddhist, Jain, Muslim, Hindu, Taoist, atheist, and perhaps Aboriginal, Indian, or Inuit.

Somewhere.

Some time.

We *are* they.

When we accept that the world is indeed a stage, an illusion with purpose, we cease blaming self or others for the conditions in our lives. When we realize we were the kings and the slaves of yesterday, our mind shifts. We become responsible for our intentions. How we think about others becomes important. The "golden rule" makes more sense. Gratitude, forgiveness, and tolerance become a part of Self replacing bitterness, resentment, and hatred. How we see ourselves and the world are forever changed.

At Parliament, it is easier to perceive this reality – the one beyond appearances, the one emanating from the soul. The differences are the outer presentation. The eyes, filled with compassion, reveal the soul. In **The Secret Doctrine**, Helena Blavatsky writes, *"That which is part of our souls is eternal...Those lives are countless, but the soul or spirit that animates us throughout these myriads of existences is the same; and though the 'book and volume' of the physical brain may forget events within the scope of one terrestrial life, the bulk of collective recollections can never desert the divine soul within us."*•

The Universal Truth in My Story
Barbara Condron

I remember in 1975, when my divinity journey began in earnest, there were people picketing a lecture given on the subject of past lives and reincarnation. History tells us it is risky to introduce new ways of thinking when the attractor field is weak. Since then, humanity has strengthened, rising to above 200, the level of courage, on Hawkins' Map of Consciousness. Evidence of that shift is apparent at events like Parliament.

The personal computer and the internet, the device and the connection, have made it possible for the forward thinkers, the sages, the old souls, regardless of their physical time on the planet, to work together. Until recently, they toiled in solitude, the only one of their kind to see, to know, to counsel. It is the end of the days of singular masters. Now, we can find our contemporaries, learn about them, meet, and as long as we are willing we can join soul forces to create a new Heaven and a new Earth. It's the rise of group consciousness.

I sometimes think of this in light of His Holiness the Dalai Lama of Tibet. When he spoke in Melbourne on the occasion of the 20th anniversary of receiving the Nobel Peace Prize, I was there. I first heard him speak during the 1993 Parliament. Time is aging both of us and it struck me how much he has done to spread the simple and positive message of the continuity of life. For decades, he has brought his message of compassion to millions around the world.

His mere presence speaks to the reality of reincarnation. Once again, an idea becomes part of the collective unconscious until its time to surface in a receptive mind.

Today, in light of this essay's subject, I wonder when His Holiness is gone, who will take his place? Whose life will speak to eternity? Who will be that change in the world? Most people look to the youth as the change. That is a very good place, and a very old one. It has brought humanity this far in evolution. To progress further, requires a change in where we look.

The new place to look is within. "Worldly people seek after all [worldly] things. Your Father in heaven knows that all of these things are also necessary for you. But you seek first the kingdom of God and his righteousness, and all of these things shall be added to you," (Matt. 6:32-33) taught one master teacher 2000 years ago.

I learned this idea and the practice of faith as a child. When I turned 22 and graduated from university, I began learning to transform faith into knowing. I became the change I would see in the world. One of the most famous soliloquies in Shakespeare's plays, includes these lines worthy of any holy work:

> "*What a piece of work is a man! how Noble in*
> *Reason? how infinite in faculty? in form and moving?*
> *how express and admirable in action,*
> *how like an Angel in apprehension,*
> *how like a God, the beauty of the world,*
> *the paragon of animals*"

Had Shakespeare studied the Four Noble Truths and Eightfold Path? Or perhaps, as some others believe, was this text a refiguring of the Biblical Psalms. Does it matter? The answer is, yes. Facts matter, as does Truth.

What is remarkable is we are able to receive Truth of our Divine and human nature from so many sources. In fact, when we know what is most important, when we have our priorities straight, our minds harmonize with Universal Law and it becomes easy to see life through the eyes of the soul.

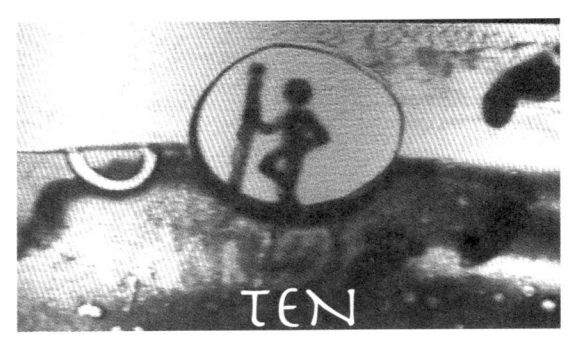

TEN
THE LAW of EVOLUTION

"I ADD TO MY UNDERSTANDING EVERY DAY"
PARABLE 1

by Paul Madar, D.D., M.B.A.

The duties of universal obligation are five, and the moral qualities by which they are carried out are three. The duties are those between ruler and subject, between parents and children, between husband and wife, between elder siblings and younger, and those in the intercourse between friends. These are the five duties of universal obligation.
Wisdom, compassion, and courage – these are the three universally recognized moral qualities of human beings. It matters not in what way people come to the exercise of these moral qualities, the result is one and the same.
–Confucius

Time

It was often a surreal experience to be keenly aware of being halfway around the world in Melbourne, Australia, and to see Dr. Sheila pop up, or Jesse Kern wave hello from down the hallway, or to run into Dr. Laurel with Elena and Dr. Pam in a side street café downtown. Having so many familiar faces around made it sometimes feel like I wasn't traveling at all. It also gave me continual reminders of the higher purpose for which our delegation came—to give the School of Metaphysics to people half a world away, and to receive new perspectives into ourselves in the process.

This journey to Australia was, I believe, a turning point for our oldest daughter, Alexandra, then weeks from turning six. We went there as a family with the intention of clarifying our ideals and our next steps in life. I went with the personal ideal of being a student of spiritual leadership so I can help others develop and maintain their inner connection. As the days unfolded I could sense especially in Alexandra an ease with travel and being in new circumstances.

Every day presented some new challenge, some new adventure, some new frustration. And we met each one and found learning and growth. Just getting on the right tram or going up the elevators or ordering food gave her little bits of authority and experience in the ambiguity of traveling in another country.

Christine and I both agree that travel is very important for our children, to expose them to the uncertainty that travel brings, and to give them ample experience meeting that uncertainty with an open mind, with humor, with grace, and with decisiveness. Learning early the art of making choices has greatly contributed to Alexandra and Vivienna having accelerated growth as well as helping them maintain their inner connection.

I think all School of Metaphysics students should travel periodically. I think travel in general has tremendous benefits for the soul. And I don't mean just traveling to and from the College of Metaphysics or other branches. I mean traveling outside the country, to a culture decidedly different from our own.

Having traveled to many countries throughout my life, I can say that every trip has changed me in remarkable ways. I have learned and practiced in my travels simple, yet profound things such as finding my way in a strange land, making friends across cultures, openness to trying new foods and customs, interpreting value differently, universal humor, expanding my perspectives, challenging belief systems, independence, autonomy, decisiveness, and so many more qualities.

Now on top of the benefits of traveling, I think traveling with a higher purpose is even more fulfilling. Going on spiritual delegations to India, to South Africa and now to Australia I had the honor of giving my time, energy and service for the benefit first of the people we met, and then for this School we all love. Of course, as I give my time and energy with higher purposes, I automatically benefit in building selflessness and service.

When I meet people in other lands I often discover bits of myself. These seeming strangers reflect back to me a side that I may not have known, or a side of me that I had forgotten. When I first met Rev. Bill Livingston of the Unity Church of Melbourne, I knew here was a very kind soul. I could instantly trust and respect him. His genuine love of people came right out, even through his Australian casual properness. As he and I talked I found out he had been sparked into studying metaphysics through reading the same series of books that sparked me, at exactly the same age—Tibetan Lama T. Lobsang Rampa's books about old Tibet. I figure there is some past life connection going on there as well between he and I. His open door policy for our family and for the School of Metaphysics to serve his congregation and borrow the church to give intuitive reports says worlds about his character.

Paul's Story via Vivi

Christine and I negotiated who would be with the girls and who would attend the Parliament sessions on what days. We had spent most of our time together with the children, touring the city and bringing them to Parliament events and sessions. Early on the last day at Parliament, I found myself blissfully solo! Christine had both girls and I eagerly set off to a morning observance having to do with Native American traditions. Well, it was cancelled. So I checked the day's events and sessions kiosk board and found another I thought would be good, something about Jain chanting. I admire Jains, and as a musician, I respect the power of chanting. Well, the presenter could barely speak English, bless his heart. He had a translator right next to him. I was straining so hard to understand him, and it was early in the morning, that I finally got up and had to leave.

I wandered back to the sessions kiosk. Looking ahead in the time slots I finally saw a session that looked interesting from the title: *The Crown Jewels of Consciousness...* and then I saw that *Dr. Barbara Condron and other teachers of the School of Metaphysics* were giving it. I thought, "Wow, I am really out of the loop!"

I went upstairs and saw Dr. Sheila near a volunteer station. I told her about it and she didn't know about it either. That was odd. She saw Dr. Barbara a little ways away and went over to talk to her about it. Well, Dr. Barbara had not heard either! It was a surprise to ALL of us.

After a bit of mustering and negotiating with Christine, who arrived soon after this with Vivienna and Alexandra, we decided I was going to be one of the assistants in this 'new' session. But the girls had other plans. Alexandra wanted to be in the session with Mama, and Vivienna wanted to ride the escalators with Dada. At just three years old, Vivi was tired and would not budge from wanting to go with me on the escalators. We had to make a decision right then, so I decided to let Christine assist in the session and I would release the scene and trust in higher order.

I felt generous, and off I went with Vivi. We watched a violinist and a guitar duo playing jazz standards around the corner from the session. We finished a giant muffin, with crumbs all over the floor, while watching. And then we went to the escalator on the second floor, leaving the stroller behind, expecting to climb the stairs, hop and run.

Vivi had, with a little coaching, taken to waving to the people going the opposite direction on the escalators at Parliament. Today was no exception. Very serious spiritual people in all sorts of robes, turbans and costumes discoursing about deep issues smiled and waved back at this disarming redhead waving and saying "HI!" to them. A camera crew filmed us coming down and Vivi dramatically jumped off the last step, gleeful as ever, with her Dad right behind her.

Going up the escalator for the twentieth time we saw another serious turban approaching. The man had a kind face, but seemed clouded by thoughts. Vivi worked her charm. When he finally saw Vivi his head lifted, his eyes got big, and he waved a big smile and said hi. I was enjoying watching how this girl could lift people with a wave and a smile.

We rounded the top and headed back down the escalator again. There was the man with the turban waiting for us.

He greeted Vivi this time with a big wave and smile. We introduced ourselves, and Ralph Singh (at left with Hezekiah Condron) said he was heading out of the Parliament, discouraged because he had hoped to bolster his sagging belief in his newest venture in life—creating spiritual storytelling CDs for kids. He had not met with many parents of small children and there were not many children around at Parliament anyway. Vivi was the youngest, and one of only a handful that were present in a consistent way.

I must have really lit up also because I have been moving toward a very similar venture in my life—creating spiritual stories and songs on CD for kids. He and I talked, exchanged biographies and contact information, and then Vivi escorted both of us up the escalator to the second floor, hand in hand with herself in the middle.

We arrived at the SOM session refreshed, talking about storytelling, as Ralph brought out a portable player and speakers to try out his recordings on Vivi. She immediately locked in on his voice and the music and gentle sound effects.

She listened, and he brightened.

She listened and he watched.

She listened, and his hope was renewed.

"She likes it!" he kept saying. "I think she likes it!"

Ralph and I talked about further connections that I knew in the storytelling world in Indiana, and when we checked in with Vivienna again, she was fast asleep in her stroller. That girl has a way about her. Generosity opens the door for Universal Law to bring people together.

In the few hours from finding the 'surprise' SOM session on the kiosk in the morning to finding a 'surprise' friend on the escalator, I saw a graceful lesson unfold. I saw once again that as I loosen my grip on my individual desires, a funny thing happens – I make space for higher purpose and Universal Law to step in. I make space for growth. As I turned my intention to serving the whole group, simply by agreeing to take Vivi to the escalators, I could see how everyone benefited more, including myself. Christine got to co-mentor within the session, Alexandra got to attend an excellent session with her Mama and all her teacher friends, Vivi got to express her wonderful qualities of cheerfulness and friendliness, Ralph confirmed new hope for his storytelling projects, and I got to eat a muffin.

Oh yes, and I grew as a father, a husband, a spiritual leader, and even as a storyteller.

A Father's Notebook

Since so much of my time was spent with the children on this trip, it seemed natural that I would write about them for this book. These are some additional brief notes I made as the journey concluded.

Feeding the Emu

I took the girls in the morning to their first-ever real train ride to a neighboring city, Ballarat, famous for its wildlife preserve and gold mining town. Vivi and Xani loved the train and the hour and a half trip flew by, literally! In the small town of Ballarat, we found the right bus and made our way to the wildlife area where kangaroos and emus wander freely. We petted and fed many kangaroos and I attempted to hand-feed an emu. Not recommended for the squeamish. I held out my hand with some feed to the giant seven-foot emu towering over us. "I come in peace," I whispered. The emu accepted the offering with a dive-bombing peck at my hand. I jumped back, feed flying, with a yelp. The girls laughed for a long time at that scene.

The girls' joy was contagious as we attracted two Chinese couples to where we were petting and feeding the kangaroos. They filmed the girls jumping like kangaroos alongside them, feeding, petting, and hugging full-size kangaroos. The girls both got to pet a joey inside his mother's pouch. They both fed and fawned on Snickers, an orphaned joey in a green fluffy makeshift pouch by the gift shop door. We collected yellow flowers across the road and ran for the bus as it began to rain.

Agape Choir

There was some beautiful music performances and inspiring and spirit-filled Agape choir. The power of humility unleashed. The leader of the choir, Rickie Beyers Beckwith, was the picture of spirit-filled humble passion, loving what she does and knowing its value to others. The girls sang the "Holy, Wholly Way" song over and over, and I didn't mind a bit.

Carnivale Spiritual
Alexandra and Vivienna were mesmerized by the Hare Krishna group's Baghavad Gita performance. They watched every bit of the inspirational exhibitions of yoga and martial arts and Vivi danced her kirtan to the modern/classical Hindu dance troupe.

Rev. Dr. Auntie Godmother Sheila
Dr. Sheila's generosity with kids shines on other continents, too! Always ready to gather the children, Dr. Sheila gave Christine and me a date night by taking both the kids at the same time for the evening. They swam, ate, played for several hours. Christine and I walked for miles through the city, sampled chocolate cake, found great coffee and watched the Fire Show on the river walk. Thank you!

Vivienna turned three
Hezekiah orchestrated a great, simple celebration with balloons, candle and cake. The girls loved it! I marvel at their energy. The parents sat in time-zone jet lag, watching balloons flying everywhere.

Buddhist Gyoto Monks
The Tibetan monks blessed items we bought for ourselves, for the girls and for the Dream Valley house at the College. The monks served as a constant spiritual presence of spiritual action. Not just talk and dialogue, but action—consistent, focused, purposeful action.

And non-attached creation. The resulting form is not the sacred part of the creation—the intention and the action are the sacred part of creation. Alexandra, especially, was captivated by the symmetry, the precision, and the concentration.

St. Kilda Beach
Jellyfish!? "Just over there is Antarctica." Sunburns! Collecting shells for the Healing Wall.

Getting around town
Seeing The Wishing Well band on the first "Golden Perfect Day" out right after we arrived. How well the girls cooperated, all things considered. We learned the short cuts in the city, over the various bridges and through tunnels. We had fun learning the public transportation system. This was all quite new.

Sacred Music Concert
Vivienna slept through the entire concert, Agape Choir and all, sprawled on my lap.

Seeing the Dalai Lama with Alexandra and Vivienna
Priceless.

Calling Papa
I called my father on his birthday from Australia. A short call, but a surprise for him and a thrill for me. I hope someday my girls will do something like that, too.∞

About the Author
Currently completing his Doctorate in Metaphysics, Paul Madar has taught, lectured and given radio and television interviews in many cities throughout the Midwest for 14 years. Paul holds a B.S. in Biology from Cornell University, an M.B.A. from Butler University. He is one of the School of Metaphysics' conductors of intuitive research. A Renaissance man, he is a multi-instrument musician, ordained minister, writer, artist, storyteller, scientist, carpenter, counselor, teacher, husband, and father of two girls.

"I ADD TO MY UNDERSTANDING EVERY DAY"

PARABLE 2
by Christine Madar, D.M., D.D..

Time & Space
One thing that surprised me about Melbourne/Australia was.......
The public transit system, the cleanliness of the city centre and how easy it is to recycle. They are also conscientious about using their water wisely. I appreciated being surrounded by people who are walking the walk, not just talking about making changes that are needed for this planet to remain healthy. Melbourne is by far the cleanest big city I have had occasion to visit.

This may sound trivial, yet it is an interesting insight I had that I can tie to practicing concentration exercises for twenty years. Australia is one of those countries that drives on the "wrong side of the road" from our American perspective. I lived in another one of those countries, Ireland, while I was in college. I remember how disorienting it was to be in a country with the traffic going in opposite directions. At times I felt almost dizzy and would get confused about where to look or walk in regards to the traffic.

I noticed in Melbourne that I adjusted easily to the change in direction of the traffic. At first I attributed it to having lived in Ireland, a bit like 'you never forget how to ride a bike'. After a few days of observing myself, and walking around the city, I discerned that it was not memory that was making it easier for me, it was attention. My concentration is much better than when I was 20 years old and therefore it is easier to adjust to anything in my environment.

Christine's Story through Alexandra and Vivi

It was Wednesday morning, December 9th.

I was sitting upstairs by the Tibetan monks and the mandala they had finished after five days of spiritual craftsmanship. It had been a whirlwind getting to the venue that morning. Including getting 15 minutes away from our shortstay apartment and realizing I had failed to put shoes on Vivienna! She was happily sitting in her stroller, quite used to being barefoot. We had to turn around, retracing our steps and get the shoes. Needless to say, we arrived at the Parliament activities much later than originally intended – I was soon to find out that the timing was perfect.

The area where the monks convened was big and spacious. Alexandra and Vivienna had room to run and play, even when a lot of people were around. They were familiar with the setting, so as soon as we arrived they took off. I was sitting quietly, watching them and a bit lost in thought about the fact that this was the last day of Parliament.

A woman sitting near me spoke up, "I think it is wonderful that you brought your children."

I watched as they tumbled over each other wrestling and laughing, seeing them through her eyes. My response was, "I remind myself that each day."

Our conversation continued. She acknowledged that it must have been a challenge to travel the distance from the USA. I mentioned that most of our time had been spent just *being* at Parliament since neither Alexandra or Vivi were willing to sit through the classes. Again, she confirmed that she thought we were doing the right thing by coming.

Her words echoed Paul's sentiments and mine. It was affirming to hear them after the crazy shoe incident that morning.

We were quiet for a while. Then I asked her if she was associated with a group or if she had come to Parliament solo. She said she was here with a few friends and they were artists. They lived in Orange County near Los Angeles.

Suddenly I asked her, "Are you the people who are creating the Sky Wheel Project?" I could see her face light up as I said, "I have been wanting to meet you this whole week!"

I introduced myself by name, saying that I had hoped to meet her at Parliament because I had something to give to her. She recognized me as a fellow Peace Ambassador. She too had coordinated a pre-Parliament event.

I gave her the last copies of the *Universal Peace Covenant* in my backpack, saying, "This belongs in your project. The world needs it."

When she saw the title and received my enthusiasm she thanked me and said "This will fit perfectly."

I went on to explain that it could have been e-mailed but I had wanted to hand it to her personally and to encourage her unique and visionary endeavor.

Soon it was time to go and we hugged. I said, "I don't know when I'll see you again but I wish you all the luck with your project. I will help spread the word."

She glanced at Alexandra and Vivienna and thanked us once again for bringing such bright lights into the Parliament setting.

Soon after Dr. Barbara Condron came and asked if I could attend the *Crown Jewels* class that she was teaching.

This is a short story, yet it speaks to the power of a clearly visualized thought and the capacity to receive.

As the coordinator of the "Living Peaceably" event in September many doors were opened for me to represent the School of Metaphysics regarding the Council for a Parliament of the World's Religions. One of those opportunities was becoming a Peace Ambassador.

Parliament then created a special Facebook page for the Peace Ambassadors to communicate before the December event took place.

One of the Peace Ambassadors that

I corresponded with briefly was Kim Garrison, co-creator of the Sky Wheel project. Kim and several artist friends are designing a satellite that will turn like a Tibetan prayer wheel as it orbits the earth (http://www.skywheel.org). They are currently gathering prayers and spiritual text from around the world to include in their project. Their goal is to launch the satellite in 2016.

I decided before leaving for Australia that I wanted to meet Kim and hand her a copy of the **Universal Peace Covenant.** I did not communicate this to her ahead of time and I did not go searching for her during my days at Parliament. I had a simple expectation that our paths would cross.

I am grateful that she spoke up and that I kept asking her questions. If I had arrived an hour earlier or ten minutes later our meeting would have been altered. I love this expression of the Universal Law of Relativity. As the laws work, our paths crossed at the perfect time.

IN ONE SPECTRAL MOMENT, I EXPERIENCED A CULMINATION OF ONE YEAR, TEN YEARS, SIXTEEN YEARS AND TWENTY YEARS OF EXPERIENCE....

Time, Space, & Self

Outstanding stories and meaningful moments from my perspective. The Closing Plenary was concluding and the emotion in the auditorium was palpable. The Dalai Lama was sitting on stage watching, as he must have hundreds or thousands of times in his years of service, pomp and circumstance that honored other people, other cultures.

As music played, the Australian girls' choir, who had sung beautifully earlier in the plenary, began to walk in pairs across the stage. Each of them was holding a banner from a pre-Parliament event. Eighty events had been hosted in 30 countries.

I started counting the banners. When I counted more than I

knew had been hanging in the Exhibition Hall my hopes began to rise. Paul said, "There it is, there is our banner." Indeed, it was the second to last to cross the stage and was within a few feet of the Dalai Lama. My eyes welled up with tears then and they do now when I recall this moment.

In the Dalai Lama's eyes, our flag was really no different than the others that had just crossed the stage. He will never know the details of the "Living Peaceably" event. This is one moment, however, that I wish every person who was part of our pre-Parliament event could have shared in person.

In one spectral moment, I experienced a culmination of one year, ten years, sixteen years and twenty years of experience and the corresponding crescendo of emotional energy.

Let me explain. In the first few days of the Parliament, I had made a special effort to find our banner in the Exhibition Hall. It was not hanging and I felt disappointed. I wondered why it was not with the others. It had been received in the Chicago office and should have been transported to Melbourne. Strangely I felt like the lack of its presence was letting down all the students who had worked so devotedly to bring "Living Peaceably" into being. I wanted the energies of all the people who signed our banner to be seen, to be felt at the Parliament.

I know the power of psychometry, which is why I left the banner hanging in the Main Room at the College of Metaphysics for two months after our event. I felt privileged to be one of the few SOM representatives actually traveling to Melbourne. I had my heart set on that banner symbolizing the importance of all the people who had not made the trip. When I mentioned that ours was not displayed some people said it didn't matter, to me it mattered a lot.

This is why I counted the banners as they streamed across the stage in the final moments of Parliament.

One year ago, in December 2008, we had been in Chicago, presenting *The INVITATION* at their pre-Parliament event. The powerful emotional energy at the conclusion of that event affected me deeply and I was moved to coordinate the "Living Peaceably" event and organize the trip to Australia. Indeed, just a few days ago we had presented *The INVITATION* at the Unity of Melbourne Church.

Ten years ago, in 1999, I was with the group of people who traveled to India with the People to People Ambassador Program. We spent several days in Dharmsala, a small town high in the Himalayan Mountains, and, the Dalai Lama's home in India. We had hand delivered a **Universal Peace Covenant** to the monks in residence. We had been in the temple where the Dalai Lama chanted. I remembered India, when our banner crossed the stage with His Holiness as a witness.

Sixteen years ago, the 100th anniversary of the first Parliament was celebrated in Chicago. Many School of Metaphysics students and teachers were part of the 8,000 people that gathered from around the world in 1993. I became a student in the School of Metaphysics in the afterglow of that Parliament. Sitting in the grand auditorium in Melbourne, Australia, I was beginning to see the timing of my entry into the School of Metaphysics through new eyes.

Twenty years ago, on December 10th, the Dalai Lama accepted his Nobel Peace Prize. I could only imagine what he has experienced in 20 years. What an honor to be in his presence, for our "Living Peaceably" event to have highlighted *The INVITATION*, and for this moment in time to exist.

I felt profound gratitude for this sequence of events.

We have a wonderful photo of Hezekiah standing next to the banner. It speaks to me of the hope of the past, present and future for peace in humanity.∞

The Universal Truth in My Story

Christine Madar

The Universal Law of Evolution ensures that we progress in learning, understanding and awareness. One of the most fulfilling experiences in life is making sense of seemingly unrelated experiences. In order to do this, you must recognize how thoughts, emotions and experiences are related to each other. Making choices to consciously grow, expand and be different increases individual evolution. As more individuals evolve, humanity progresses as a whole. Gratitude is a natural expression of the fulfillment of the Law of Evolution.•

Christine has a gift for connecting people with the resources they need. She has earned her Doctorate of Metaphysics, is an ordained minister in the Interfaith Church of Metaphysics, and serves as one of the intuitive reporters for the School of Metaphysics. She received her B.A. degree in Anthropology from Colorado College, her advanced training as a massage therapist from the Boulder College of Massage Therapy, and has long been fascinated by how the Laws of Relativity and Infinity work in people's lives. In addition to organizing international delegations and major peace events at the College of Metaphysics, she teaches the correspondence teachers as well as the College's healing class. She is a wife and mother of two great souls, ages three and six.

"I ADD TO MY UNDERSTANDING EVERY DAY"
PARABLE 3
by Sheila Benjamin

Walking in the Footsteps of Mother Teresa of Calcutta

Do you remember playing dress up when you were a kid? Did you ever think that what you were doing was playing out your soul's assignment for this lifetime?

I have learned throughout my studies in metaphysics that the Soul reveals itself in the roles that we play when alone between the ages of zero to seven years of age. The doorway to subconscious mind is left open for the soul to shine through and show itself. It is important for us to remember these events in our lives, which can help us understand our soul's purpose. It is also important that we provide positive and inspirational stimuli for the children who are around us.

During these formulative years, I played bank teller and ballerina. I also was very much in love with my religious practices that I was learning. I loved the nuns who were my teachers. I can remember thinking at the age of six that I was marrying Jesus as I made my First Holy Communion. I collected holy cards like some kids collect magic cards, baseball cards, and so forth.

Throughout my life, I have been inspired by individuals who have dedicated their life to service. People like Gandhi, Pope John Paul II, His Holiness the Dalai Lama and Mother Teresa. I was creating my life's mission each time I visualized my life to be in the spirit of these great people. I knew that what they did, they did out of love, out of passion, out of devotion and were not at all concerned if others in return recognized them for what they did.

They were humble.
They were dedicated.
They were my heroes.

We all need great people in our lives to look up to, to emulate, to reach toward. Mother Teresa has been such a person in my life. I used her as an example to remind myself to smile at others knowing that it was a way of giving my love to them. Her life was a perfect example of someone who was living the golden rule in every step that she took.

I can remember when my nephew was about eight (he's 23 now) and he got his first computer. We were looking up thoughts about peace, people who symbolized peace and so forth. I remember that Mother Teresa was one of these people we read about.

Michael, my nephew, turned to me with the innocence of youth on his face and sincerity in his heart, and said, "Auntie Sheila, you are one of these people."

I received his thoughts into my heart. Yes, my life had become one with seeking truth, love and light.

For the past four years, I have portrayed Mother Teresa in a Living Prayer called *The Invitation*. I have called the spirit of Mother Teresa of Calcutta to myself as I wrap a simple white cotton cloth with three blue stripes sewn along the edges around my body. The garment is very similar to the one Mother Teresa wore each day for more than 40 years. I receive her spirit as I hold a rosary in my hands and recite the words that she spoke when she accepted the Nobel Peace

Prize.

Her life has been an inspiration to me for many years of my life, so when Dr. Barbara Condron, the creator and director of *The Invitation*, asked me if I wanted to be a part of the Peace Dome presentation, I said, "Yes!"

When she asked if I wanted to bring Mother Teresa, I felt honored while acknowledging that it was a perfect fit. Dr. Barbara knew it also.

It was easy for me to say the words of Mother Teresa with meaning, emotion and spirit, because in my life I have real experiences that I was able to call upon. I have worked with the elderly in nursing homes, with children who need an adult in their life, and with the mentally ill; all people who need someone to care.

I have not become a nun – at least not in this lifetime – however I have devoted my life to serving others. I have worked with the sick, the lonely, and the poor in spirit. I have taught others to become more connected to their own inner self.

When we gave *The Invitation* at the Pre-Parliament event in Chicago a woman knelt down in front of me and thanked me. She was paying homage to the spirit of Mother Teresa that was brought to life through me.

My life continues to be enriched because of my place in *The Invitation*. I am reminded to share my life. I think of this each time Mother Teresa talks about witnessing the Hindu woman, with eight children of her own, sharing her food with her neighbors, a hungry Moslem family.

I am reminded that people are always more important than things or time, and that the smile is the beginning of love.

Find someone or a group of someones in your world who are inspiring to you. Create an image as to how you can bring them to life in your everyday activities. You will find that you become what you imagine.∞

About the Author

Dr. Sheila Benjamin was born in Chicago, Illinois. Her parents were Catholics and raised her with a strong religious education. She learned to use her life and her senses as an instrument in which to see God in all. Her mother taught her to live occurring to the Golden Rule. Even so, she was disturbed when confronted with other's afflictions. This avoidance bothered her, and as she aged she chose to place herself in a service position as a Recreational Therapist. She continues to work with children today who have been diagnosed on the Autism spectrum and is able to teach them the simple truths of sharing, caring, and cooperating. She often sees herself as a Universal Aunt, and treats all children as if they were her own.

IT IS IMPORTANT THAT WE PROVIDE POSITIVE AND INSPIRATIONAL STIMULI FOR THE CHILDREN WHO ARE AROUND US

I have known Paul and Christine Madar for almost two decades. I have watched them establish an internal commitment to knowing Self, meet, fall in love, and then invite very wise souls into their lives to ceate a family. The result is one of the most beautiful families I have ever seen - beautiful both inside and out.

Christine and Paul have ideals, like most parents, to afford the best for their girls. They share parenting in a way worthy of emulating. Yet, what distinguishes them is more than the result of upper middle class values, ethics and standard of living. Although both of these highly educated people could live anywhere in the world and provide high dollar schooling for their daughters, they choose to forge a wholistic way of education.

Both Madars are trained in intuitive research; Paul as a conductor and Christine as an intuitive reporter. They understand the existence of the soul, and as ministers are vigilant to its needs. They realize their first responsibility is as teachers, examples of conscious living. They are raising their daughters at the College of Metaphysics in Missouri so they can have the advantages of living with people of different races, cultures, and backgrounds, and the nurturing that comes from living in nature. Tree limbs replace desks and the rising and setting sun, clocks. These girls are learning the responsibility of freedom.

*It is a perfect way to teach evolution. I have watched Alexandra captivated by her dad's portrayal of His Holiness the Dalai Lama. She knows all the words to **The INVITATION** at age six. I look forward to seeing the effect such high mindedness has on the choices she makes in life.*

Many people noted the strong family presence the Madars emanate. Some of them began wishing they had shared the Parliament with the youth in their family. Kim put it in words, "I think it is wonderful that you brought your children." When more people follow the Madars' example, we will all function more perfectly in harmony with this law that governs spiritual progression in our universe.

ELEVEN
THE LAW of PROSPERITY

"I RECEIVE THE WEALTH OF THE UNIVERSE."

by Hezekiah Condron

*With her comes all good things,
and She carries in Her arms
wealth beyond counting.
I rejoiced with love for all people,
as I could see Sophia in their hearts,
guiding them.
What I learned with great effort
I now share freely;
I do not hoard Her wealth for myself.
She is an inexhaustible treasure for mankind;
She blesses the world with Supreme wisdom,
and allows all people to realize
their unity with God.
–Wisdom of Solomon*

My journey began over a year ago when I attended a PreParliament of the World's Religions event in Chicago, Illinois. We were able to present *The INVITATION*. I had a wonderful experience there and was looking forward to many more like it. I later found out that several people from the School of Metaphysics intended to go to the Council for a Parliament of the World's Religions in Australia and that I would be able to go as well.

When we hosted our own PreParliament event at the College of Metaphysics, I had a great time. I was one of the official photographers. I met many interesting people including Will Bowen, author of the **Complaint Free World** and **Complaint Free Relationships**, and his daughter Lia, who is one year younger than me and who I have become good friends with. The PreParliament event heightened my anticipation of going to Australia.

A few weeks later, my parents and I flew from Kansas City to Denver to Los Angeles to Melbourne. We left KC at 8:30 am Sunday November 29 and arrived in Melbourne at 9:30 a.m. Tuesday, December 1. I can now say, I know what it is to time travel.

Here are parts of the journal I kept during our trip.

Hezekiah's Daily Journal

Tuesday, December 1, 2009
I loved flying.
I realized that this was the longest I had spent not touching the Earth.

Because of the time change we arrived around 9:30 am Tuesday. We spent two hours going through customs and getting our luggage. Then we met up with Tad Messenger who drove us around town. I thought it was very interesting how the steering wheel was on the right side similar to Europe and Japan. I was amazed by how much like home, Australia looks. And I loved it.

Tad took us to a place called Queen Victoria Market. The market had every imaginable kind of food. It consisted of a series of individual

DREAMTIME

vendor shops – each selling anything form smooothies and packaged foods to fresh meats, cheeses, seafood, and fruits and vegetables. I became inspired and bought enough food to make a delicious meal for myself and my parents. We had fish, green beans and carrots, rigatoni-type pasta with cheddar cheese and basil pesto on the side. I cooked this meal for my parents to thank them for allowing me to come along on the trip. It was delicious.

Our apartment is beautiful. It has a fully functional kitchen, a stereo with CD player, a phone-tv-dvd player. It has an impressive view with a balcony 21 floors above the city. The three rooms have stark colors in the form of red-browns, whites, tans and blacks.

After we ate dinner, I went to bed and was asleep sometime between 11 and 11:40 pm Australian time. Except for a couple hours on the plane, we had been awake for I don't know how many hours.

Wednesday, December 2, 2009
I woke up at 7 am this morning.

This was BEACH DAY! We met the Madars in the lobby. I had not seen Christine or either of her children since they departed from the college many days earlier. We all walked through the city together. Melbourne is incredibly beautiful. We walked on a bridge over the Yarra River. It flows through downtown Melbourne.

We then caught a tram - a cross between a bus and a train. We traveled to St. Kilda Beach arriving about 10:30 am. There were only a few people there. As it warmed up, more and more people flocked to the beach. It is winter at home in the middle of the United States and it is summer in Australia.

Thursday December 3, 2009

I awoke and went with my parents to the breakfast gathering in Tad's apartment a couple floors above ours. We ate food with Tad, Jesse Reece, Jesse Kern, Drs. Sheila, Pam and Laurel and the Madar family. It was a bring a dish, just like at home, so we brought granola that we had bought the day before at the market. We had fresh fruit - strawberries, pineapple, kiwi, and bananas. Yoghurt, very big here. Potatoes and toast. It was quite a feast!

We were meeting to discuss the Parliament and *THE INVITATION*. We decided to meet each day around 5 or 6 pm to touch bases, share and set goals for the next day. Several of the people are volunteering at Parliament.

....We walked to the Exhibition Center about 3:45, received our programs, and planned the next day's activities. Tomorrow, I am going to attend a film about medicinal plants, a workshop on Naga chants and the *Breath of Life* observance. Mom and I will go to the grocery store sometime tomorrow because I am guest chef for a dinner party tomorrow night. The menu is: Beef Stroganoff, Green Beans, & French Bread. I plan to prescreen *Seventh Generation - The Construction of a Healing Wall* here in Australia during the dinner.

The Parliament officially started at 7:30 pm. The Opening Plenary was amazing. It was a beautiful ceremony in which several religious leaders of great eminence spoke, giving blessings for the days ahead. There are over 5000 people at Parliament from 75 countries or more. Everywhere you go there are Buddhists or Sikhs or New Thought or Jains or Hindu or Jews or Christians or Pagans or Indigenous peoples. Many speakers, singers, and dancers took their turn on stage tonight, speaking eloquently about the various ways we can work together to make the world a better place. It was very inspiring. I look forward to learning more over the next 6 days.

One thing I learned today was:
The variety of peoples from around the world who come to Parliament.

My prayer tonight is:
Dear God, help me have a great interfaith experience over the Parliament of the World's Religions and help me make many new friends.
Amen.

Friday, December 4, 2009

We attended the Parliament of the World's Religions.

Today I felt sick. I woke up with a sore throat which persisted for several hours.

Dad went ahead and later Mom and I attended a movie on the medicinal use of plants called *Numen: The Nature of Plants* which I greatly enjoyed.

I wasn't feeling any better at lunchtime, so I decided to stay with Dad while Mom went out in the city to buy the groceries for supper. Dad and I attended a panel called "Mother Nature Don't Do Bail Outs." It was about the health of the earth and what we can do to help the earth stay healthy and clean. It was a youth session which was very nice. One of the speakers was an Aborigine who played his digeridu very well.

Today was a health day. Mom bought fresh sage, ginger, and garlic to make the tea for my cold that was recommended in the *Numen* film. I can tell it's already making a difference.

One thing I learned today was:

I learned more about the medicinal powers of plants. I found it incredible that I could use them to help better my health and help others to do so, too. I will share this on my website (indigo-chef.com). My mom's going to see about getting the film, **Numen**, so we can share it with college students.

Another thing I learned was the sheer magnitude and richness of the worships and talks going on at any one time during the Parliament. It is huge!

My prayer tonight is:

Dear God, thank you for my parents and friends and the new friends I am making. Help me to feel better tomorrow and feel stronger.

Amen.

Saturday, December 5, 2009
Today I felt better when I woke up.
The healing projections, sleep, vitamins, and herbal tea had improved my health greatly. I like to be healthy so getting sick is a big deal for me.

We went to the Parliament. There we came across some Tibetan monks who were creating a sand mandala. We watched them, listened to their chants, and took pictures of their mandala for a while before moving on.

A man named Terrence who had just come from a divine feminine workshop walked up to me, shook my hand and introduced himself. He told me he sensed a great deal of the divine feminine in me and congratulated me on coming to the Parliament at such a tender age. He asked if I was 16 yet. I told him I was 14 which he found even more impressive. He also introduced himself to my Mom who had been filming our interaction.

Terrence (pictured below) is a Roman Catholic priest from Canada who 12 years before had a realization of interfaith and began reading and studying other religions. He gave me a dvd which was an interpretation of the Golden Rule in several faiths. I gave him a business card and a copy of **Why does the Dalai Lama Matter to You**, my first full-length film which I completed last summer.

I felt honored that he walked up to me and talked to me. I was pleased to get to know him. He invited us to a youth panel (bottom picture) which was most enjoyable. Terrence encouraged everyone to sing a Christian children's song called *"Down in my heart"*. He sang a special and spiritual rendition including "I got the love of Jesus, Krishna, Buddha, Divine Feminine Lakhsmi - down in my heart" - I learned a great deal about how to think more positively.

My cold was coming back and I was starting to feel tired. Then I ran into Stanley Krippner!

Dr. Krippner is a well-traveled and accomplished professor in the field of consciousness. He teaches at Saybrook Graduate School in California and helped found the International Association for the Study of Dreams (IASD). I met him at the IASD conference last June in Chicago. He was my first interview for the film I'm now making called *The Dream Mystery*.

He introduced me to his friend, Aris. I was so pleased to see Stanley (at far right, with aris and my parents), I felt better instantly! He told me he would be speaking Monday at 11:30 am in Room 102. I hurried off to tell Mom the good news. When she learned that Stanley was here and he would be speaking she was so happy and excited that it redoubled my enjoyment. Together we headed to lunch.

We met up with Dr. Sheila who was volunteering, and saw my dad. I told them both the story of how I saw Stanley. We ate lunch then went to the Carnivale Spiritual. It was like an Indian talent show. It had amazing dancing, singing, yoga, martial arts, and a theatrical performance of the ***Gita***. I enjoyed this. The ***Gita*** is one of my favorite - if not my favorite holy work. During the Carnivale, I met up with the Madars. I was happy to see them but not as happy as Alexandra was to see me. She was beaming! I get to see that about 2 or 3 times a week. She was beaming!

There were Indian dancers, twin yoga masters, and a martial artist who performed with two swords. A swami who has been doing the Carnival for 30 years gave a lesson on consciousness in the middle. I really like the ***Gita***. It was my favorite part.

We got to hear the Agape choice and sang several religious songs. My mom and I thoroughly enjoyed. "O let me love, let me love, in a holy, wholly way" was one great song. Rickie Byers-Beckwith was the choir director and lead voice. Twenty members of the choir made the trip and about 60+ others joined on at Parliament. She called it the CPWR Village Choir!

Dad and I ate a great catered dinner of fish and chips, pizza, lasagna, oriental dumplings, salad and a myriad of desserts. It was as good as any fine dining restaurant. Then we met Mom and everyone at the entrance to the Exhibition Hall where they were discussing plans for *The INVITATION* the next day.

One thing I learned today was:
How much I like the *Gita* and how easy it is for me to feel better when I am around people I really like.

My prayer tonight is:
Dear God, thank you for a great day! Especially for the Gita play. Help me be more like you every day.
Amen.

Sunday, December 6, 2009
My parents and I woke up and boarded a tram which was heading toward the Unity Church where *The INVITATION* would be held today. At stop 65, we dismounted the tram. We proceeded to walk several blocks uphill looking for the church. By the time we got to the next tram stop, we figured we must be on the wrong side of the street. We headed back.

We were tired and thirsty by the time Jesse Reece appeared from a side street to guide us to the church. Dr. Christine had sent him to look for us because she sensed we were lost or needing assistance.

By the time we arrived, I was hungry. There was lots of food there and the peaches were the best I've ever eaten. I played with Alexandra and Vivienna. The church was full and buzzing with many from Parliament. The minister, Rev. Livingston, was very happy to see his church so full.

The INVITATION went well, except for a few times when some of the actors forgot their lines. The new addition this time was a movie Paul Madar created which helped to introduce the audience to the laureates in *The INVITATION*. He had been working on it for a month and brought it to Australia to finish. A couple days earlier he had lost the audio - mysterious, and my mom gave him some ideas that might salvage his efforts. Her ideas gave him what he needed and he came through with a great short film that set the tone.

Jesse Kern was the new edition to the cast. Despite the fact that he had very little time to prepare Martin Luther King, Jr. He made a valiant effort to bring Dr. King to us. John Harrison, the man who played Dr. King from the beginning of *The INVITATION* was unable to come to Australia.

People seemed moved. I could tell by watching them that they'd never seen anything like it before. I filmed the performance, something I greatly enjoyed doing. Giving *The INVITATION* at Melbourne Unity was an asset to the church, the School of Metaphysics and to Parliament because we acted in a way Parliament can evolve - going to the people, going into the cities and making friends - "hearing each other", like the Parliament's motto says.

There was an Aborigine named Jeremy who taught after *The INVITATION*. He was the same man I saw the day before on a panel Dad and I went to at Parliament! He spoke at length about the Aboriginal culture. Then he played the digeridu. At one point he had us close our eyes while he played a Native American instrument that had been given to him so we could experience the music more fully without judging with our eyes. When he finished talking, we left the church.

I said goodbye to Rev. Livingston. Knowing I was American, he asked if I could teach him how to blow a kiss. I did.

There were mulberries growing near the church. They were the biggest I'd ever seen and tasted delicious. After snacking, we boarded a bus which took us back to the city near the Exhibition Center.

One thing I learned today was:
I learned more about Unity Church. I also appreciated seeing Steven Alpert (right) at *The INVITATION*, I had taken his Interfaith online class for five weeks before we came to Parliament. It taught about different religions, their beliefs and practices.

Monday, December 7, 2009
Mom and I watched an Inuit film in the morning, had lunch, then we attended Dr. Stanley Krippner's presentation in the afternoon. He and another lady talked about spiritualism. He talked about African religions in Brazil. He has traveled all over the world teaching and learning.

He talked about the one thing coffee plantation slaves never gave up was their religion. They would practice it secretly. They have an ethical way of life based on patience, tolerance, and kindness. They believe people are good in their core and worthy of love and respect. They believe in reincarnation, the wisdom of God. Life is for growth and evolution.

We came back early so Mom and Dad could prepare and rest for tomorrow. I really like being here. I went out on the balcony and just watched the moon come up and the busy streets below. We are 21 floors up and it's a great view. From my parent's room we can even see the ocean. I am grateful.

One thing I learned today was:
How important supporting someone is.

Tuesday December 8, 2009
Mom and I got up earlier than usual so we could get to the Parliament before Dad started his presentation at 8 am. It was raining so I let Mom use my jacket as an umbrella while we hurried to the exhibition center. We arrived just a few minutes before his presentation began.

There were about 27 people when my dad began. Within minutes of him starting the room reached over 50 people. By the time he ended there were almost 70 people, not counting SOM students or volunteers.

I had never seen or heard of a SOM presentation, workshop or seminar in my lifetime that had done so well. He taught *The Still Mind, Emptiness, Divine Love* in a simple and effective manner that anyone could understand and that people greatly enjoyed. I filmed and took pictures of the event. I was happy for daddy and the students of the School of Metaphysics.

Later that day, my mother was on a panel of women presenting "THE SEARCH FOR INNER PEACE: Multifaith Views from Women around the World." As part of her presentation she showed a condensed version of the documentary I made on the *Healing Wall* at the Peace Dome. She represented the Christian tradition amongst Buddhist, Jew, Sikh, Pagan, Hindu, and Muslim viewpoints.

One thing I learned today was:
How many different kinds of people desire to learn about metaphysics.

My prayer tonight is:
 Dear God, thank you for all the people I have been able to meet here in Australia. All the new friends I am making. And for helping Mom and Dad today.
 Amen.

Wednesday, December 9, 2009

Thinking that our breakfast with the Dalai Lama was today, I woke myself up extremely early. The alarm went off at 6 am. We walked to the Exhibition center arriving just in time for the sunrise morning Sahana given by Gurukuru Khalsa. A traditional Sikh morning prayer. There were musicians who gave kirtan as well. I enjoyed this music. I've liked all the music I've heard at Parliament.

After the prayer, Dad and I walked back to the apartment to retrieve my camera which I had accidentally left there.

When we came back to Parliament, we discovered to our surprise and delight, that a notice had been posted saying that Mom would get to present her lecture on *The Crown Jewels of Consciousness - Three Universal Spiritual Practices*. It was a great example of exponential notation, you know - Powers of 10 - the way it spread. Mom said it was the Universal Laws in action and a testimony to Universal Mind.

She enlisted the help of Drs. Daniel, Laurel, Sheila, Pam, and Christine in teaching dreams. In this way, they all got to present their knowledge, which I thought was a genius idea on Mom's part. This way everyone could contribute what they had to offer. A lot of people wanted to know about SOM.

Within minutes of Mom finishing her presentation, it was time for the four Tibetan monks who had been creating a sand mandala for days, to destroy their creation. I spoke briefly with a man studying to be a Catholic priest. I talked with him and gave him one of my business cards. He had been recently studying the Bible and knew a lot about my namesake. "Hezekiah is one of three good kings in the Bible," he said.

When the time came to dissolve the sand mandala, the Tibetan who was coordinating the event asked for two young volunteers. At the insistence of Dr. Sheila and Rev. Paul, I volunteered, walking into the center area and standing with him. A girl, she was either Mideastern or Indian, also volunteered. She was several years younger than me. The Tibetan man had us hold two hornlike instruments. They were about seven feet long.

The mandala was dissolved. The sand scooped into a vase and then the monks carried the sand to the river. We carried the horns after them. People followed in procession to the footbridge where the monks poured most of the sand into the river.

After we returned inside the building, the monks gave out the rest of the sand inside small packets. Then we hurried to the plenary auditorium where His Holiness himself would be speaking.

As soon as we entered the auditorium, I made a beeline for the seats I knew I wanted - just below the media, meaning the best view. This was the Closing Plenary. It was hard to imagine this was the close of Parliament.

Alexandra came to sit on my lap during part of the closing which I thought was very sweet.

Many people spoke at length before His Holiness was brought on stage. There were farewell blessings in many traditions. He spoke on world peace for about 30 minutes. I recorded his entire talk while Mom took pictures. Alexandra also got to see him talk although Vivi was sleeping. It was the fourth time I had the opportunity to hear him. His talk stood out to me as the best part of the entire Parliament.

An Aboriginal descendent named Joy welcomed him and presented him with a gift in the form of a large plant and animal skin. She was very funny as he tried to figure out exactly what she had given him. He exclaimed, "It's moving!" as the plant and animal skin in his hands flopped around. He settled for laying the plant across the chair. Auntie Joy unfolded the animal skin and placed it on his lap. The audience laughed with sympathy for him. It was like someone eating ice cream and offering it to someone who is lactose intolerant, you know what I mean?

Auntie Joy and others completed the Plenary, then we all went to the footbridge. They brought out all the banners and Christine spotted ours from the Living Peaceably event. I got my picture taken with the two girls who held the banner.

Everyone was given journey stones made by Aborigines. I will give mine to the Healing Wall.

After the picture at the bridge was taken I went with Pam, Chris, Alex, and Viv while the rest of our company trammed to the Unity Church to offer the first intuitive reports in Australia - and on a continent outside the U.S.!

We went to the food court. I ordered another lamb wrap and cucumbers to cool it down. Pam also got one. All of us except Dr. Christine had gelatin. I had cookies and cream. It was good. Then we walked across the river, saw a black swan, and went to a park with sand sculptures then returned to the apartment. I introduced Dr. Christine to *Avatar: The Last Airbender*, a cartoon story, which she deemed worthy of showing to her children.

Today's Lessons:
I immensely enjoyed learning from the Dalai Lama a fourth time.
I loved helping with the dissolving of the sand mandala.
I am greatly pleased with the Parliament and glad I am in Australia!

My prayer tonight is:
Dear God, thank you for this trip to Australia and if it is meant to be let me return again someday.
Amen.

Thursday, December 10, 2009

Today, we woke up early and walked to the exhibition center again. The Parliament was over and this time I was having breakfast with the Dalai Lama (opposite page) to celebrate the 20th anniversary of his receiving the Nobel Peace Prize. Breakfast was held in the same room the Indian Carnivale had been several days before. There were dozens of tables set for eight guests each. The Tibetan organizers said 1440 places were available. Mom saw that number as quite Biblical.

Orange juice and apple kiwi juice were on the table as well as various pastries in a wire vessel in the center of each table. At each person's place sat a cup filled with muesli, topped with sweet vanilla yoghurt and finished with blackberries and blackberry juice.

Several waiters and waitresses moved around, serving tea and coffee. Later, they served the main course of spinach-mushroom frittata with skewed tofu and fresh vegetables. Baby tomatoes and portobello mushroom were served with a creamy sauce that was delicious. A string quartet played for us.

A film consisting of a series of pictures about the Dalai Lama's life prepared us for the man who would join us soon.

His Holiness arrived and was greeted warmly by the guests and Auntie Joy Murphy Wandin. He spoke on truth and peace through justice as well as human rights. It was different from what I'd heard him talk about before. Mom filmed and I took pictures this time.

After breakfast, Tad and I walked back to the apartment while my parents toured Melbourne.

On the way to the apartments, Tad and I ran into Jesse Reece. We talked about what we'd been doing that day. Jesse said he went up the Skydec and to the glass ledge where you can step out at 83 floors. Then Tad and I proceeded to the apartments. We talked about gemstones and opals. I learned that all opals came from Australia and the most valuable are those that come from Lightning Ridge. Those are considered to have a value slightly less than precious stones. He also told me that the only true jade comes from Burma. The rest is jadeite. Once we had reached the apartment, we met up with Dr. Sheila, Jesse Kern, and the Madars. We took the tram to St. Kilda's beach where we waded, picked up shells and rocks, made sand castles and played with plastic figurines.

Tad, Sheila and Jesse returned early. Sometime later the Madars and I also headed back but only after a powerful wind kicked up and turned the beach into a sandstorm. We had to walk through the rain some of the way back. When I got back to the apartment, my parents were already there.

Daddy went out and bought steak for me which mommy then grilled with sauteed mushrooms, macaroni with Tasmania cheddar cheese, and fruit.

After dinner, I did some journaling with my mom, then headed to the Madar's apartment. Sheila and I had agreed to spend time with Vivienna and Alexandra so that Christine and Paul could spend some time alone together. We took the girls swimming. When we got back, we all changed. Alexandra and Vivienna took a bath. Sheila and I popped popcorn. Then we all sat down and watched **Avatar: The Last Airbender** again.

We watched the same episode we had watched the previous night which annoyed Alexandra somewhat but which I was grateful for. It allowed her to better understand and assimilate the episode. I plan on showing each episode to her at least a few times before moving on to the next. Christine and Paul returned and I took them to my apartment so they could say goodbye to my parents.

Things I learned today:
I appreciated hearing about human rights for the Aborigines.
Peace through justice from the Dalai Lama.
I appreciated spending time with my friends and getting to go the beach one last time.

Friday, December 11, 2009
Today we slept in until 8 o'clock.
We wanted time to site-see before leaving Melbourne. About 10 o'clock we walked to Federation Square. We visited the Natural Opal Mining Company Store. We found it at 119 Swansea Street. It was very fancy, filled with display cases of fossils and statues of ancient plants and animals. The opal jewelry there was breathtaking.

I learned that the company mines 95% of Australia's opals. I also learned that only a small percentage of all opals are black which makes them one of the most valuable varieties. We had coupons for a free opal pin which we acquired at our apartment. It was a tiny gold colored kangaroo with a small opal set into the pendant. I found out that the more valuable Australia opals, are those with red shot, through with blue and green. Normal ones of blue and green are plentiful. Red in the blue and green, are more valuable.

After the opal store, we went to St. Paul's Cathedral, an episcopal church. It was an enormous church with vaulted ceilings about three stories high and stained glass. A man was tuning the piano and I saw my first pipe organ – it was about 12 feet across and a story tall.

I knelt where Pope John

Paul II prayed and I prayed, lit a candle and left a $5 donation. My prayer:

How can I help educate the world - about life, health, the human mind?

I was asking for guidance.

John Paul II's prayer was for Unity in the Christian religion. We bought a few souvenirs and Christmas presents for my friends.

Across the street, we saw several choirs of kids singing Christmas songs while we searched for a place to eat. I filmed one choir while Dad found a restaurant called Time Out. I had pancakes with bacon and hash-browns. They served a grilled banana on top - it was very sweet. Mom ordered pita bread, cucumber and olive dips. I had this several times and liked it a lot. The food was different than its American counterparts. No less enjoyable.

When we left the restaurant we went to the ACMI - the Australian Center of Moving Images. There I played the newest computer games, learned the history of media, communication, film, animation, and telecommunications over the past 150 years. It was awesome. I had never heard or seen anything like it. It had a broad, worldwide view of the development of media - not just Hollywood and the U.S.

There were several video games that people had created that illustrated the state of the art. Mom took footage of the records of the first moon landing for my Healing Wall film. She explained how this event drew the world together in 1969.

Mom, Dad, and I made a flip book. They had machines that took pictures - probably video over the span of 5 seconds. You moved around while the camera photographed you. The film was then taken into freeze frames, printed and placed into a flipbook which you could buy. It was fun!

I played a game with a robot that was problem solving that I would like to buy. I enjoyed it.

After the movement center, we watched a street performer. This is common in Melbourne. This week we saw a violinist, a drummer, a flutist playing on the sidewalks. It makes for a festive atmosphere and good attitude on the part of people.

The city had a very relaxed and pleasant vibration, different from most cities in America. People were friendly and helpful. It was enjoyable hearing them speak English with Australian or British accents. Some of the words I learned new meanings for -lift for elevator, rubbish for trash, lou for toilet, Hungry Jack for Burger King (We figured this name change had to do with Australia being tied to Great Britain, the queen and all. They also have McDonalds which advertises their coffee drinks like Starbucks in the States. These similarities, yet differences were quite illuminating.)

Melbourne is a port city on the Antarctic Ocean and the Yarrow River flows through it. The water gives a moving energy to the city and cleanses the air. We were living on the 21st floor, so we had a great view of the city day and night.

We took the trolley around the downtown area, then returned to begin packing. We managed to store our treasures and I went to sleep about 9:30 and got 5 1/2 hours of sleep.

We woke at 3 am to travel to the airport with Sheila, Laurel, Elena, and Jesse Kern. That's the beginning of the journey home....

Also I ate at Subway in Melbourne today! That was quite something for the Indigo Chef (indigo-chef.com) – my new website for families on living a healthy life.

The Day Recovered -- The Flight Home
December 12th

This was the algebraic day.
We left on Flight 25 Quantas from Melbourne on Saturday, December 12 at 6 am. We arrived at Auckland, New Zealand at 11:30 am local time, a three-hour flight and - two hour time change. We were at Auckland for four hours. New Zealand is beautiful - islands with rolling hills of green trees, vibrant colors. We left Auckland at 3:30 pm local time on our way to Los Angeles. That was an 11 1/2 hour flight across the International dateline so we arrived in Los Angeles at 6:30 am SATURDAY, DECEMBER 12th!

Looking at the date and time, it appears like it took a half hour to go from Australia to LA.! This is the day we "lost" when we left the United States Sunday night at 11 pm and arrived in Australia at 8:30 am on TUESDAY! And people think time traveling is a myth or science fiction! Time is an illusion of mankind's creativity.

On the flight home, I watched two episodes of Man vs. Wild, the animated movie, Up, slept for a couple hours and ate a meal. We arrived in LA at 6:30 am and waited at the airport until 12:05 when we flew Midwest direct to KC. I slept in the airport for an hour and a half.

The most memorable video I saw on the trip home was *Kung Fu Inc.*, a documentary on a new evolution of Shaolin Kung Fu. The monks train to be part of an elite squad which performs around the world.

Mom says the movie is a good example of an observation I made this week about human nature. I said humans have a basic urge to better themselves and their condition. The Shaolin monks in the film are examples of this. One learned the new techniques so he could travel. Another practiced breaking swords on his head so he could be chosen to perform. I learned more about monks, where the disciplines come from and why.

From LA to KC, it was a cloudy day when we took off then we flew above the clouds and it was beautiful and sunny. For a while, we saw the Rockies and a sand desert and fields of crop circles and plains before entering clouds again a couple hundred miles outside Kansas City.

Several times in the past week I would exclaim "We're in Australia!"

And more than once I told my parents, "Thank you, parents, for bringing me here!"

I am blessed.

I made a very good choice, a fortunate birth.

December 13, 2009

When we got to the KC Airport, Matt Valois was there to greet us. He helped us pick up our luggage and then drove us to the KC School of Metaphysics to pick up our car. Kansas City had gotten a good snowfall but now it was heating up. We stayed at the school a little while and got on the road about 7 p.m. and arrived home at 11:58 pm on Saturday. Sixteen hours by the clock since we'd left Melbourne. Travel time, counting layovers in New Zealand and California, was actually about 30 hours.

My mom let me off at the lane gate so I could run the rest of the way home, something I like to do when I return from trips. There weren't many people awake except for Jonathan, a grad teacher, and Sam, our Lhasa apso, who greeted us warmly. It is great to be back!

My Memories...
Something I will always remember about this trip is the many new people I met and friends I made.

My favorite place...
The Beach on the Antarctic Ocean, and the Exhibition Center and Melbourne in general.

Something I learned...
How to be more outgoing and make many friends.

If I'd had more time...
I would have seen some of the plant and animal life and maybe even gone to the conference at Sydney and to Ayers Rock. I think I'll go to Australia again later in my life.∞

The Universal Truth in My Story
Hezekiah Condron

It was incredible traveling to another country that was so much like home. The fact that so many people I know and love were there with me made it more enjoyable. I enjoyed meeting new people and seeing people I already knew there, such as Stanley Krippner and the Dalai Lama. Melbourne was so beautiful. Every person we met was friendly, talkative and willing to help. It was the golden rule in action! I realized friendliness begins with your own attitude.•

D
R
E
A
M
T
I
M
E

In summer 2009, Hezekiah submitted a proposal for a presentation at the Melbourne Parliament. Here is what he submitted.

Title of Program:

21st CENTURY GRAFFITI
Creating The Healing Wall for kids and those who love them

Description:
From 4 am December 31, 2008 through 4 am January 1, 2009, Hezekiah Condron participated in an annual Peace Vigil praying for peace as each time zone welcomes the new year. He was one of five who completed the entire marathon by reciting the 577-word Universal Peace Covenant 33 times. Hezekiah is 14 years old. This is his story.

HEZEKIAH'S PURPOSE FOR GOING TO AUSTRALIA

"TO PRESENT A PROGRAM ON MAKING PEACE AND TO MEET MANY NEW PEOPLE WITH THE PURPOSE OF CONTRIBUTING TO THE WORLD."

His program is designed for young people and those who love them. A young filmmaker and budding storyteller, Kie will present a short documentary he created to tell the story of the Peace Dome. He will share his experiences of growing up on the College of Metaphysics campus in the United States where he lives with his parents and a consistently changing number of people of all ages and backgrounds. He will explain how children have been a part of the development of the Peace Dome and its Healing Wall since the beginning.

"The Healing Wall is the whole world brought together in one place," says Hezekiah. The Healing Wall is an 18 foot by 9 foot relief map of the world created on the Eastern retaining wall of the Peace Dome. Native stones are being collected from around the world with the idea of placing them in the wall three years from now. Kie wants to invite you to participate in making this dream a reality.

How does your program relate to the 2009 Parliament theme: Make a World of Difference: Hearing each other, Healing the earth?

By bringing the peoples of the world together, to create and manifest a common goal, we can practice peace. The Universal Peace Covenant states, "Living Peaceably begins by thinking peacefully." We hope to receive people from every continent when we put the native stones from around the world in place in the Healing Wall.

How does your program relate to the following goals of the Parliament:

The Healing Wall is the first wall of its kind. It will bring people together and that will make a better world. It will strengthen our community by making friends from around the world. Just touching the Healing Wall, even before the stones are there, transforms people.

How do the content, format and design of your program help to achieve these goals?

Through pictures, music, and stories. Hezekiah hopes to lead people in a Circle of Love like the ones we practice at the Peace Dome and perhaps lead everyone in reading the Universal Peace Covenant, the document read at the Peace Dome every morning at 5:30 a.m. central time.

Who do you predict your primary audience will be? Why?

People of all ages, because we want to leave a better world for our children's children.

Biography
Hezekiah Condron is a 14-year-old who lives at the College of Metaphysics in Missouri. He decided to come to Australia when he attended the PreParliament Event in Chicago. Kie studies creative writing, history, and algebra, is learning piano and Kung Fu. He has been taking pictures since he was 4 and filming since age 6. His films include a pictoral rendition of his dad's book The Emptiness Sutra, *which he narrates, and* Why does the Dalai Lama Matter to You?, *a documentary about why people come to see His Holiness, and the "Indigo Chef" series teaching kids healthy eating and cooking.* •

In August, Hezekiah received a kind letter from the CPWR program chairs informing him that his proposal would not be among those presented in Melbourne. The cover email was quite supportive and he took the decision in stride.

I watched him continue to work on the Healing Wall film, discovering footage that the adults around him had believed lost and suffering technological challenges even up to the end. He never faltered in his willingness to see the film through. He brought to life through pictures and stories, the story of the Healing Wall adding to the historical records of the Peace Dome.

His determination deserved recognition and so we condensed the film into just over six minutes so I might share it as part of the ten minutes I was being afforded as part of a panel on peace. Hezekiah and his film were well received. His program on making peace was shared, even if in a slightly different way than first visualized. Hezekiah learned there are many avenues through which to create. He is now looking forward to the next Parliament of the World's Religions, often asking if the city has been chosen. By 2015, he will be 20, and I look forward to who he will become and what he will want to offer.

Watching Hezekiah during the Melbourne Parliament was like observing a flower opening. The beauty of his Spirit was magnetic. He ended up being a walking program on making peace and his secondary goal "to meet new people with the purpose of contributing to the world" was fulfilled again and again. The following story illustrates it best.

When we arrived back at the College there was a message that a woman named Nina had called and wanted to talk to Hezekiah. I told him, "That's Nina Meyerhoff! She's the woman who leads the Youth Spirit Council that Terrence introduced you to."

Nina is president and founder of Children of the Earth. She is presently forming The World Spirit Youth Council to "activate youth around the world to unite as a movement in the face of recognizing spirit as the positive force for social change and world peace." The youth programs have met in Japan, Nepal, Switzerland and Thailand, and were represented at Parliament.

When Kie returned Nina's call, she graciously invited him to their conferences later in the year. Kie is eager to travel again. It is his openness that enables him to receive the wealth of the universe.

ᵀᴴᴱ LAW of ABUNDANCE

"I CREATE PLENTY FOR EVERYONE."

by Barbara Condron, DM, DD

*The winds of God's grace
are always blowing;
it is for us
to raise our sails.*
–Ramakrishna

Wednesday, December 9, 2009 9:10 a.m.

"Dr. Barbara, did you know you're giving a presentation this morning?" Sheila Benjamin asks in a matter-of-fact way. The importance of her question is belied by the manner in its delivery.

Puzzled, because the words she speaks do not match her thoughts, I say, "I beg your pardon?" My brain hears the words. My mind doesn't understand them so I don't think I've heard her correctly. "What do you mean, Sheila?"

"You're on the board for 11." I'm in shock, so many thoughts are rushing through my emotions, like grains of sand seeking their place through the funnel of an hourglass. "Paul Madar told me."

It is the last morning of the Parliament of the World's Religions. I am eager to drink in every last moment, the people, the sights and sounds of travelers who have migrated for a short time to commune with one another. Every one is someone I want to meet. Every presentation is one worthy of attendance and I find myself again thinking that Parliament is my occasional taste of what the dream of the matured College of Metaphysics will be, – a place where people from all cultures, faiths, and traditions come together to learn from shared wisdom. Here is the reality of Homo Spiritus, Spiritual Man, and I want to receive it fully so it can change me, transforming my giving into a higher form.

Daniel, Hezekiah, and I have managed to get to the Melbourne Convention Center, together, and in time to attend the Sunrise Morning Sadhana with Gurukirn Khalsa, a Sikh minister. I am pleased that we can experience this form of worship together. It is a perfect way to begin this day.

On the way there, Hezekiah discovers he's forgotten his camera. This is unusual since photography and filmmaking is such a big part of his life. A short version of his ***Seven Generations*** film premiered the day before. He also knows the Tibetan Monks plan to dissolve the mandala they have been constructing over the duration of the Parliament in the early afternoon before the closing plenary. Kie has faithfully taken pictures each day as the mandala appeared before us, and this will be the completion of their rite.

I am dismayed. I have managed to assist Kie each day, and in the light of this development, I feel in the rush of the morning, I've let him down. I am also looking forward to being present on this final day of Parliament since one thing or another has seemed to keep me somewhere else more often than I wanted. Thankfully, Daniel senses my inner conflict and volunteers to go back to the apartment with Kie to retrieve the camera after the sadhana. They have already departed and will probably be gone for 45 minutes or so.

Sheila's words sink in. "How does he know?"

I am completely bewildered. I have given my offering to Parliament the day before as part of a women's panel on *Multifaith Views of Peace.* Perhaps he has his days mixed up. That's easy to do when you travel halfway around the world with two vivacious and personable redheads, ages 2 and 5.

"He said he saw it on the board." I can see the image in Sheila's mind, the legacy of years of practice in thought transference.

"Take me there," I reply.

I follow Sheila to the kiosk boards situated at the top of the escalators where they have been easily visible to those arriving or departing the second floor of the conferences. Each day, additions and other changes in schedules appear on the board, offering an updated and immediate announcement of the day's offerings. These are in addition to the 390-page book, listing all the panels, presentations, films, and plenaries of the parliament.

My eyes travel through the listings. There it is, in between a *Report on the Indigenous Assembly* and *Closeness to G-d.*

The CROWN JEWELS of CONSCIOUSNESS - Three Universal Spiritual Practices
Barbara Condron and other teachers from the School of Metaphysics....
   11.30-1.00 pm   Room 108

The hand of God is upon this from the beginning. I can see the Universal Laws at work. Room 108 is the same room my husband Daniel used for his ***Still Mind, Emptiness, Divine Love*** observance 24 hours earlier. It is the room we have just come from, next to the space the Tibetan Monks have been making sacred with daily chanting and kriya yoga.

My mind focuses on the title. ***The Crown Jewels of Consciousness*** is the proposal I sent, upon her request, to Grove Harris, CPWR

Program Director, just two weeks earlier. Have I missed an email communication from her about this presentation? It is certainly possible what with the Thanksgiving holiday just before we departed the States. Questions pour into my mind, emotions stir.

I take a deep breath, ordering my thoughts. I am so honored, and thrilled. I know I do not have the proposal or notes with me today, and I know I don't require them. I will be speaking on the principles I have lived throughout my adult life. It will all come together, as if by divine plan, just as this opportunity has unexpectedly arisen. What is important now is gathering those who will share this good fortune – the *other teachers from the School of Metaphysics.*

Turning to Sheila, I ask, "Do you know where everyone is this morning?"

"We'll find them," she replies with the confidence I most admire in her.

"Let's send a mental broadcast." And so we do.

Within one hour, every one in our delegation who can be, is present, and participating in this spontaneous emergence of Spirit. Several times as events of that morning unfold, I give thanks for Spirit's part in guiding Paul Madar to be the tool for our awakening, lest we all have slept through it! I give thanks for Sheila being present to receive his discovery, and for the divine connection that drew us immediately together so we might manifest a miracle!

Earlier that week

The story of how this interactive session came into being is an example of the Universal Laws in motion. You'll find the strength that arises from the Law of Relativity, the joy that connects Believing and Knowing, and the humor that comes through the Law of Proper Perspective. Some will read this story and call it fate. Others will see it as luck. I recognize it as a tale of fortune in the truest sense of the word – the workings of the Universal Law of Abundance in our lives.

The title of the presentation *The Crown Jewels of Consciousness - Three Universal Spiritual Practices* fits well with Australia. I don't realize the irony in it until after we are in the country for a few days. The nation is a part of the British crown, a different notion for one raised in "the colonies". Even the environs of the Melbourne Convention Center where parliament is being held speak of the idea. Located directly across the street, is the "Crown" Casino!

Each day we walk by the gambling house on our way to the Parliament of the World's Religions and on our way back home to the apartment we are renting for the ten days of our stay. Early on, I make the mistake of attempting to navigate a short cut through the casino that a parliament volunteer has suggested. She spoke of a shopping area filled with Christmas trees that the younger children in our delegation had enjoyed. What transpires when we follow her advice is a complete surprise.

We enter into a maze of cafes, cloakrooms, and lounging areas, looking for the shops and never finding them. We arrive at a place where there is no way through except by all the slot machines; gaming machines I'm told they are now called.

As 14-year-old Hezekiah and I start to move through the room, a well-dressed security man stops us. "How old are you?" he approaches Hezekiah directly.

The man is intimidating, although not much larger in size than Kie. Hezekiah looks in my direction. I nod, encouraging him to respond to the man.

"Fourteen."

"I'm sorry you cannot enter the casino," the man replies with an authority that says he is being polite in stopping us.

As strange as it may sound, age restrictions never crossed my mind. In my naiveté, it didn't occur to me that we might get lost in the building or that there might be areas Kie wouldn't be able to enter because of his age. So, here we are, trying to find the way out of a gambling den on the way to a gathering of holy people! Evidence for sure that God has a sense of humor.

The irony is clear and it alleviates any anxiety in me arising from the man thinking Kie and I intended to do something illegal.

"Is there any way through?" I ask. Expecting the security man to offer directions, I explain, "We're trying to get to the south side of the building, the convention side entrance."

More kindly, he shakes his head, "No, sorry. You'll have to go back the way you came."

"Really!" I am quite surprised. As we walk away, I note what I have learned and I have to respect the cunning design of the building. In doing so I realize all the hallways lead to the gambling room! It makes perfect sense as I reflect upon the purpose of the establishment. It also gives me cause to reflect on why young people like Hezekiah are not welcomed here.

What is it we - adults - do not want them to see, to experience, to learn in places like this?

Having no "stake" in the activities here, I find the questions easy to answer. Some come to rouse the senses, to experience giddy highs. Some come to dull the senses, to drink and "lose" their troubles. Some come seeking to fill an emptiness inside by finding temporary companionship because they are lonely. Some come helplessly hoping to pay bills created through ignorance or purposeful neglect. Some come to "have a good time", to risk making a reputation while others risk destroying their own. Yes, it is a good thing we spare our youth these things for they are reflective of the poverty in humanity's Spirit that Martin Luther King, Jr. spoke of so eloquently fifty years ago in the U.S., where a few seek to profit from the weaknesses of the many and sorrows are revealed in the light of day.

Across the street is a different world. Oh, there is still an atmosphere of gambling - meeting people from different countries who speak languages foreign to your own, who dress differently, think differently, and worship differently. The stakes here are much higher.

In the Melbourne Convention Center over 6000 have gathered to share. They have come together to give and to receive. They have come in abundance, because they are wealthy in Spirit, because they want others to share in that abundance. This venue welcomes all people, of all ages, countries, backgrounds, class levels and religious faiths. The Parliament of the World's Religions is a microscopic picture of what the world is now, with these people, in this time, and in this space.

To some, it represents only .00001 percent of the world's population. For me, Parliament is the future of the world.

It is an image worth seeing, experiencing, learning – at every age. That is an image of abundance.

Universal Abundance Truths taught in the 1950s

Abundance is a spiritual concept. Like beauty, it is borne within the Mind of the beholder.

When I was young, I never wanted for anything. I was cared for every day by people who loved me. I had a warm, safe place to sleep, healthy food, and good fellowship with several hundred church people I learned to call "Sister" and "Brother". These people, who were no blood relation to me, were people I could trust, people I could go to should I ever be in need, and they would respond. My life was blessed.

My mother taught me to pray for others before praying for myself. Sometimes, we prayed for a blessing to come into a person's life. Sometimes, we prayed for someone to be healed. Sometimes, we prayed for the family of someone who had died. Sometimes, we prayed for the dead person's soul. Prayer taught me how to hold another's welfare in mind.

"If you can't say something good about somebody," she'd say, "then you shouldn't say anything at all." That made me thoughtful. With some people, this was easy, because a lot of good things to say came to mind! With others, I might find myself quiet for a very long time. I learned to study people, to evaluate with fairness and honesty. I learned how to look for potential in a person, for the real wealth that exists in the soul. Quite often in my praying for others, I found answers for myself, too.

Kindness is the quality that fosters abundance.

My father taught me to always do my best. He admired excellence, and in my desire to please him, I learned how to excel, to stretch beyond my means. He taught me to give completely, not holding anything back, to expect that things would always work out for the best. My dad taught me to trust in the infallible workings of Universal Law. I learned as I give, so I receive.

Universal reciprocity is the action of abundance.

My grandmother taught me to ask God's help and guidance. She, my grandfather, and my parents all lived in the same household until I was 10 years old. She told me God had a plan for my life and if I would merely trust him he would lead me to fulfill that plan. She prayed for me every day of her life, and when she was gone from this earth I felt the absence of those prayers. My grandmother introduced me to God. God through the brilliant hues in a sunset. God in the song of a mockingbird and the fragrance of wild roses. She allowed space for mystery when we gazed at the stars in the night sky, and from her, I learned that miracles are all around us when we have the eyes to see.

Appreciation is grace in abundance.

My grandfather taught me to do the right thing. If I met someone who was hungry, I should feed him. If I met someone who was lonely, I should befriend her. If I met someone who was hurting, I should ease his pain. If I met someone who was lying, I should tell her the truth. From him, I learned that in thought and deed, I carry the Lord in my heart so as to bring His presence everywhere.

Benevolence is the mercy of abundance.

As I grew older and went to public school, I began learning not everyone experienced the blessings I did, and not everyone saw the world in the same light. This was puzzling to me, then confusing for a number of years. I didn't understand why people couldn't get along better, why there were wars, poverty, and injustice when there was obviously plenty to go around if people just cared enough to share.

Sharing our good fortune was something my family always did. We did not have a great deal of anything material. I was the daughter of a minister and granddaughter of an evangelist. In the 1950s and 60s, congregations used their funds to build churches and ministers had other means for income. Ours was the hospitality industry. We owned and operated a modest-sized motel. So we provided a home away from home for people. That's the attitude we had. I remember many nights when the bell would ring at 2 or 3 am, and Dad would get up to answer the door, offering the boarder the room at significant discount because of the late hour.

Every Christmas, we delivered cans of roasted pecans to the needy families to provide some nourishing holiday cheer and as a way to let them know someone thought of them, and cared. Money put aside throughout the year bought these, and however many hams we could afford, for the most deserving. I remember the tears, and thank you's and "Praise the Lord!"s. I learned at an early age what it felt like to be generous.

I attribute my early training in abundance to my family's faith tradition. The heart of Christianity rests on the two commandments Jesus taught: first, *Love the Lord your God with all your heart, with all your mind, with all your soul*, then *love your neighbor as yourself.*

This parable is more than an autobiographical sketch. It is how it came to be that **other teachers of the School of Metaphysics** were provided a platform to speak during the Parliament of the World's Religions.

March 2009
Kindness fosters Abundance

The Council for a Parliament of the World's Religions (CPWR) called for proposals in mid-2008. They were due in early spring the following year. Attending and performing at the PreParliament event in Chicago in December 2008 fanned the flames of our desire to take *The INVITATION* down under. Being in the energy field that is Parliament brought back wonderful memories of spiritual communion within and with others. My heart longed for that quality of interaction on a global scale again.

When Christine Madar announced she would head the delegation to Melbourne, I was thrilled. I knew it would bring an update for her of an experience ten years earlier as well as give the School of Metaphysics a unified presence in a country we had been dreaming of visiting since that People to People delegation went to India.

Inertia set in during the winter months and it seemed we, as a group, were dragging our feet on the arrangements to travel down under. It was more the financial investment required than the time away from work, family, responsibilities. In the end, providence opened for us with economical flights that within 45 whirlwind minutes made our decision for us. Once we had committed to the trip, to my way of thinking, proposals naturally should follow.

Daniel was the first to submit his proposals, and fittingly, he was the first to receive a positive response. The clear sight developed through global travel throughout his life and over 30 years of discipline, service and teaching in the United States, have made his life his message. Speaking at Parliament would bring ***The Still Mind, Emptiness, Divine Love*** teaching into the world-at-large and the program chairs recognized its value. (As a side note, I remember Daniel telling me that a woman who spoke with him after the teaching said that she had been looking for a presentation on love, and that Daniel's was one of only two she had found listed out of the 1500 programs offered during the week. I am still contemplating what that means.)

I knew the cast of ***The INVITATION*** was making the trip. I also knew all of them were seasoned teachers, engaging public speakers, and in some cases writers. With only days left to apply, I asked if they intended to submit proposals. None had at that point, so I encouraged them to do so. Having known these people since they were undergraduates, I knew they would bring a wealth, clarity, and wisdom to the purpose of the gathering, aiding the council to attain its goals.

The proposals they created reflect their individuality and the place group consciousness holds in the workings of the Law of Abundance. Each focused the power of the mind upon a question and an answer that would nurture anyone desiring a harmonious, kinder world. Follow me, as I quote from their writings to illustrate the cooperative nature of abundance available to us all.

"If someone from another planet looked down upon earth, would they view humanity as essentially good or evil? In a world which seems to always have war, poverty, and hunger, are there solutions that work?" These questions open Dr. Laurel Clark's One Picture is Worth a Thousand Words proposal. Laurel's keen discerning ability, taps into the line of thinking every reasoner at some point produces. Her life of education and service has made it clear that the answers

rest within our faith traditions. *"To solve the world's problems,"* she writes, *"begins with the recognition that we are essentially divine."*

Dr. Pam Blosser suggests how internal conflicts that keep us from receiving that divinity can be resolved. In **How to Think Like a Boddhisatva**, she encourages us to appreciate the unfolding of life through forgiveness and gratitude. *"An intentional thought for the goodness of all concerned then becomes the avenue for uniting with others,"* she writes. *"Mystics have known and practiced this reality for centuries through unified prayers, mantras, chants and meditation, and scientists are now recognizing as truth."* Her aim is to bring out the boddhisatva, the apostle, within each individual.

Rev. Paul Madar's proposal **Our Common Ground: The Structure of the Mind** introduces a means to rethink what historically we have allowed to separate us as humans—faith, nationality, politics, culture, class, gender and economics. *"The strata, energy essence and material of the mind reveal our common construction and the tangible nature of our thoughts,"* he writes. *"Learning the universal structure of the Mind and how all minds are intrinsically inter-connected provides the opportunity to discover a deeper foundation of common ground."*

While Paul focuses on adult education, his wife Christine addresses how adult attitudes shape the attitudes children adopt. In **Developing the Virtue of Honest Communication from Birth: The Bridge to Peace**, Christine teaches that how we communicate is as valuable as what we communicate. *"Children need the virtue of honesty as part of their foundation of consciousness to develop good reasoning skills, to communicate clearly for understanding, and to foster inner peace,"* she writes. She places the responsibility on the shoulders of the adults in our societies, observing that when adults model honest communication, they are able to guide children to do the same.

To illustrate this power, Dr. Sheila Benjamin describes "**Peacemakers**, *an interactive program designed to help children make changes within themselves, within their relationships with others, and in their relationship with the world."* For twelve months, adults and children came to the Peace Dome on the campus of the College of Metaphysics to study Nobel Peace Prize Laureates. Their lessons of love, respect, friendship, smiling, service, and purpose - often in the face of inhumanities - afford the virtuous models children need.

Laurel's *Creating a Personal Vision for Peace* serves as the means for anyone to live a life worthy of emulation. Passing on the story of how a group of spiritual teachers, ages 18 – 70, from different faiths, some belonging to no religion, gathered together in interfaith and educational dialogue for nearly a year to discuss, research, and compose the Universal Peace Covenant is inspiring to all who receive it. It is the story of *"a universal urge to understand how we can live harmoniously together on this earth."*

It is easy to see how these people offer solutions to the real problems in our world. Encouraging them to submit proposals for consideration arose from my natural faculty for thinking of others. I have seen many people limit their abundance by thinking *for* others. This is one of the biggest challenges human beings face in their journey up the spiritual ladder. Thinking *for* others occurs in a busy mind focused on the thinker. Thinking *of* others arises in the space of a still mind ready and willing to be of service to others.

This is the great irony of abundance. I found myself encouraging others when I had yet to reconcile myself to what I had to offer! This uncertainty, in what I had to give, would play a key role in what was to come.

Universal Reciprocity activates Abundance

In the end, I submitted two proposals. The first was titled ***The GABRIEL FACTOR: Dream Interpretation as a Gateway to Higher Consciousness.*** It began: *"The presence that is Gabriel has endured in the human experience for centuries. In the 6th century BC, Gabriel aided the Hebrew Daniel in interpreting his dreams. It was Gabriel who appeared in the dreams of Zechariah, father of John the Baptizer, and Mary, the mother of Jesus, to foretell the destinies of their progeny. In 610, Gabriel enters Mohammed's dreams, the beginning of what, over the next two decades, will evolve to become The Koran. Gabriel is "the bearer of God's secret messages to His chosen ones," the Archangel of Dreams, Premonitions and Clairvoyance."*

This presentation was designed in three, half-hour increments. First, reporting the common images that appear in dreams received from people around the world and offering insight into the shifts in global consciousness they indicate, would be given in lecture format. Second, this would be followed by a question-answer period. Third, time and space allowing, an interactive workshop given to smaller breakout groups led by qualified faculty from the College would afford attendees experience with dream interpretation.

Once decided, I felt very confident in this proposal. It was not the one of my heart, as you will read about shortly, it was the one of my mind. This proposal addressed the single most important learning in my life which opened my mind, and minds of thousands of students, to the Truth in all Holy Scriptures – the Universal Language of Mind, the language of God.

I was raised in a family who talked with God every day. They expected God to hear their prayers, and they expected God to speak to them. So I learned how to listen. I also learned how to doubt my own ears. In my young adult years, while seeking to reconcile that doubt, I learned the value of entraining head and heart. That wealth I owe to mastering two distinct consciousness experiences: state and content. It is the state of mind that allows us to experience and recall a dream. It is the content of mind that enables us to discern its meaning. **The Talmud** says, *"a dream uninterpreted is like a letter unopened."* I understand this, and I know the sequence of events in thought that unlocks the dream for the dreamer. This is what I wanted to share with those at Parliament.

Dreams also gave the perfect opportunity to open the floor to an interactive workshop where members of our delegation schooled in the art and science of dream interpretation could hear and respond to individuals' questions and comments. This is a form we had practiced for five years as we presented a day-long transformative experience called POWERS of TEN at colleges and universities in the U.S. I imagined *The Gabriel Factor* would be similar in its construction.

Time passed. The organizers said we would be notified in early summer. Days came and went. Daniel received his acceptance letter. More time passed. In mid-September, I received a correspondence from two of the program chairs. The letter began by thanking me for the proposal and appreciating commitment to the Parliament. Then it went on to say,

> "We deeply regret that we have not been able to include the program proposal mentioned above in the Parliament. Thank you for the patience you have had with us as we assemble the program. Please know that the length of time for which we considered your proposal is an indication of the great respect we hold for your work....."

The letter encouraged attendance and participation at Parliament in the many venues of discussions, open space, and interactions with people one meets. I remembered these well from the 1993 Parliament and the burden on my heart lightened a bit.

I was nevertheless disappointed. There was no desire to deny this. In my mind, *The Gabriel Factor* represented the best that the School of Metaphysics offers to the world, and it was not quite acceptable in a venue I thought most compatible. Was my perception that distorted? This troubled me for days. I kept thinking about it, wanting to respond.

I had to clear my mind of any resentment or acrimony. Empathy for the program designers did not allow space for ill will in me because I had often been the one in a judgement seat. I had no idea the task the programmers had in front of them, nor the space or particulars of what they wanted to transpire. I just knew this proposal was not, in the present moment, going to happen.

I printed out the letter, and would reread it at some point in the day, meditating on what I might have done differently, better, clearer. I was so convinced of the value of what we offer, particularly to this group of people, and the need for it worldwide, that it was difficult to just let it go. Almost two weeks later, my sight cleared enough to see something in their letter I had missed.

> "Knowledge is vital to the interfaith movement, we will alert you should a formal speaking opportunity become available....."

This meant the possibility was open. How quickly, I had shut the door in my own face! I needed to acknowledge this open door, to inform them we were willing and able to respond when called.

"I am heartened to hear that this program remains open to your consideration should another presenter be unable to meet their obligation," I wrote. "I believe the exploration of dreams is a topic that deserves recognition in Melbourne and I hope you have included it in your program choices. Dreams have played a major role in every culture and religion on the planet. The personal experience of dreams is often the means by which spiritual leaders are called to serve.

"We are each individually connected to the Divine Source. Listening to our dreams centers the Self. Listening to others' dreams connects soul and spirit, forming community. For this reason the discussion of dreams is harmonious with this Parliament's theme of 'Hearing each other, Healing the earth.' This Parliament will be enriched by any program allowing for others to be in the presence of dreams."

I affirmed our interest in participating should available space become open, expressed thanks for their work, and acknowledged the challenges they were meeting with grace and humility.

Having neutralized the charges in my thinking, I could let it be and rest at peace knowing I had done everything I knew how to do.

Appreciation is the Grace of Abundance

I had sent a second proposal. This was the one of my heart.

When I thought of presenting in Melbourne, my mind kept returning to the subject of my workshop in 1993. In that year, I had recently completed writing a book called **Kundalini Rising**. One reviewer described it as *"a scholarly fusion of myth, legend, Biblical, historical, scientific, and metaphysical data...revealing the qualities of mysticism which relate to the processing of the Kundalini experience to the heights of its inherent ecstasy."*

Since then, I have continued to concentrate, meditate, and visualize for the purpose of greater revelation concerning this powerful mental energy. My husband Daniel and I have created a means to intuitively discern the transference of energies within and between the major chakras linking mind and body as part of the Intuitive Prosearch Department at the College of Metaphysics. The annual Kundalini Rising Spiritual Focus Session has afforded a place to share this wisdom with others from around the world.

My inner level research has brought a series of Kundalini experiences which I am coming closer each day to being capable of describing. It is this work that I wanted to share in Melbourne. I wanted to update what I had given 14 years before.

Yet, each time I tried to describe my thoughts, His Holiness the Dalai Lama of Tibet got in the way!

The Dalai Lama
My affection for the Dalai Lama is an impulse of Spirit.

At the 1993 Parliament of the World's Religions in Chicago, I stood three feet from him and my consciousness was changed. I did not yet know the history of the Dalai Lama, and had a collegiate acquaintance with the Buddhist religion. For me, being in the presence of the Dalai Lama was an experience of shaktipat, an energetic transfer of creative energy from teacher to disciple, the manifestation of Kundalini.

His Holiness was invited to close Parliament on the tenth day. He arrived a few days earlier to teach classes to select groups. Through what I can only attribute to the Universal Laws acting on my behalf, I learned he was meeting with Buddhist monks and Catholic nuns in one of the upper floors of the Palmer House, away from the activity of Parliament. This information was important to me for two reasons: first, it made me aware of the Dalai Lama's earnest desire to bring together in dialogue those from different religions, and second, it enabled that transference of energy when we met face to face.

Years passed. In the spring of 2007, when I traveled to Chicago to speak at the University there, I learned His Holiness was offering a public address in Millennial Park. My husband, our 12-year-old son, and I joined the thousands who came to hear his address on ***Finding Inner Peace in a World Full of Turmoil***. I came as a mother. It was our son's first experience with His Holiness.

That autumn, we traveled to Indiana University-Bloomington, the learning institute where the Dalai Lama's brother had taught for many years after leaving Tibet to seek refuge in America. The Dalai Lama was teaching from ***Atisha's Lamp on the Path to Enlightenment***. Here I was a student, eager to be, to absorb, to transform.

My fourth meeting was in the summer of 2008 in Madison, Wisconsin, where His Holiness taught meditation. When I heard that this teaching was to include Tenshug – the long life ceremony for the teacher – I knew I wanted to be there, to offer my energy, my support. There are a few people walking the earth who the world truly needs. They are people whose vibratory pattern, both in who they are and what they present, cause our world to be a more evolved, compassionate place. The Dalai Lama is one of these people. For this reason, I want to assist Him in being healthy and whole.

So I went to Madison. For Him. For me. For the world. For you. The days I have spent in the presence of Jetsun Jamphel Ngawang Lobsang Yeshe Tenzin Gyatso, the man who many call a living Buddha, have strengthened the truth of the living Christ in me. I have been writing a book about this for three years.

This is how it came to be that I finally submitted a proposal to the 2009 CPWR committee entitled: ***Best of Both Worlds: A Christian Woman Meets the Dalai Lama***.

My Christian background prepared me well to perceive the inherent partnership in the teachings of the Buddha and the Christ. In my proposal, I wrote, *"The teachings of karma meet Jesus' admonition that we reap what we sow. What separates us, from Self and each other, are the imperfections in our judgements, often emotional in nature. The Christ's teaching to remove the plank in our own eye mirrors the Buddha's counsel for each of us to direct ourselves first to what is proper, then to teach others; thus a wise man will not suffer. The evolution from suffering to compassion to love is the neutralizing factor in the consciousness of humanity. Bringing together the best of Eastern and Western spiritual teachings reveals to us truth on new levels."*

Each successive time of being in the Dalai Lama's presence, the relationship between love and compassion took on a mathematical form in my mind. As I wrote this proposal, I knew I was ready to teach the "Star", a form that came into focus largely as a result of attending His Holiness' 2007 teachings at Indiana University on Bodhichitta, the awakened mind. The Sacred Star is a Taraka Yoga form for emotional intelligence that aids in neutralizing false judgements and prejudice. It identifies six emotional doorways through which energy flows. Each doorway allows mental energy to travel into the physical plane creating opportunities for love and compassion to unite in personal transformation.

It would ultimately be this proposal that would be the stimulus for my contact with Amelia Sunyata Perkins, Honna Eichler, and Grove Harris, all program organizers at the world headquarters of CPWR in Chicago.

October 2009

In late October, only weeks before Parliament, I had no word concerning my second proposal so I wrote to the Chicago office. I shared with them our plans to give *The INVITATION* at Melbourne Unity and our hopes that Dean Lawrence Carter of Morehouse College in Atlanta might portray Dr. Martin Luther King. Then I mentioned that I had only heard about one of proposals for Melbourne. Could they advise me on the status of the second?

Within the week, I received an invitation to participate on a panel titled *The Search for Inner Peace: Multifaith Views from Women around the World.* This panel would include views from female leaders in the Jewish, Buddhist, Hindu, Muslim, Sikh, Pagan and Christian traditions. (This story is told in Chapter 13.) Since thought is cause, I could see my desire to receive an abundance for SOM people to engage the world at Parliament had transfigured into receiving an abundance of co-presenting with a wonderful group of women, global in reach, a group that kept growing until it reached 10! Their kindness and generous spirit was a blessing, and the reciprocity between us filled the room that day with people of all faiths, from around the world. That panel was a manifestation of many my lifelong dreams. The standing room only crowd was a testimony to the Universal Laws in action.

Although I was grateful for this invitation, it did not satisfy my yearning for people attending Parliament to hear from those in our delegation. This part of the creation was yet to be fulfilled.

One week after agreeing to sit on the panel, I received an email from Program Director Grove Harris, offering a place to speak. I was so happy. I knew my prayers and thought projections of goodness for all concerned arising from the Gabriel proposal had been heard!

> "We'd like you to offer a session on your book, which could also serve as a gathering point for people from the School of Metaphysics at the Parliament."

Here it was! This was the open door for those who submitted proposals to have a voice at Parliament. I was thrilled! The original seed idea was continuing to thrive. Perhaps it was God's will for us to share our wisdom in this way.

Upon Grove's suggestion I revised my proposal. She encouraged me to create a new title that might be "more targeted". I was not certain of her meaning, so I meditated, seeking inner guidance. After some time of intuitive breathing, an image appeared within my mind of three overlapping circles, the central image being the flower of life, only instead of the flower this was a jewel. I heard the familiar chant, "Om Mani Padme Hum". My head was clear, my heart whole. All the years of study and practice, of experience and understanding, of Kundalini awakened and arisen, united in that moment. Jesus's words *"you know not the hour or the day when the son of man will appear"* drifted through my consciousness like leaves on a gentle breeze and the smile of my heart lifted to my lips.

"All hail the jewel in the lotus!"

This is the proposal I started to write:

The CROWN JEWELS OF CONSCIOUSNESS
Three Universal Spiritual Practices

The triune nature of reality echoes through the Holy scriptures of the world's religions. Brahm the Creator, Vishnu the Preserver, and Shiva the Transformer reflect this for the Hindu. For the Christian, it is the Father, the Son, and the Holy Spirit. For the Buddhist, the trinity is the Buddha, the Dharma and the Sangha, the community. The trinity of creation expresses in all our endeavors - father, mother, and child; three expressions of love - Eros, philio, and agape; life, death, and resurrection.

Creation finds its highest expression through three practices taught in some form by all religions. These are concentration, meditation, and visualization. These mental postures illumine the mind and purify the body preparing the Self as a channel for the Divine. Since 1975, Dr. Barbara Condron has taught these "crown jewels of consciousness" to people young and old, from many walks of life, and many religious faiths. For Parliament, she has chosen three exercises designed to strengthen the individual's spiritual experience.

First, the exalted instrument for tuning the mind is presented. In the West, this is called the star of David or the Seal of Solomon. In the East, it is known as the Sri Yantra. This form centers the attention, freeing consciousness from the confines of the physical world allowing mind to transcend the limitations of the physical senses and produce the concentration that Jesus spoke of as "the narrow path" and Gautama taught as "the dharma".

Second, meditation is the science of harmonizing the Conscious Mind and Subconscious Minds and attuning them to Superconscious Mind. Dr. Condron will teach "The Star", a geometric illustration of love and compassion that came into focus largely as a result of attending His Holiness the 14th Dalai Lama's 2007 teachings at Indiana University on Bodhichitta, the awakened mind. It identifies six emotional doorways that allow mental energy to travel into the physical plane creating opportunities for personal transformation as consciousness aligns.

Third, the mind's creative power, Kundalini, finds its greatest expression through visualization. Visions and dreams can unite in the "dream consciousness circuit" where every conscious thought reflects the mind of its creator and every nighttime thought brings revelation from the Real Self. Time allowing, participants will break into groups for dreamwork with teachers from the School of Metaphysics located in the United States.

When I sat down to respond to Grove, I told her I appreciated her counsel and her offer for a place for our teachers to assist. I was gratified and fulfilled. It seemed my complete image of plenty for all was coming to pass.

I waited to hear a confirmation and notification of when this might be scheduled. Instead, I received a brief email from Grove acknowledging my acceptance of the place on the peace panel. It had no mention of the *"Crown Jewels"* proposal.

I did not hear from Grove before I left the States. I believed that the panel was to be my venue during Parliament. I arrived in Australia grateful, and expecting nothing more. I received the opportunity the universe saw fit to afford me with grace. No one else knew this story. Like Mary, I was keeping these things in my heart, where my greatest learning transpired.

Now, you know why no one knew about this session and why I was confused when Sheila told me I was on the board as a speaker.

Benevolence is the mercy of abundance
Wednesday, December 9, 2009 9:10 a.m.

If we had had more time for conscious planning, we probably would have developed common goals to accomplish; we would have spread the word as we did for Daniel's observance and the panel on peace. It would have been just as satisfying, the road there would have merely been a different one.

I followed my outline, introducing the concepts of the three jewels of consciousness: concentration, the ability to focus the mind's attention at will, meditation, the specialized form of concentration employed in the service of knowing one's Creator, and visualization, the capacity to create with thought through harmonizing with Universal Law. I drew the Sacred Star, the geometric form found in cultures and religions around the world. Then I introduced the spiritual teachers in their midst and encouraged those attending to move into groups for the question and answer session.

Because everything happened so quickly – two hours from learning that the ***Crown Jewels of Consciousness*** was scheduled, to actually offering it – I didn't recognize that this was the last interactive event for all us. This was the final time period allotted for giving and receiving with others. Considering what we afford, we were perfectly placed. The session, particularly the smaller groups, encouraged integration of ideas received all week into useful and deeper thought and people were grateful.

Watching the five groups reflected to me a simple and profound fact – those present were able to be face-to-face and engaged with half of the psi counselors currently on the planet! The level of metaphysical teaching was evident. I chose the doctors to convene these groups for many reasons. They are examples of the education of the whole Mind that the school provides. They are students and teachers, three past presidents, a current president and chairman of the board of directors. They are psi counselors who know how to connect on all levels with people.

Immediately, I saw them harmonize with people from many religions, backgrounds, and nationalities. They were living examples of what Spiritual education brings – the high-mindedness that comes from practicing concentration, meditation, and visualization every day through all experiences.

A few weeks after we returned from Australia, I sat down with each of the leaders asking them about the people they met. Here are their parables of the Universal Laws.

SEARCHING
Dr. Sheila Benjamin

The people in my group were searching.
There was a young man who sticks out in my mind particularly because he had just recently sold all of his belongings. He is from the United States, and he had come to Australia searching for who he

is and what his next step is. Through the interaction with the group, he realized that there is a place in the United States, in his home country, where he can find all the answers.

"I want to visit sacred sites," he said.

"When you are in the United States, you can come to the Peace Dome and visit us there because we have answers to your questions," I told him.

I'm expecting to hear from him. I believe he'll research our sites because he is definitely hungry for knowledge to feed his spirit. By the time we parted, it was like his thirst had been quenched.

There was another young girl from Europe who had a lot to say. She revealed many dreams. As I taught how the Universal Language of Mind works and what the dream was telling her, her own dreams answered questions about what was going on in her life. She could see that the interpretation definitely made sense and it was connected to her life.

That was the theme of the people who were there. They were looking for something and all of them thought it was the best session they had come to. I think it was because they received individual attention and their questions were answered.

There are many people walking the planet Earth who desire peace, security, and love. When one disciplines their thoughts through concentration, visualization and meditation, you know that you're always connected to the Source, to God, to love and that is who you are.

When I was searching, I found the School of Metaphysics. My soul was thirsty for love. I could love others; I couldn't love myself. That's probably the greatest thing study gave me, is my own kind of sense of centeredness, and so it's given me a greater opportunity to serve other people. It's given me peace which is what I desire most.

LETTING GO
Dr. Christine Madar

What arose pretty quickly in our group were questions about emotions.

There was one gentleman, who's from, I believe, Denmark. He was asking some pretty good thought-provoking questions about consciousness and concentration. As the talking continued, the whole group ended up talking about grief. That was the collective theme.

This man asked a question about being able to concentrate when your emotions are fluctuating, whether it's really a lot of joy or really, really depressed. He was kind of a little bit of the devil's advocate. "Sounds good, undivided attention," he said. "Sounds really good, but when you have all the emotional stuff, then what?"

So I answered him, "With the practice you learn to be able to be still with whatever comes your way."

So then he tosses back to me, "That sounds really nice, but what if your loved ones dies? One of your parents die, or a child dies?" He didn't quite know who he was asking. It was perfect Law of Attraction. I received his question and said, with full authority and equanimity, "I knew this experience with the stillbirth of our first child."

I told of that journey. "I have experienced the death of a child. I know I went the whole gamut of emotions. I know that because I studied concentration exercises I was able to: Number One, fully experience the emotions. Number Two, remember who I was through it. I can sit here today, completely telling you that I'm grateful for that experience and 100% back that up."

What this did was open the door for all these other people to relate their experiences.

"My parents died this year and I've had visitations," one woman from Florida said. She said both of her parents had passed away within six months of one another. She'd dreamed of them. She was at peace with their deaths because of the dreams, however her siblings were still in a lot of emotional turmoil and she felt bad about that.

"I don't know how to reconcile that," she told us. "Sometimes I feel like I should still feel bad." That interesting little guilt.

So the idea of the visitation dreams, even just affirming to her that they are real, gave her a way to be at peace with them. She had had psychic or lucid intuitive dreams throughout her life, so I talked to her about the reason why she is like that. It made sense that she was giving and receiving with her parents after they died. There was the understanding, the openness that she has now of her mind.

There was a younger gal in her twenties who was from Canada and studying in Melbourne. She was studying a psychology kind of program, psychosomatic – how thoughts and emotions affect the body. Her father had died three years ago. So she wanted to know about that.

It's that wonderful "Ah!" You know it, you know why it's happening, and yet to experience the Universal Law of Attraction like that was really beautiful. Ours was the grief program, and I thought I handled it pretty well.

Afterwards, the younger gal sitting next to me came up to me. She gave me a hug, and she said that she could tell that I knew what I was talking about. She really appreciated it. The connecting theme was concentration. It was the first thing Dr. Condron mentioned – undivided attention, concentration. People don't even know that they can concentrate through emotional fluxes in life, and that when you know how to concentrate, you're still going to have that emotional flux. Your understanding of it is going to be different.

ENLIGHTENMENT
Dr. Pam Blosser

The people who were in my group were interested in learning about how to become enlightened. I talked about the divisions of the mind and what it's like to be connected to the subconscious mind, what it's like to be connected to the Superconscious mind, what it's like to be whole-minded.

They had been so filled with other types of information during the Parliament that this was a time of connecting everything together. It was like organizing all the things they'd had in the week. They'd been going to different classes and getting the universals that they didn't realize they'd gotten. Now, we could pick out the universals.

It was the basic metaphysics taught in the First Cycle of School of Metaphysics lessons, actually in the first few months: – the mind, how you know when you're connected to your subconscious mind, which is purpose. We talked about how to have a purpose in your life. I see the subconscious mind as being focused on process. When you have an expanded vision of your ideals and you're thinking more globally and expanded, that's when you're acting more from your Superconscious mind.

I did talk about ideal, purpose, activity --- that that's one way to be whole-minded. It's a simple way that people can understand how to bring all their mind together. I talked about the relationship between the conscious and subconscious minds; the relationship between the different divisions of mind. This was the discussion because these were the questions they had.

They wanted to learn how to be enlightened. That was what they were wanting. One woman came up to me afterwards and said it was the best session she'd been to through the whole thing. It was on the last day, the last one, right before the closing plenary.

The Dalai Lama said in his closing speech, "The philosophies may be different, but many of the practices are the same" so there's definitely a commonality of different religions. Until the Parliament, all the religions were separate in everybody's mind. The Parliament was the beginning of bringing people together, giving us the opportunity to see that we're not so different. That brings all these people's minds together which becomes even more powerful.

I think of Malcolm Gladwell's **The Tipping Point** and what a powerful force Parliament is in the world.

RECEIVING THE INNER URGE
Dr. Laurel Clark

My group was really interested in understanding how to receive from Subconscious or Superconscious Mind. One woman asked about a dream, then as we talked about the dream that got into a discussion about intuition.

There was a man, who I think is probably Aborigine, who had

very clear intuitive experiences when he was younger. He said he used to be guided by an inner voice, but he wasn't hearing that voice so much anymore. He really wanted to get that back. This led into a discussion about undivided attention and what happens when people get their attention all involved in brain chatter, being busy all the time, being on cell phones.

I gave the example that people will be one place and texting somewhere else. Everybody resonated with that in terms of this being a puzzle factor that they hadn't even thought about before. They could see how, when their attention is directed outward, then they don't listen inwardly anymore. There were other people who were nodding and agreeing with that.

Somebody asked what we teach in the lessons that teaches people how to develop intuition and bring it back or cultivate it. I talked some about the order of the Essential Life Skills and the exercises that develop them. It's not that you have the ability to concentrate or you don't have the ability to concentrate. It's something that you can develop.

I suggested to one man that he spend some time every day in silence, where he's not involving his mind in lots of different things at the same time. He liked the idea of that.

Later that day, after the Dalai Lama spoke at the plenary, the woman who had asked about a dream came up to me and asked, "Can I ask about a dream of my husband's? He has this recurring dream." She made a point of finding me in a crowd of thousands.

I really appreciate what you've been teaching recently about the order of concentration and meditation and then visualization because what I realize is that is how I've led my life. I didn't go to college with a goal about my career. I expected that somehow by being in college I would find out what I was supposed to do and at that stage in my life I didn't really have a concept of it. I actually learned how to meditate for the first time while I was in college before I became a student in the School of Metaphysics.

I have a very firm memory as a child being in kindergarten having an experience in school which was really troubling. There were some kids who were laughing, ridiculing a boy because he wanted to play with a dollhouse. I felt bad for him, and I wanted to help him. I remember lying in bed at night and thanking God that I was a girl and I didn't have to deal with that.

Then, after I had that thought that arose from within me, I had this brain thought, "Wait a minute, you don't even believe in God!"

I wasn't raised with a religion, so that experience was very profound because it was a direct experience of listening first. The exercises in the School of Metaphysics have helped me to not only understand that process but to have control of it. To know what to listen to. I feel it's saved my life in a lot of ways. Learning how to know what it is that I'm even listening to, whether its an inner voice I'm listening to or if it's brain chatter, or if it's somebody else's thoughts.

Over a period of time before I became a student at the School of Metaphysics, I just probably would have thought I was psychotic because I heard voices in my head. What I know now is that sometimes it's all of those. Learning how to concentrate, to cause my outer mind to be still, has enabled me to be aware of what I need to listen to. That has enabled me to know what to do with that inner voice which has always happened in my life in response to what it is that I'm trying to do.

The awareness of the concept of "Seek ye first" didn't come first in my life. I attribute a lot of that to not being raised with a religion. Even that idea – "the kingdom of heaven" – I wasn't taught that as a child.

I was definitely taught that in the realm of humanity one has a certain responsibility to be considerate of other people. There's something that my mother used to say in kind of singsong voice that her mother had said to her. It's from a poem:

"Straight is the line of duty.
Curved is the line of beauty.
Follow the straight line and
you will see the curved line will ever follow thee."

I don't even remember what I was doing when that came into my mind! But it was so loud in my mind that I know that thought was obviously something important to her, and it was something that I received. I think that was secular, really. I think I probably need to give that some more thought.

I know the Law of Attraction definitely operates with the inner urge. I'm thinking in terms of people having not only the urge to listen but having that be the guiding force. One of the things I've seen with people who've studied at the School of Metaphysics is it's almost like there are two camps. There are people coming to the study because there's something consciously they're not very clear about. Then there are other people – for instance, someone who's been in college, they realize they really don't want to go to college anymore but they don't know what they want to do. They're seeking that inner wisdom. They're aware enough, or open enough, to a kind of inner self so the truth is based on that more than the outer mind. Maybe that is "seek ye first."

I haven't done everything I want to do with my life, but if I died today, I would die with really a deep sense of peace that I have not only been fulfilled but fulfilled what I think I've been called to do. I don't have the doubts that a lot of people my age do, thinking, "what have I done with my life? It's half over." I don't have any of that and I really attribute that to listening first and making choices in response to that. That's what practicing the crown jewels of consciousness has meant to me.

CONNECTEDNESS
Dr. Daniel Condron

Since the group I'd guided had already learned what the three crown jewels are, I started by saying, "Okay, you can ask me any question you want about anything that's been discussed: concentration, meditation, visualization. It was also mentioned we teach dreams in the School of Metaphysics, so if you have any dreams you want to be interpreted I will answer those. Any questions you'd like to ask."

Each one asked a question. There was a couple of them with dreams, and one woman asked about an experience.

"Well, what about if it's not a dream but you kind of go inside?" she asked.

I said, "Why don't you describe it."

"It was when I was in college and I was studying for a test at the library and it was kind of late at night, and I was by myself. All of a sudden I felt this black come over me. This black, deep black, and then I seemed to go inside with it deeper and deeper and then I went to the light. There was a light that I experienced. I felt kind of afraid of it and then coming back."

I explained that this experience occurred when she was – or at least at the point of beginning to – discovering her own inner light. She needed to explore that more. It told her who she really is.

Then I told her some more things, and she began tearing up and crying a bit. She said, "Oh, I didn't realize there was so much there inside of me." And so it reached her very deeply. I reached out and touched her arm, and she was really appreciative about it. In fact, she's studying religions at some college and I ended up giving her a copy of **The Secret Code of Revelation**. I gave to her because I thought this would be very beneficial to help her with her studies.

The people in my group all seemed to be very interested in learning. All wanted to use the opportunity provided for them by having me present, where there was a person where they could specifically ask a question. That seemed to be very important or on their mind. They all seemed very interested in asking questions and receiving whatever I had to offer. They seemed to be grateful for what I offered them.

It seemed like their mental images were operating. The mental images were very clear to me, so I could just see inside the mental images. I saw exactly not only what the mental picture was that they were offering, but also what their needs were behind that, and I was able to offer them their needs.

There were a couple of dreams. I was able to follow along and just see the mental images. I was able to perceive exactly what they were saying and what they needed to hear. I offered truth to them. It was very fulfilling, very successful, very useful to the people present, I believe.

I see concentration, meditation, and visualization having a beneficial effect on me every day in my life in the present moment.

It's an ongoing process with me because my soul growth and spiritual development, my enlightenment is a never ending story. It just keeps growing and growing, greater. Concentration is the ability to focus the attention on a single ideal or thought and then meditation is the stilling the mind to receive the answer to our prayers or what we receive from the high self or inner self.

So the two together create the ability for us to get the mind more still or with less and less thoughts until we know the space between our thoughts. In the space between our thoughts, we know who we are beyond brain thoughts and even mind thoughts. Then, in that space and then from that space, we can consciously choose thoughts. This is the beginning of power because it is true – a universal truth – that thought is cause. It's how the whole universe was created, with thoughts.

Once we master our own thoughts and consciously choose them from the point of space, then we become master of our universe and master of what we create in our life, and master of what we draw to us and master of what we become.

A thought is a visualized image or a thought form so therefore choosing thoughts consciously means to choose or to create a visualized image thought form and speak it out as words in the life. Those are the keys to creation, the keys to enlightenment, the keys to knowing self and knowing the whole self and becoming who we really are, which I continue to use every day.

A Miracle

It was there all the time.

That's the thought I turned over in my mind for days afterward. Abundance is there all the time. The Universal Laws always function perfectly. God is present. *"Seek the Lord, while he may be found,"* says **Isaiah** 55. We use that chapter from the Old Testament of the **Bible** to convey the ideal and purpose of the School of Metaphysics.

The day of the ***Crown Jewels*** was so full! Decidedly, a day of great wealth. Immediately following our presentation, we joined the Tibetan Monks who were just feet away. They were scheduled to dissolve their mandala masterpiece at 1 p.m. To do so, they asked for two young people to assist. With Sheila's and Paul's encouragement, Hezekiah stepped forward. He and a lovely girl, a few years younger, carried the longhorn in procession from the second floor of the convention hall outside to the bridge over the Yarra River where the monks emptied the sand from their labor, returning it to the sea.

What a memorable experience for our son! The boy who has been in the presence of His Holiness' teachings three times and who created a film titled **Why Does the Dalai Lama Matter to You?** became an honorary monk that day, maturing in spirit before our eyes. This, just minutes before he would hear His Holiness speak during the closing plenary.

Hours later this day concluded by giving the first Intuitive Reports outside the United States for our new friends at Melbourne Unity Church. What fulfilling abundance for all!

It happened so quickly, I didn't get an opportunity to look through my Parliament materials again until we returned to the apartment late that night. Someone had said **The Crown Jewels...** was listed in the supplementary pages. These were the ones printed after the book went to press and given out separately. As I scanned the pages, I found the listing. My eyes rested on it for some time. It took a while for me to believe my own eyes.

How could I have missed this? How could all of us have missed it? What were the odds? I knew I had not read over the materials in detail, and I received my lesson of care-full-ness. I reflected upon how I had spent my time since arriving in Melbourne. Helping Hezekiah document his daily experiences, preparing for **THE INVITATION** and the peace panel, plus giving and receiving at Parliament filled my days. I was sleeping only a few hours a night. It was a function of abundance itself that I remained clueless.

I think of *"The Crown Jewels of Consciousness"* session as a miracle in our lives. It manifested beyond my conscious determination and intention, and in a manner that allowed the truth of our abundance to make itself known. I received because I trusted God and the infallible workings of Universal Law. It was a function of law that at the right place and right time, Paul Madar was looking for a session to attend and, as he describes it, "I saw '***The Crown Jewels of Consciousness***'. That sounded like something I'd want to attend. Then, wait! ***Barbara Condron and teachers from the School of Metaphysics!***" Then Paul told Sheila and Sheila told me. The rest is our-story! It sounds like a fictional story line. The beauty is, it happened. The topic of this session, who and how it was presented, the timing of it, and how it came into the world speaks to how miracles come into our lives every day.

Most spiritual belief systems include the three jewels. The content of consciousness is universal in that way. The state of consciousness, however, is the product of an individual's disciplined mind. The ideas alone are insufficient for lasting transformation. If ideas were sufficient for a (w)holy state of consciousness, we would be creating a different planet as the great thinkers of the past and of today have imagined.

Every master teacher of consciousness has taught a practical application for ideas, the uniting of the state of consciousness with the content of consciousness. Once the teacher leaves the planet, how long that practical application endures speaks to the evolution of the human being. The evolution of religion - of high-minded ideals – is important, and I think that is what this gathering is all about. When the universals are appreciated, we live abundantly, creating the next steps in fulfilling the promise of eternal life.

All we need to do is open our hearts, clear our minds, and invite the Holy Spirit to guide our thoughts and actions. ∞

I THINK OF
"THE CROWN JEWELS OF CONSCIOUSNESS"
SESSION AS A MIRACLE IN OUR LIVES.

IT MANIFESTED BEYOND MY CONSCIOUS
DETERMINATION AND INTENTION,
AND IN A MANNER THAT ALLOWED
THE TRUTH OF OUR ABUNDANCE TO
MAKE ITSELF KNOWN.

The Universal Truth in My Story
Barbara Condron

As one gives, so one receives.

As a teacher, I've learned the secret of abundance. The education began by giving without expecting anything in return from the student. Once this practice became a part of Self, the freedom to expect the return from the riches of the Universe opened to me. This return was more than replenishing energetic coffers. This was perceiving the connectedness throughout the Universe that makes every individual equal in the eyes of the Creator. We are all made of the same substance – spiritually and materially. Our bodies are made mostly of water and a collection of several dozen minerals all fashioned through a spiritual intelligence that continues to mystify the greatest scientific minds. The secret of abundance rests in the mind of its maker.

As one gives, so one receives.

After many years of seeing the cause and effect in giving and receiving, something wonderful happened in my mind. The two began to merge. Giving and receiving no longer happened between me and someone else. Giving and receiving occurred within Self. It was a simple realization that made me Whole. As I give with joy and wisdom, joy and wisdom are mine! That is the secret the teacher comes to know.

As one gives, so one receives.

Abundance is the mark of a mental creator. One who teaches others, through thought and deed, to give universally and to receive in like measure, knows the Truth of abundance.

As one gives, so one receives.

That is the education life provides when a teacher teaches teachers.•

DREAMTIME

ᵀᴴₑ LAW of COMPLETION

"I AM COMMITTED TO BECOMING FULLY ENLIGHTENED."

by Barbara Condron, DM, DD

*One Nature,
perfect and pervading,
circulates in all natures.
One Reality,
all-knowing,
contains within itself all realities.
The one moon is reflected
wherever there is a sheet of water,
And all the moons in all the waters
are embraced within the one moon.
The embodied Truth of all the Buddhas
enters into my own being.
And my own being is found in union with theirs.
–Yung-Chia*

The 1993 Parliament of the World's Religions changed me.

I spoke on the topic of *Spiritual Initiation: Gateways to Transcendent Consciousness,* receiving much more than I gave.

Eight thousand people from all over the world came together in Chicago, the site of the first Parliament in 1893. I met people I had only read about. I forged relationships which stretched a decade to the dedication of the World's Peace Dome on the College of Metaphysics campus in 2003. I deepened relationships with the spiritual students and teachers who attended with me, bringing the School of Metaphysics teachings of the Universal Laws and Truths to the Parliament.

I realized there were others who sensed the Truth of the coming days of Co-creation – what we at the School of Metaphysics have known since 1973 as the dawning of Intuitive, Spiritual Man. Ushering in that Light is the purpose of the school.

I remember Barbara Marx Hubbard speaking on the essence of creative life during one of the evening plenaries where all attendees come together. I was captivated. Many of the words from her mouth, I had spoken. I had just turned 40 at the time, and she was of the generation before me. I admired her thinking and by the time the last day rolled around, I came out of my shyness into humility so I could approach her and give her a copy of **Kundalini Rising**, the book I had just completed on mastering creative energies.

Gerald Barney of the Millennium Institute was another I remember. He spoke to the need for change for a sustainable future. His work carried him around the world, advising businesses and governments of their projected futures based upon the statistics at the time. I was drawn to Gerald because he approached vision scientifically. He advocated reasonably seeking steps toward a desired goal as a replacement for the dispiriting heaviness of reacting to circumstances. For instance, he focused on population growth, asking simple questions. At the rate of its population growth, could a country feed its own people today? In 10 years? In 50 years? Simple questions, that in these days of scientific ingenuity, can have simple answers as long as the reasoning in that populace is sound. Because people make the answers complicated, we find Parliaments of this nature a helpful requirement for humanity to progress. At SOM, we teach the universal dynamics of group consciousness that can be applied anywhere at any time by anyone so I attended each of Gerald's presentations.

There is much learned in the interaction between human beings, and most of it does not have to do with statistical data, rather it has to do with principles taught by the spiritual masters throughout time. Buddhism teaches that when one can move the heart of the self, the heart of the society moves. That's why Gerald, Barbara, and it seemed all of us came to Parliament that year.

I watched Barbara Fields and Jim Kenney, and saw the Tao of leadership in action. Lao-tzu's words come to mind, *"True leaders are hardly known to their followers. ... When the work's done right, with no fuss or boasting, ordinary people say, 'Oh, we did it'."*

The Parliament of the People, an idea I heard attributed to Barbara Fields, empowered everyone who wanted to participate a voice. It gave people a chance to choose between eating and communion, since it was held in a large ballroom during lunch time. The timing made it a wonderful symbolic action. Those of us who chose communion with like minds, found our spirits fed and our bodies at peace. Communion meant something deeper, more fulfilling than eating physical food. Communion was spiritual.

I saw the radiance on Barbara's face the last afternoon as she stood on the sidelines watching the crowds who gathered at Millennial Park to receive His Holiness the 14th Dalai Lama of Tibet. Most of us thought it would be 100 years before the next Parliament and so felt deeply the gratitude of being there to experience it.

Those days were the first time I was in the presence of the Dalai Lama, an initiation that would become a part of my maturing in head and heart over the next 17 years. What he has stimulated within me since that meeting is chronicled in **A Christian Woman Meets the Dalai Lama**, a book I have been writing for three years now. In 1993, I did not foresee the place that work would have in my speaking during the 2009 Parliament. In the end, it does.

Peace is an idea whose time has come

I think the most proactive thought form to arise in my consciousness from the '93 Parliament was the need for a declaration of Peace, a concept of what peace is, rather than a negation of what it is not.

This came in response came to a document presented at Parliament which had been signed by 143 religious leaders. I remember reading that these people came from Baha'i, Brahmanism, Brahma Kumaris, Buddhism, Christianity, Hinduism, Indigenous, Interfaith, Islam, Jainism, Judaism, Native American, Neo-Pagan, Sikhism, Taoism, Theosophist, Unitarian Universalist and Zoroastrian religions. I remember the sting that the fledgling International Church of Metaphysics was not among them. I remember that from that disappointment came a greater light of awareness that would guide my decision-making through the coming decade.

The document that premiered at the Chicago Parliament is called **Towards a Global Ethic**. It was intended to be "an initial statement of a group of rules for living on which all of the world's religions can agree." The initial draft was written by Swiss Catholic priest Hans Kung in the early 1990s. He had two purposes. He wanted to describe what the world religions have in common rather than what separates them, and he hoped to establish a beginning minimal code of rules of behavior everyone could accept. I remember being encouraged and inspired by the thought that people from around the world could agree on universal tenets. Then I read the document.

"The world is in agony," it begins. It goes on to describe the pain, the fear, the death in the world. Then it condemns abuse, poverty, injustice, violence. Then the affirmations begin for a global ethical code, the establishment of a few core thinking principles – *"we must treat others as we wish others to treat us"* – and many descriptions of what *not* to do – *"live for ourselves alone, exploit in any way, oppress, injure, torture, kill, steal"*.

On many levels, the document marked the great progress of humanity up to the second millennium. It helped me to identify the evolutionary development of the animalistic nature in man into the human(e) nature. Whether from a theological, psychological, sociological, or anthropological point of view, the *Global Ethic* helped me to accept it for what it is on its own merits – a statement of human consciousness about human consciousness.

The more I read it, the more my spirit declined.

As I shared it with others, I saw the effect of the words. I saw people shrink away from the very first sentence, thus missing what was to come. I saw people become impassioned by the "wrongs" the document focused upon. I saw some dismiss the "bad" parts and focus on the "good". As I observed my own response and that of others, I noted the Law of Duality sinking into the extremes of physical polarity. I saw the limitations of human consciousness, and the seeds for its remedy were sown in mine.

I was awakened.

And I was moved.

I had been meditating for 18 years, teaching Mind and the Universal Laws that govern creation to anyone who wanted to learn for almost as long. Before that, I was raised in a wholesome environment by Christian parents in middle class 1950s America. I learned early how to think in ideals, and education in Mind taught me how to wield the power of reason. In all those years, I had learned that opinion rises from the outer mind and environment. Truth comes from inside the individual, whether rich or poor, master or servant, saint or sinner. Truth rises in the consciousness from within Self.

I, you, – we serve to stimulate one another through our interactions. I learned that in every situation, whether I am acting as teacher or student, parent or child, young or old, artist or scientist, what is constant is the reality that I Am that I Am. This is true for me and it is true for you. We are whole and complete as I AM. So the most I could hope for was to be a stimulus, a tool, a means by which my whole Self could engage other whole Selves.

I had watched countless, well-meaning individuals in my youthful years, attempt to impress their truth upon others. It was as if they believed the lack of confidence they held in their own ideas would somehow be dispelled when they convinced someone else of its worthiness. I saw it with some of the Christians in the churches I grew up in, then I saw it with teachers and fellow students at school. Later, I would be able to recognize it in public figures – politicians, spokespeople, CEOs, and the like.

Humanity can try to impart, imprint, impress, or otherwise force the truth to be known by others and every time it will fail. This is why polarity thinking which has widely populated spiritual literature and teachings is limited in its capacity for whole understanding.

When I read *Towards a Global Ethic*, I understood the importance of the document and that it symbolized an amazing step forward for all of humanity. The establishment of common goals is essential whenever two or more are gathered. And, in truth, all religions share basic and fundamental ideals. The signing of the **Global Ethic** by such a diverse group of religious leaders, and so many of them, was a beginning for some. For me, it was an ending.

Towards a Global Ethic, says *"Earth cannot be changed for the better unless the consciousness of individuals is changed first."* It's a statement in the negative sense and its Truth is Thought is Cause, and the Physical its Manifest Likeness. It is the Twin Verses spoken by the Buddha in his Sermon at Bernares. It is the reality I had come to know as that intuitive grasp of Truth that comes from within. This is the Truth that is universal. The Truth, Jesus addresses when he says, *"I Am the Truth, the Way, and the Life, no one comes to the Father but by me."*

When a change begins within the individual it permeates every thought, every word, every action. This change does not require external motivations, be they laws, sanctions, financial incentives, or even friendships. These are in use and have been in use for millennia, and the world has been slow to change. There had to be a complete way to express the Truths in all religions, the Truths the **Global Ethic** was supporting. When the inner urge, the Spirit of Self is heeded, when it is whole or holy, the physical world is transcended. The limits fall away. Jesus taught this as, *"Seek ye first the Kingdom of Heaven and all else will be added unto you."*

The **Global Ethic** opened my mind to a clearer understanding of the Law of Duality. If presenting people with a document of polarities – do this, not that – directed their minds to think in "do-this, not-that" terms, then what kind of document would direct their minds to a whole picture? The *Global Ethic* made me wonder what a whole-minded document defining peace might read like.

I knew people whose consciousness was spiritual. Some of them I had read about and studied throughout my life, during my time at university and through my activities with the School of Metaphysics, a non-for-profit educational institute for higher learning. Others I knew personally. I was surrounded by people invested in soul growth and spiritual progression. They were learning to be teachers of spirit, "fishers of men" Jesus called them. They had come together over time and space in America and were all teaching at SOMs around the country. We regularly met in conference so I began to encouraged our leaders to work with their students and teachers to research and meditate on peace, then bring their ideas together.

During those days, the *Global Ethic* proved to be the catalyst for a greater resonance – the work of the founding fathers of the United States. The connections between the establishment of the government of this country which drew upon the best systems existing in the 1700s, including that of the native American Six Nations Confederacy, and the work the School of Metaphysics exists to perform, has been in the consciousness of this 501(c)(3) educational institute since its beginnings. In the nine months required for the *Universal Peace Covenant* to come forward, the correspondences with the minds of Benjamin Franklin, Thomas Jefferson, John Adams, George Washington, and the like were apparent. What our founding fathers had begun by creating a republican form of government, where freedom to choose (and be personally accountable for that choice) is the law of the land, would be supported and enriched by a document that would declare the consciousness choices which sustain that republic. The *Universal Peace Covenant* seeks to be that document.

In 577-words, the *Universal Peace Covenant* contains only two negations. One, is the affirmation that *"government and laws cannot heal the heart"* and two, [peace] *"is not made in documents but in the minds and hearts of men and women."* Both statements point to the individual responsibility that enables people to exercise freedoms with the whole in mind. The other 550 or so words express the highest thoughts created throughout time and space, drawing upon Truths expressed by thinkers from Lao Tzu to Victor Hugo to Eleanor Roosevelt to the founding fathers themselves.

The *Universal Peace Covenant* paved the way for the Peace Dome to be dedicated in 2003. "A Moment of Peace" at 1 pm on October 11, 2003 was proclaimed by 13 mayors, two U.S. governors, and one nation's president. This was the moment when people on every continent, including scientists in Antarctica, joined in reading the covenant as One Voice.

I grew up with television. The power of radio in humanity's life had caused a common ear in humanity. Television was training humanity's collective eye. Dedication Day, I was privileged to introduce the recitation of the *Universal Peace Covenant*. I stood with others at the top of the Peace Dome second story ramp, above the relief map of the world. I watched the words drifting on the wind and a long-held desire manifested. As a child in the 1960s, I wondered if what I saw on television – from Mickey Mouse cartoons to the Vietnam War – kept going out into space. Was it possible other intelligent life somewhere "out there" was receiving what we humans were projecting? Bear in mind, this was before computer graphics made such ideas commonplace through sci-fi television and movies.

As I watched the birth of cable TV, then the internet, the stakes grew higher. Now the loudness of our planet was amplified by increasing numbers. Knowing how I could be disturbed and even alarmed by what I virtually see and hear, I could only imagine the same would be true for some unsuspecting space traveler caught in the electromagnetic waves we broadcast. By that time, science was saying the waves continue on – indefinitely.

I was chagrined. I made a conscious choice to produce moments, worthy of broadcasting, that might help neutralize some of the offensive and short-sighted creations humans are capable of fantasizing, enacting, and broadcasting into space. "The Moment of Peace" was one of these.

"World peace begins within ourselves." Hundreds of voices created the waves moving out into space. They carried who we are on this blue planet to any receiver, and my heart moved up to my throat.

Years later, in 2010, the year I am writing this, I open to the final page of a *Newsweek* magazine. There I see a picture of what I had seen in my mind as a child with a headline that reads: "What are They Watching on Alpha Centauri?" At the bottom of the page a small part of the earth is seen. Rising arcs move out into space measuring recent to distant times. The closest arc, representing where Alpha Centauri is in relationship to Earth, is receiving the first season of the television shows "*Lost*" and "*The Apprentice*". The farthest arc, 400 trillion miles from Earth, is just now receiving FDR's first televised presidential speech. Between these two come all the shows from "*The Twilight Zone*" to "*MASH*" to 24-hour news broadcasts and shows around the world.

Perhaps you think it odd that I take all this personally. Perhaps that is how religious thought sensitizes consciousness. My thought is, in a connected universe, it is personal. My thoughts and actions affect you to the extent you allow, and yours affect me in like kind.

I made a difference the day we dedicated a dome on the College of Metaphysics campus as a universal site for peace, and so did thousands of like-minded individuals who read the **Universal Peace Covenant**. I live what anthropologist Margaret Mead is often quoted as observing: *"Never underestimate the power of a small group of individuals to change the world. For indeed it is all that ever has."*

The Peace Dome was born.
What would it become?

The tile mandala at the center of the first floor measures its progress by marking the lineage of people who come here. Many of them have witnessed eight Nobel Peace Laureates brought to life through **The INVITATION**. After dedication, **The INVITATION** became a heartbeat, a pulse of lives worth examining. I tell the story of how this play came to be in a book titled **Peacemaking: Nine Lessons in Changing Yourself, Your Relationships, and Your World**.

The INVITATION has grown to be a powerful force in my life. It would unite me with Parliament in 2008, as Christine describes in Chapter 6. The Chicago premiere of the play opened the door for us to travel to Australia. It seems a bit illogical to me now that I didn't realize my commitment to attend arose from my peace work until just a few weeks before going to Melbourne. Telling the story here makes it seem so obvious. However, as revelations of a mystical nature seem to operate beyond physical laws of the universe, the profound ways the concept of peace has shaped my life to this point would prove to be a significant illumination for me.

"We have inherited a big house," Martin Luther King, Jr. stated in his Nobel Peace Prize acceptance speech, *"a great 'world house' in which we have to live together - black and white, Easterners and Westerners, Gentiles and Jews, Catholics and Protestants, Moslem and Hindu, a family unduly separated in ideas, culture, and interests who, because we can never again live without each other, must learn, somehow, in this one big world, to live with each other."* I grasped this ideal even as a child. The necessity for its practice has come to light in my adult years. *"This means that more and more our loyalties must become ecumenical rather than sectional. We must now give an overriding loyalty to mankind as a whole in order to preserve the best in our individual societies."*

Each time I heard Dr. King's words, it was like spring rain upon tender buds in my consciousness. My mind was opening, flourishing by contemplating "the art of living together as brothers." Our family has lived this truth for decades, sharing our lives with an ever-changing student and teacher population at the college. What the Peace Dome birthed in me was the realization of how the True Reality I live might become a universal reality for all people on the planet.

Over the past decade, I have come to view the work we do through the Peace Dome as the evolution of the Interfaith Church of Metaphysics (ICOM). When it was initiated in 1977, the "International Church of Metaphysics" described the spiritual movement resulting from the School of Metaphysics educational program of study. After our individual and collective experiences at the '93 Parliament, our governing boards elected to replace "International" with "Interfaith" as it was seen to more closely reflect the consciousness we offered in the world. ICOM was never intended to create a new religion, for sufficient spiritual practices already exist for global consciousness evolution. Once I accepted this simple fact, it was easy for me to acknowledge ICOM's absence in the signing of the *Global Ethic*. What is needed is education and practice of the Universal Truths which already exist in the collective consciousness of our species, a personal insight of the ecumenical.

Those who, over the course of years exercise their minds daily through concentration, meditation, and visualization, experience this natural unfolding of spirit in consciousness. Its intrinsic value arises as the eye of perception – be it described as the Tibetan Buddhist wisdom eye, the Western theosophist's third eye, the Christian single eye – opens to see a new heaven and new earth. The open mind experiences omniscient vision, and the universal connections in all Holy Scriptures is perceived. This mental action works in my Mind every day.

I have observed that this same mental action produces expansion and enlightenment in every case where it is implemented. The mental action is receiving a vision from the inner mind. The key is in receiving. Receiving is the esoteric teaching in every religious tradition on the planet. It is accomplished first by producing the still mind, a concept and practice that my husband, Daniel, has invested his consciousness in perfecting.

When the vision is received in the outermost level of consciousness, this means it has presence on all inner levels. This is the experience of avatar, the descent from heaven to earth. Then it is the duty of the physicalized Conscious Mind to interpret what has been received.

What happens in that moment, sets one's destiny because the choice made determines the Self's course on earth, in heaven; –and sometimes in hell. Now the mind must remain disciplined, the mind's inner light steady, so the action can be chosen that will best align with the vision. The result is the whole mind is entrained, and ascension can be realized.

"If thine eye be single, thy body will be filled with light," taught Jesus who became the Christ. Religious examples of this action abound in the world's Holy Scripture: Mahavira, Arjuna and Krishna, Lao Tzu, Zoroaster, Guatama the Buddha, Queztlcoatl, Jesus the Christ, Guru Nanak, Baha'u'llah, and others prove the model we can follow. Their lives and their words teach us how to live an enlightened existence. We can imitate one, or receive from all, and that is the gift of interfaith.

It was when I received an email from a program associate at the Parliament that I came to fully realize how profoundly the ecumenical reality of peace work has permeated my consciousness.

How One Moment Changes Everything
October 28, 2009

It is 2 a.m. when I start checking emails. There it is. The subject line reads: "Invitation to the 2009 Parliament." I note my body has inhaled at the sight of it and I am now holding my breath. I click the mouse to open the electronic letter.

The beginning is positive, "Greetings from the Council! It is great to be in contact with you - I've heard wonderful things about you and your long-standing involvement with the Parliament from Amelia."

Months earlier, I had submitted two presentation proposals for the 2009 Parliament of the World's Religions which is to be held in Melbourne, Australia. One focused on dreams and dream interpretation, the area of my expertise which I have found most valuable to religious studies, had been gently rejected in late summer. Now it is near the end of October, just seven weeks from the gathering, and my second offering has yet to receive a response.

I begin exhaling.

> "In view of the fact that you will be at the Melbourne Parliament and have such extensive expertise with both the Parliament and East and West relations, I am pleased to extend a special invitation to sit on a unique panel."

A panel! I will be able to meet others from around the world! What an amazing opportunity. My gratitude and joy include a shadow of disappointment in having a weaker voice than in 1993 Parliament when I was younger and less experienced. This imagined hurt, born from my own unfulfilled desire, threatens to distract me from the good in this situation.

I know this dragon. I have slain his brothers dozens of times in recent years. I am unfairly judging the present by the past, expecting, hoping for an equal or larger area of influence in keeping with the wisdom I have gained. Noting the need to direct my mind into the present, I remove the plank marring my vision from the beauty of this moment, and purify my own thinking. I chastise my separate self for even the hint of belittling others by failing to honor my place among them. Would I decrease their opportunity to speak in favor of lengthening my own? No, I would not. By Self-correcting the egoic tendency I affirm that my influence is a personal responsibility, my own to choose. Forgiving the distraction, neutralizes the hurt.

Now, the what-if dragon rears its head, pulling a train of thoughts into the future. "Extensive expertise", it says. My mind starts to wonder, what is expected of me? My openness betrays me, as doubts about my qualifications enter my mind. This trip to Australia will be the first time I have left the North American continent. I have only recently procured my first passport. Inner plane realities aside, in the physical world I have not been much of a world traveler. This

Lernaean Hydra is growing more heads! In that moment, I don't see all the people from around the world I have befriended, taught, and served. I am only seeing the abyss of what is not.

Neutralizing this train of thought is put to the side as I still my mind to receive more.

> The panel is titled, 'The Search for Inner Peace: Multifaith Views from Women around the World' and incorporates views from female leaders in the Jewish, Buddhist, Hindu, Muslim, Sikh, Pagan and Christian traditions.

I am astounded. Here is a culmination of what I have been studying, teaching, and living all my life – bringing people of all faiths, all backgrounds, all countries together. This one line pulls together the unity of all religious teachings in what I know as interfaith. Such a group will most assuredly invite the presence of the Holy Spirit. To receive the light these practitioners of faith will shine upon the human condition is a godsend. To be afforded a voice within this group is a blessing.

And the subject matter, peace! How perfect for someone who lives 300 feet away from the world's Peace Dome. The resonance of this invitation with my work of the past 17 years is clear to me. The 1993 Parliament's influence upon my thinking has everything to do with my dedication to illuminating a visualized seed thought of peace that is accessible to all people. That seed thought is the ***Universal Peace Covenant***.

In this light, my doubts of worthiness fade.

I review the list of religions. No interfaith. The process of elimination points to this invitation being predicated on my tradition being Christianity, the faith of my youth, not Interfaith, the work of my adult years. I hold my breath and keep reading.

> It will be a special program because it will span two time slots, filling both the Engage and Open Space time allotment. You, along with the other panelists in this presentation, will each provide your insights on how your tradition has contributed to finding inner peace.

I feel my solar plexus chakra reverse its direction and energy starts pouring out of my adrenal glands. I watch as a sudden emotional urge to flee takes hold of my thoughts. "Your tradition." If that tradition is Christianity, who am I to represent an entire faith? Catholics and Protestants, Quakers and Lutherans. The Evangelicals of my youth come into my mind. Can I speak for them? Can I represent people who condemn Buddhists as atheists, the Hindu as transmigrationists, and Catholics as idol worshippers? Can I represent, in good conscience, a religion that has championed fighting and dying for freedom in the name of God and country? A nation that, in the present climate, is denounced in many parts of the world as purveyors of the inhumane rather than peacekeepers? I consciously stop the flow of ideas realizing I am examining my own thoughts of what it means to be Christian.

> You are welcome to share some of your expertise on east and west relations and understanding of one another. In the second section, there will be a conversation between the panelists with each other and the audience.

Here, is the permission I need. In these first moments of receiving these ideas, it occurs to me that the person writing the email, is honoring what I know from experience - "your expertise" – more than I am. All at once my mind opens and 56 years of questions and answers, seeking and finding, reconciliation and illumination appear before me. This shift in perspective is like moving through a wormhole in space from one location to another light years away.

Years of concentration practice, enable me to hold my attention steady through the extremes. Being free from these pairs of opposites, as the **Bhagavad Gita** describes them, affords me the complete image of what I might bring to this panel. It is easy for me to see that I will need more time to reconcile the thoughts this letter is stirring.

> Please let me know if you would be willing to contribute to this panel. Your contribution would really add an edge to the presentation on the whole.

"Add an edge"? What does that mean? Fear is rising in my Mind. It is talking to me, "Who am I to speak for Christianity?" I am much more equipped to speak for interfaith, for the metaphysical perspective that is the pursuit of all religious thought. I know that had Honna's invitation been for an Interfaith representative, I would be in a very different place mentally and emotionally right now.

I know I will say "yes" to this invitation. I know it is the right thing for me to do. On these counts, I am certain. I also know that to say "yes" to this offer means clearing my conscience. For my own integrity, I need to do this work of honesty before giving my reply.

I close the computer and sit in half-lotus on the floor of my small study. I lift my eyes, looking out into the night sky. Nights are rarely black here on the campus of the College of Metaphysics. Away from the artificial lights of cities, the moons and stars give the domed-sky life.

I want to say yes. Without reservation. I know to do so I must calm the windstorm in my head and comfort the yearning of my heart. This is the craft I have spent my life thus far mastering. I first calm my solar plexus, urging it to begin returning energy back into mind instead of pulling it out into the body to be wasted in fueling my turmoil.

My mind clearing, my heart becomes lighter. I affirm there is nothing to fear. Only my own undisciplined imagination will bring me harm. Like Mary receiving good news from Gabriel, I affirm that in this moment, at this place, I have found favor with God.

I focus my mind on the rise and fall of my breath. Breathing in. Breathing out. Receiving light. Giving light. Welcoming God. Abiding with God. Inspiring Spirit. Holifying Spirit. Each breath is a tide, cleansing the thoughts that are temporary in nature and revealing those of greater permanence.

Emotions calm. Mental thoughts settle. The outer mind harmonizes, creating the familiar resonance to Superconsciousness which years of daily meditation bring.

Mind so aligned, I choose the prayer Jesus taught as my dhyana. I choose these words because they express the thoughts of one who is a Christ. The passage is recorded in the New Testament of the **Bible**, in the sixth chapter of ***Matthew***.

Our Father,
    The images in the prayer come to my mind. Their meaning in the Universal Language of Mind fills my consciousness.
    I come as the Real Self, whole and complete.

Who art in Heaven ... I honor the Divine plan for my maturing as creator.

Hallowed be thy name ... Claiming this spiritual birthright,

Thy kingdom come ... I receive the Maker's blessing.

Thy will be done ... I surrender to this highest purpose, manifesting the creator's likeness

On earth ... with every thought, and
...*as it is in Heaven.* ... giving thanks for the Spirit that fills me

Give us this day our daily bread ... May the choice before me fulfill this purpose

And forgive us our debts ... both human and divine.
as we forgive our debtors ... May my intention be clear,

And lead us not into temptation ... guiding thought and action
but deliver us from evil ... in the light of understanding

For thine is the kingdom, and the power, and the glory ... for the goodness of ALL concerned.

Forever. ... In timeless eternity of the ever-present now
Amen ... So be it.

In the glow of the early morning dawn a light flickers. Is it a star? A planet? It moves to the left, then up, to the right. Some call these lights unidentified flying objects (UFOs). Some see them as falling stars. This light is not falling. It is moving.

I see it as the Christ light. It reminds me of who I am. *"Ye are the Light of the world!"* Jesus taught his disciples. It reminds me of where I have come from and where I am to go. I close my eyes, carrying the image of the Sacred Star into meditation. I chant the sound of creation until its silence pervades my consciousness.

After some time, my vision clears.

I have my answer.

When I return to the computer, the time reads 3:33. I open Honna's email, click reply, and type....

> Dear Honna,
>
> I am honored to receive your invitation to be on this panel and happy to accept. I feel it will be a wonderful opportunity to share the interfaith studies and practices taught at the College of Metaphysics and lived at the Peace Dome here in the Midwest United States. I welcome the opportunity to learn from others in this distinguished venue and am grateful....
>
> Again, thank you and the programming committees for extending this gracious opportunity to me.
>
> May peace be with you all ways,
>
> Barbara

I click "send", then step off a mountaintop, beginning my ascension from the abyss.

The Calling

When I land, I am three months old.

My grandfather takes me in his arms before a crowd of 5000 in Atlanta, Georgia. He prays that my life will be dedicated to the Lord. I had been a colicky baby until then. After that, my mother said I was happy.

My grandfather was a faith-healing evangelist. A contemporary of Billy Graham and Oral Roberts, he was featured with them in a July 1950 article in **Look** magazine. As long as I knew him, he always said he did nothing of his own power. He always felt the Lord had called him to do this soul-saving. Only by the grace of God was he able to aid others. He said it was the power of the Holy Ghost moving through him that healed others.

It was that power my grandfather called upon to dedicate my life to the Lord. He would never learn that the power he wielded has a long-standing tradition in the Hindu tradition. Shaktipat, the transference of kundalini energy, is considered an act of grace on the part of the guru-teacher and cannot be imposed by force. On that night in Atlanta, a transcendent purpose for my life was set. Mine would not be an ordinary life.

As a child, my mind was open, friendly, and loving. I talked with my Spirit guide. I remembered dreams. I read people's minds. I knew when people were telling the truth and when they weren't. Early on, classmates would seek me out for counsel.

I spoke in tongues at 10. Stopped going to church when I was 12. I saw auras at 15 and remembered precognitive dreams at 18. At 20, I experienced a dramatic non-dreaming astral projection experience. I didn't really understand these experiences. I just knew I had them. When I shared them with friends, I learned how uncommon they were. When I worked up the courage to talk to my parents, minister, teachers, even college professors, they were interested yet had no light to shed.

By 22, I no longer saw a point to living. I had graduated from the University of Missouri, and could see no future. I experienced what Buddhist scriptures call the emptiness yet lacked the spiritual education to know it. Three months later, I began studying Mind and consciousness at the School of Metaphysics. There I embarked on a disciplined course of study focused on three practices for the evolution of consciousness: Concentration taught as prayer,

Meditation taught as stillness, and Visualization taught as dreams and visions. These are the crown jewels of consciousness, the three universal practices taught in every religion. Once mastered, a fourth practice, the activation of Kundalini, brings illumination in the creator and the created.

I began to realize Kundalini was the power my grandfather experienced. He called it "God's electricity." He experienced its effects, often fasting and praying, seeking divine guidance for its best use. His was a life built on faith, so he did not believe or understand many of my experiences. In my early adult years, I finally came to realize I received the Kundalini power early on with little instruction for its conscious cultivation. That lack did not keep it from flowing through me, driving me toward enlightenment about everyone and everything. It nurtured in me an insatiable curiosity that caused me to excel in any endeavor. Believing was meant to lead somewhere. It was not an end. It was a beginning, for improvement, for betterment, for perfecting the Self. I wanted to know God.

I began teaching the practical application of metaphysics in September 1975 just three months after I began formal study. The inherent urge to teach, to pass on wisdom, is strong in those who hear the calling. It was natural for me to receive the activity of the SOM as "teachers, teaching teachers." Finally, after years of self-doubt and recrimination, fueled by questions that seemed to have no answers, I felt like I was living a more wholesome life.

In my desire to represent Christianity in Truth, I came across a book my grandfather wrote called **Divine Deliverance**. He described his calling at age 9, the sins of his youth, and his conversion to God at 18. *"I knew that when I gave my heart to God I must begin preaching,"* he wrote, and so he did. Once I was born, he imagined that I would follow in his footsteps and, more than he ever knew, I have.

All of these thoughts rise as a result of accepting Parliament's invitation. The crux of my moral dilemma of representing Christianity at Parliament had everything to do with understanding Self, and my relationship with God and with humanity. Little did I suspect that when I submitted my proposal months before, it would produce a revelatory grasp of the religion of my childhood.

People like my grandfather, who believe in an authoritarian, even punishing God, have a difficult time suffering that which is foreign to their experience and thinking. I spent my 20s, challenging and strengthening my own convictions, all the while thinking I was trying to get my grandfather to see that what I was studying and practicing was not the work of the devil. Eventually, the only thing we seemed not to see eye-to-eye on was our interpretations of Jesus as a savior. He maintained a separateness of Self and that Messiah which I had dissolved in my consciousness through prayer, meditation, and service. I saw Jesus as representing my commitment to becoming fully enlightened. Ironically, my attachment to my grandfather accepting his only granddaughter's life choices, produced my own understanding of what it means to worship the One Living God.

Through this self-reflection, I found part of my answer to the question, "Who am I to represent the Christian faith?" Now, I could see that my duty was to speak from the teaching of the Christ, according to the understanding in my heart, and to do so to the best of my ability. This soul-searching was the entraining of my Mind into Spirit. I knew, when the appropriate time came, that the Holy Spirit would also reveal to me the right words to say.

Genesis

In 1979, I was nearing the completion of doctoral studies. One day we were studying the third chapter of the **Book of Genesis**. My eyes had been opened four years earlier to a deeper meaning of these scriptures from my youth. I learned how to see the story of creation as an allegory, figuratively. The Lord, the man, woman, and snake all took on meanings outside the narrative. The literal translation of text had caused me problems even as a child. I remember asking my parents, why didn't the woman die when she ate the fruit from the tree? Their answer was, she did,– eventually. That's a simple illustration of the level of pure unquestioning faith, even superstition, around me when I was growing up. There was something within me that reached higher, that aspired toward a more benevolent, even mystical Christianity.

In the early years, my search was challenging. My questions were sincere, and not, as my family chose to believe, a rebellion against them and their church. I continued to attend church long after they stopped. I was seeking to resolve the conflicts of my heart arising from mixed signals stemming from partial truths. How could God be loving, yet let children die? Why was a baby born with a disease that ends its life while a mean person is allowed a long life of cruelty? Why did God punish those trying to do the right thing while tyrants are allowed freedom to cause the suffering of others? I wanted to know the truth. I believed it was possible to experience the truth. It made sense that there are Universal Truths and our perceptions of those Truths, what the Buddhists call Absolute Truth and Relative Truth. Jesus taught, *"The truth will set you free."*

In my metaphysics study, I had a framework from which to view higher truth. I was gratified to find its application in the faith of my youth. All I needed to do was open my mind. The passage reads:

3:1 Now the serpent was more subtle than all the wild beasts that the Lord God had made. And the serpent said to the woman, Truly has God said that you shall not eat of any tree of the garden?

:2 And the woman said to the serpent, We may eat of the fruit of all the trees of the garden; :3 but of the fruit of the tree which is in the midst of the garden, God has said, You shall not eat of it, neither shall you touch it, lest you die.

:4 And the serpent said to the woman, You shall not surely die;

:5 For God knows that in the day you eat of it, your eyes shall be opened, and you shall be like gods, knowing good and evil.

Thirty years ago, when this passage was first interpreted for me in the Universal Language of Mind, I realized I had been so caught up in the descent – the fall of man – that I had failed to receive the complete thought. Until then, my view of God was critical, sometimes accusatory and judgmental. I lived the first 22 years of my life in the shadow of the tree of knowledge, alternatingly afraid of not making the right choice and increasingly indifferent to the idea that such a thing even existed. If the Lord didn't want the man and woman to eat of the trees in the middle of the garden, then he wouldn't have put temptation in front of them. To do so was tantamount to putting matches before a child and telling him not to touch them. In my youth, I remained resolute that there had to be a greater truth.

Metaphysical **Bible** interpretation gave me a way to begin ascending. Eric Butterworth's **Discover the Power Within You** presented a God closer to the one I knew in my heart existed. This God was no longer distant or separate. *"For God knows that in the day you eat of it, your eyes shall be opened, and you shall be like gods, knowing good and evil."* Experience opens the Mind's perception to the polarities in life. My family had tried to shield me from the experiences of the physical world. They wanted to protect me from harm. Not knowing how to teach me to neutralize it, they only knew to try to warn me away through fear, guilt, and chastisement. I could see this, so my journey of gratitude, forgiveness, and tolerance began.

Reading the **Bible** in images, then interpreting those images into words, opened my eyes. What we choose to see determines the world we make. This is not the creator of an undisciplined mind, the vengeful god who punishes or the critical god who condemns, or even the benevolent god who is comforting. Using the godlike sight affords the capacity to understand the cause and effect relationships in our world. It is expressed in the truth of the Biblical golden rule *"do unto others as you would have them do unto you,"* taught in some form by every major religion. Existing in Superconscious Mind transcends those relationships revealing a greater Truth taught by my native American ancestors, "We are one in the Spirit."

On that day in 1979, my consciousness resurrected. I received the Truth of being made "in the likeness and image of God". I became more dedicated to bodhichitta, cultivating the wisdom in my consciousness by aiding others to relieve their suffering. I affirmed Universal Truths in my life.

I AM a teacher in the cause of realization that I AM a Master.

I live the truth that he who teaches learns.

I interpret dreams and Holy Scriptures from around the world.

I commit myself to understanding the Power of Divine Consciousness, the power of grace, of revelation.

I contend with divine and human beings and my life is spared.

It is Kundalini that urges us to know Self as Creator. Noted Western psychologist C.G. Jung wrote, *"When you succeed in the awakening of Kundalini, so that she starts to move out of her mere potentiality, you necessarily start a world which is totally different from our world; it is a world of eternity."*

That is the world my Christian grandfather gave to me, a world I felt called to bring to the Parliament of the World's Religions.

Revelation

In the weeks before addressing the peace panel, I thought deeply about the first half of my life's journey. I knew I needed full illumination of why this opportunity had come my way. Without it, I would be no better than the hypocrites, the Pharisees, of my youth. With it, I would come to understand the greatness of the faith tradition of my birth.

That illumination I found in the last book of the **Bible** - *The Revelation of St. John the Divine.*

The ***Book of Revelation*** is rich with imagery. When read with physical eyes solely, it brings the stuff of nightmares - war, pestilence, famine, death, destruction. It is unattractive and remains a mystery most do not even want to hear. When read metaphysically, as a guide for Self-realization, it becomes the most extensive textbook for spiritual ascension ever written. This is the way I understand the book. Its imagery is alive in my consciousness anytime I seek revelatory insight. I am committed to the spread of the Truth it affords, so I teach its interpretation and am now assembling a multimedia presentation of the text. I had to admit, yes, I am qualified to speak on behalf of Christianity at the Parliament of the World's Religions.

After I accepted Honna's invitation, I spent weeks evaluating my early beliefs and what I had come to know about Christhood. I knew I had unconditionally claimed my Christhood in 1998 when my mother died. I knew my life was spared by grace when I walked away from a death-defying car wreck in 2005. I knew I had stood looking at the Peace Dome a few months later, and in a moment of illumination, realized that I no longer believed in hell. Even with all the transitions in consciousness throughout my life, even accepting that we create our own hell or heaven, I still believed that hell had a separate existence until that day.

These kinds of thoughts are not easy for me to write. I am aware that many Christians may condemn me as a blasphemer because such thoughts trouble them. I have compassion for them, for I have known the troubled heart. I remember being taught as a child, to pray that Jesus would come into my heart, and it would be so, only to have those I loved doubt that my prayers were answered. It took a broad range of life experiences to realize my restlessness was not the result of a battle for my heart and soul and life between Jesus the good and Satan the bad. These were the fearful imaginings of my family. My restlessness was a passion for spiritual transcendence.

The Multifaith Panel on Peace

Elisheva Salamo (Jewish), Jessi Kaur (Sikh), Chang Wu Shi (Buddhist), Anisa Buckley (Islam), Prabhu Duneja (Hindu), Jem Jembia, Michelle Mueller (Pagan), Barbara Condron (Christian), Chang Shen Shi (Buddhist), Pritpal Kaur from Tony Blair's foundation.

The part of me that believed that Jesus could come into my heart, that he could dictate my thinking and rule my conduct, was present from the beginning. I gave my heart to Jesus when I was five, and then, in a strange way, I progressively hid the fact for years. When I went to school I learned to hide my faith lest I be ridiculed, laughed at or ostracized. I was ashamed, just like the man and woman in the garden, and for years did not feel at home in the religious or the secular worlds.

Studying metaphysics, removed the stigma in my own mind and by the time I studied **Revelation** in the advanced course of study, it was like finding the Holy Grail. **Revelation**, Chapter 5, came into my mind many times as I balanced accounts concerning my representing Christianity. John is caught up to Heaven where he sees the throne of God, the four living creatures, the 24 elders, and the sea of glass before the throne. God sits on the throne holding a scroll with seven seals. No one on heaven or on earth is worthy to open it. John weeps.

As I redefine what I think it means to represent the Christian faith, I am clearing my consciousness in every level of Mind. I am *"cleansed in the blood of the lamb"*, not in some physicalized gothic sense of animal sacrificing compatible with ideas of the Holy "Ghost", rather in a spiritualized metaphorical sense of unveiling the Truth in innocence that is the Holy Spirit. Through the effort, illumination of Christ's teachings, Buddha's teachings, and Krishna's teachings manifest. I know what John means when he writes, *"Then thousands of angels proclaim, 'Worthy is the lamb that was slain to receive power, and riches, and wisdom, and strength, and honor and glory, and blessing'."*

My grandfather always told me the Lord had his hand on my life. My grandmother told me how they had prayed and God had sent an angel from heaven to the family. My father told me he never worried about me because he knew I was in God's hands. My mother told me God had great plans for my life, that's why he had given me many talents. In the vernacular of our church, this meant I had a calling, a higher purpose than one I would ever be able to conceive with my physical mind.

At last, I understood why I received this seat, on this panel, at this time. It was not of my conscious making, yet totally the result of conscious choices in living, a complete image of existence, – neither-either, yet both.

"I AM Aleph and Tau, the beginning and the end, the first and the last."

The opportunity had arisen by my own hand and by the hands of many. In prayer and meditation, I surrendered all that I AM to the Lord so the Holy Spirit might use my lips to speak, my hands to write.

"The grace of our Lord Jesus Christ be with you all, all you Holy ones. Amen."

I COME AS A VOICE OF CONSCIENCE AND OF REASON.

The Peace Panel Address
Tuesday, December 9, 2009 Melbourne, Australia
I am honored to be in your esteemed company this day.

At the 1993 Parliament, a daily part of the gathering was a noontime Parliament of the People. We had the opportunity to meet in groups like this to dialogue, to ask questions and to listen, to give and to receive.

A document which ultimately came from that Parliament - the **Universal Peace Covenant** says - *"The open exchange of ideas is necessary for discovery, for well-being, for growth, for progress whether within one person or among many."*

I am humbled to have been chosen as a voice for Christianity at this Parliament of the World's Religions.

Some Christians might take exception to my representing Christianity today. Having come from a place of separation in faith I can understand such a viewpoint.

Yet, as I contemplated my thoughts for today, it occurred that my religious journey is similar to that of a man I have grown to admire and hold in high regard. That man is Mohandas K. Gandhi. Gandhi's mother was a devout Jain who gave him the discipline and virtue of a moral compass. It was in his young adult years while studying in England that he was introduced to the **Bhagavad Gita** and the **Bible**, and the world of Universal Truth opened to him.

I began with the **Bible**, and when I studied at the School of Metaphysics in America, I learned of the **Bhagavad Gita** and the teachings of the Jain, the **Tao**, the **Dhammapada,** and others. As my heart filled, my mind opened and my eyes could see the connections between all the great religions. Just yesterday, in a youth session I attended with my son, a young speaker said, "If I ask someone in the front of the room to direct me to the exit, she will tell me to turn around and walk 30 paces. If I ask someone in the back of the room where the exit is, he will say turn to my right and walk 6 steps. Others will give other directions, according to their relative position, and all will be correct from their point of view. The exit remains what it is and where it is." So it is with soul growth and spiritual progression. There are many paths to one destination. Revering them all is Interfaith, and this is the religion of my middle years.

Christianity is the religion of my incarnation, given to me by my family as a guide for my Spirit and a Light on my path in this world. My life was dedicated to the Lord when I was three months old during a tent revival conducted by my grandfather, a faith healing evangelist. The Christianity of my youth is a very personal religion, one of conversion, of change. It asks that you invite Lord Jesus into your heart so he may transform you.

In our efforts for world peace, the first world and the last is Self. We have only to learn to live with Self, to make peace with Self and our Maker. So we must desire to transform the human spirit, to reclaim our divinity. This is the message of Lord Jesus.

And so the responsibility of a Christian begins with being a Christ.

The responsibility of a Buddhist begins with being a Buddha.

The responsibility of a Hindu begins with being a Krishna.

So I come to you today as a Christ, a Buddha, a Krishna, anointed with the responsibility of the dozens whose vision is the Universal Peace Covenant, the hundreds whose efforts sustain its life, and the thousands whose breath intones the words like a prayer.

I come not because I am an authority on the religions which grew from the teachings of the great masters, rather it is because I am willing to receive the truth they lived.

I come as a voice of conscience and of reason.

When Jesus was born, the story goes, the angels proclaimed, "Peace on earth, goodwill toward men." Jesus came in peace. This is where the consciousness of the Christian begins. Because most find their daily peace disrupted, the first stage on the path is learning to live in gratitude and prayer. By seeking to forgive, we learn to love our neighbor as we love ourselves which brings peace into the world. This change of Reconciliation is the first stage, the transfiguration of the heart.

Through his life and teaching as recorded in the gospels, Jesus lives the Resurrection of consciousness. This is stage two.

Stage three is the Revelation of Jesus the Christ which brings the New Heaven and the New Earth. The Revelation is to be the experience of every thinker. We must, as Gandhi so succinctly conveyed, "Be the change we would see."

At an excellent session on the *Faces of Peace*, Dr. Homi Dhalla, a Zoroastrian priest, observed that *"if we do not teach peace to our youth, someone will teach them violence."* For this reason, we invite you to participate in the great work of peace education.

Toward this end, I share part of my son's newest film on the making of the Healing Wall. On the retaining wall of the Peace Dome is a relief map of the world that awaits your loving participation so it may be transformed into a Healing Wall, a fulfillment of our potential, both human and divine.

Each morning at 5:30 a.m. faculty and students at the College of Metaphysics come to the Peace Dome to recite the **Universal Peace Covenant**. It is a heartbeat for peace in this new age, for truly "Living peaceably begins by thinking peacefully." We invite people of all faiths to join us.∞

300

DREAMTIME

PARABLES OF UNIVERSAL LAW

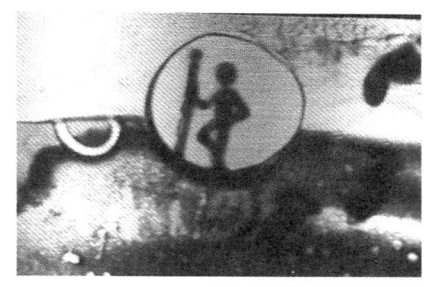

"It is good.
My world is alive,"
Baiame said.

Yhi took his hand and called in a golden voice to all the things she had brought to life.

"This is the land of Baiame. It is yours forever, to enjoy. Baiame is the Great Spirit. He will guard you and listen to your requests. I have nearly finished my work, so you must listen to my words."

"I shall send you the seasons of summer and winter – summer with warmth which ripens fruit ready for eating, winter for sleeping while the cold winds sweep through the world and blow away the refuse of summer. These are changes that I shall send you. There are other changes that will happen to you, the creatures of my love.

"Soon I shall leave you and live far above in the sky. When you die your bodies will remain here, but your spirits will come to live with me."

–adapted from *Aboriginal Myths, Legends, & Fables*
by A.W. Reed.

Acknowledgements and Blessings

To those who rekindled in 1993, the Spirit of 1893 that is the Council for a Parliament of the World's Religions, twenty years after the founding of the School of Metaphysics. To Dirk Ficca, executive director of CPWR, who led the world to come together in Melbourne (2009) and who invited THE INVITATION to Chicago in 2008,–your soul is magnified by the equanimity in your heart and the clear-sightedness in your head. It was from your invitation, we made this journey down under. To Amelia, Honna, and Grove, as a student once wrote to me, I write now to you, "Thank you for your service. Signed: The World."

To the friendships we are building around the world, much gratitude. Our hearts sing in our meeting and the song it makes lingers in our minds, through us the world is a friendly place. To the people of Melbourne who bid us "No worries!" we will spread the joy of your hospitality until we return.

To His Holiness the 14th Dalai Lama whose wise choice to leave his homeland so he could receive the world is a model of manifesting the Sacred Star in all its manifestations, particularly forgiveness, tolerance, and kindness. Your presence is always with us. To seven other Nobel Laureates for bringing together souls who have known each other before and whose lives continue to change others into infinity.

To J.R. for receiving the vision of what would become the School of Metaphysics and being fearless in upholding a candle in the darkness following two world wars in this Kali Yuga, thanks giving for a teacher of Mind. To my fellow students and teachers for making simple choices in a world of plenty, you inspire me to improve, to be better than my best each day. To Laurel, Sheila, Pam, and Tad, your grasp of Holy work is an inspiration to all you meet. To Christine and Paul, your pioneering spirit keeps the home light burning for everyone. To Laurie for your great love of life, people, and God. To Jesse Reece and Jesse Kern, for your willingness to learn and to teach through example. To Erin and Elena for your generous natures. To Alexandra, Vivienna, and Hezekiah, the youngest mahatmas among us, live long and prosper in this land that the Lord gives you to tend.

To spiritual partner on the path to eternity, my husband Daniel, keeper of the still mind, divine love beyond time and space. It is Daniel whose phrases are quoted here to describe the action of each Universal Law. He distilled them on the occasion of our son Hezekiah's Community Blessing Ceremony in the Peace Dome, on the occasion of his thirteenth birthday. They perfectly describe the consciousness of each Law and deserved to be known by all.

In Lak'ech Ala K'in, me-me. –Barbara Condron

THE LAWS

One The Law of Existence	Seven The Law of Relativity
Two The Law of Free Will	Eight The Law of Believing & Knowing
Three The Law of Duality	Nine The Law of Proper Perspective
Four The Law of Cause and Effect	Ten The Law of Evolution
Five The Law of Attraction	Eleven The Law of Prosperity
Six The Law of Infinity	Twelve The Law of Abundance

Thirteen The Law of Completion

THE PARABLES

I AM told by Dr. Daniel R. Condron
I Make Conscious Choices
    Parable 1 told by Erin Collins
    Parable 2 told by Dr. Sheila Benjamin
    Parable 3 told by The INVITATION cast
I Value the Aggressive & Receptive
    Parable 1 told & photographed by Elena Dubinski
    Parable 2 told by Dr. Sheila Benjamin
I Discipline My Mind
    Parable 1 told by Dr. Pam Blosser
    Parable 2 told by Jesse Aaron Kern
I Am Open and Loving told by Tad Messenger
I Expand my Consciousness told by Dr. Christine Madar
I Am Connected with All told by Dr. Laurel Clark
I Learn in Every Activity
    Parable 1 told by Jesse Loren Reece
    Parable 2 told by Laurie J. Biswell
The Permanent and Lasting is Most Important told by B. Condron
I Add to my Understanding Every Day
    Parable 1 told by Paul Madar
    Parable 2 told by Christine Madar
    Parable 3 told by Sheila Benjamin
I Receive the Wealth from the Universe told by Hezekiah Condron
I Create Plenty for Everyone told by Barbara Condron
I Am Committed to Becoming Fully Enlightened told by B. Condron

END NOTES for learning more

Introduction

MacBeth by William Shakespeare, THE COMPLETE WORKS OF SHAKESPEARE. Updated Fourth Edition. Edited by David Bevington. 2000 pp. New York : Longman, 1997. ISBN 0-321-01254-2 (hbk.)

The Dhammapada, Sermon at Bernares given by Guatama the Buddha, by Eknath Easwaran, Nilgiri Press, 2nd Ed. 2007. ISBN-10: 1586380206

Dreamtime Aboriginal stories of life and creation by A.W. Reed

Parliament of the World's Religions online www.parliamentofreligions.org

Power v. Force by Dr. David Hawkins, Veritas Publishing; 1st edition (June 1, 1995), 2002 Hay House publisher. ISBN-10: 0964326116

The Silver Cord 2005 SOM Productions, School of Metaphysics, Windyville, MO 65783 USA

www.sacred-texts.com

The World's Wisdom by Philip Novak, HarperCollins Publishers, 1995, ISBN 0-066341-3

Two Suns Rising by Jonathan Star, Bantam Books, 1991, ISBN: 0-553-07391-5

One

Book of Matthew, Bible online www.biblegateway.com

Universal Language of Mind: Book of Matthew Interpreted by Dr. Daniel R. Condron, SOM Publishing, 1994 ISBN: 0944386156

Course in Miracles online acim.org | Foundation for Inner Peace • PO Box 598 • Mill Valley, CA 94942-0598

Association for Global New Thought | 220 Santa Anita Rd | Santa Barbara, CA 93105 online www.agnt.org

Sri Chinmoy online www.srichinmoy.org
en.wikipedia.org/wiki/Sri_Chinmoy

Two

Tao Te Ching translated by Gai-Fu Feng, Jane English, Vintage, 1st ed. 1989. ISBN-10: 0679724346.

Council for a Parliament of the World's Religions vision: online www.parliamentofreligions.org

Melbourne Unity Church online http://www.unitymelbourne.org.au

The INVITATION created by Dr. Barbara Condron, 2004 dvd, script ©2007 SOM Publishing, School of Metaphysics

A Life Worth Examining created by Paul Madar, 2009, SOM Productions, School of Metaphysics

The Universal Peace Covenant created by spiritual teachers School of Metaphysics 1996-97.

The Peace Dome online www. peacedome.org

Three
Traditional African Proverb

Tibetan Buddhist Sand Mandala www.asia.si.edu/exhibitions/online/mandala/faq.htm

AGAPE Choir online www.agapelive.com

Four
Sikh Teachings of Adi Granth online www.sikhs.org
Genpo Roshi, the founder of the Big Mind Big Heart Process online www.bigmind.org

Margareta Dahlin Johahnsson, pastor of Peace Lutheran Church in Danville, CA Peace Lutheran Church • 3201 Camino Tassajara • Danville, CA 94506

musician and founder of Inner Harmony, Michael Stillwater • online www.innerharmony.com

How to Raise an Indigo Child by Barbara Condron, 2002, SOM Publishing, ISBN-10: 0944386296

Compassion Rising Michael Fitzgerald online www.compassionrising.com

Colin Lee, a young man who, as a minister and the head of Shift International | www.shiftinternational.net

Weston Pew with the Sacred Door Trail, the only sacred trail on the North American continent | www.thesacreddoortrail.com

Five
: *Lightning Ridge Opal Mine online http://www.opals.net.au/*

Edgar Cayce online www.edgarcayce.org

First Opinion: Wholistic Health Care in the 21st Century by Barbara Condron, 1998, SOM Publishing, ISBN-10: 0944386180

Chief Oren Lyons (right) from the Onondaga Tribe of the Iroquois (French) Nation online en.wikipedia.org/wiki/Oren_Lyons

Peacemaking – Nine Lessons for Changing Yourself, Your Relationships, and Your World by Dr. Barbara Condron, 2003, SOM Publishing, ISBN-10: 0944386318

Seventh Generation DVD on the Peace Dome Healing Wall

Six
: *Eithei Dogen Moon in a Dewdrop: Writings of a Zen Master Dogen*

A Complaint Free World by Wil Bowen, 2007, Doubleday, ,ISBN-10: 0385524587 online http://oaks.nvg.org/dogen-quotations.html

Rev. John Strickland, a Unity Minister in Atlanta, GA www.atlantaunity.org

Seven
: *Sioux prayer online www.angelfire.com/md/elanmichaels/SiouxPrayer.html*

Jyorei healers online www.jyorei.org/

Dr. Homi Dhalla who is the Founder and President of the World Zarathusti Cultural Foundation

World Peace Prayer Society, Masahisa Goi, online www.worldpeace.org

Indigenous musician and story-teller Jeremy Donovan online www.jeremydonovan.com.au

Nine
: *Spiriteul Carnivale online www.spiritualcarnival.com.au*

Power of Prayer around the World, Peace Dome, College of Metaphysics, Missouri, USA

Peace is first a state of mind. Peace affords the greatest opportunity for growth and learning which leads to personal happiness. Self-direction promotes inner peace and therefore leads to outer peace. We vow to heal ourselves through forgiveness, gratitude, and prayer. We commit to causing each and every day to be a fulfillment of our potential, both human and divine.

Peace is active, the motion of silence, of faith, of accord, of service. It is not made in documents but in the minds and hearts of men and women. Peace is built through communication. The open exchange of ideas is necessary for discovery, for well-being, for growth, for progress whether within one person or among many. We vow to speak with sagacity, listen with equanimity, both free of prejudice, thus we will come to know that peace is liberty in tranquillity.

Peace is achieved by those who fulfill their part of a greater plan. Peace and security are attained by those societies where the individuals work closely to serve the common good of the whole. Peaceful coexistence between nations is the reflection of man's inner tranquillity magnified. Enlightened service to our fellowman brings peace to the one serving, and to the one receiving. We vow to live in peace by embracing truths that apply to us all.

Living peaceably begins by thinking peacefully. We stand on the threshold of peace-filled understanding. We come together, all of humanity, young and old of all cultures from all nations. We vow to stand together as citizens of the Earth knowing that every question has an answer, every issue a resolution. As we stand, united in common purpose, we hereby commit ourselves in thought and action so we might know the power of peace in our lifetimes.

Peace be with us all ways. May Peace Prevail On Earth.

--created by Spiritual Teachers in the School of Metaphysics 1996-7

DREAMTIME

THE SCHOOL OF METAPHYSICS

is a 501(c)(3) educational institute teaching the intuitive, spiritual potential of individuals through a four-tiered course of study and continuing education programs in the field of consciousness development. To learn more visit us on the internet or contact us at the School of Metaphysics World Headquarters, Windyville, Missouri 65783 USA.

About SOM study programs, intuitive research, books & recordings
visit www.som.org

About dreams including open campus, membership & scholar program
visit www.dreamschool.org

About our peace work including the Universal Peace Covenant, proclamation for the Universal Hour of Peace, and The INVITATION
visit www.peacedome.org

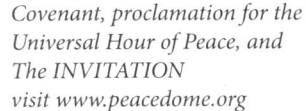

For progress on
The Healing Wall
visit www.healingwall.org